The Book of Glass

Gustav Weiss

The Book of Glass

Translated by Janet Seligman

Barrie & Jenkins

London

First published 1971 in Great Britain
by Barrie & Jenkins
2 Clement's Inn, London WC 2
© 1966 by Verlag Ullstein GmbH, Berlin
English translation © 1971 by Pall Mall Press Ltd, London
All rights reserved
SBN 214 65111 8
Printed in Germany by Gerhard Stalling AG, Oldenburg

Contents

A note on the plan of the book

This book sets out to trace two broad lines of development — overlapping in time — which the author hopes will explain the history of glass more satisfactorily than the usual division into Antiquity, Middle Ages and Modern Times.

The first section deals with the earliest glass in Egypt and the Near East, and follows the spread of glassmaking, until the ancient tradition finally spent itself in Europe north of the Alps.

The second section, too, beginning in the countries where glass was first made, extends from the Islamic East, through the Renaissance in Europe and ends with the activities of the modern Scandinavian glass-designers.

The third chapter outlines the technical and scientific developments which span the whole course of glassmaking.

The typological tables bring together a selection of dated glasses chosen to characterise the formal repertoire of individual periods. The scale (1:6) of these examples remains unchanged throughout the book.

The lists of signatures are divided as to master glass-cutters (page 192), diamond-engravers and stipplers (page 158), glass-painters (page 155) and glassmakers of the Art Nouveau period (page 280).

Foreword

This book has been written as an introduction and a guide to the world of glass. It is a world which can offer a lifetime of investigation and rewarding discovery and which, happily, is still continually being enriched by findings which fall into widely divergent categories.

The past offers inexhaustible opportunities to the inquirer. To discover it is a form of self-knowledge and therefore by no means fruitless.

Glass was a product of the countries of the eastern Mediterranean. Like so much else, it was taken over by western civilisation and has remained until modern times intimately linked with the mutations of that civilisation.

Glass is the work of men and reflects the individuality of its creator and the spirit of its age. Yet we know practically nothing of the glassmakers themselves and their fortunes. The sixteenth and seventeenth centuries are the earliest periods from which we have names and a few biographical details. Only occasionally did makers sign their wares, so that stylistic comparison is the principal means of identifying a piece. This requires wide experience based on personal examination of specimens.

Since earliest times glass, the man-made substance, has been compared with crystal, the pure creation of nature. Works in crystal were the forerunners of cut glass. The Venetians gave the name *cristallo* to their best glass, as did the Bohemians, while the English use the phrase 'brilliant' cutting. To this very day — despite our greater knowledge of crystallography — the word crystal betokens the noblest glass. And it is, after all, right that this should be so, for crystal is the natural model for transparency and the play of light and colour — the very properties of the material with which the glassmaker gains his effects. Art and technique, manual skill and creative fantasy formed a unity in handmade glass. The glasses of different periods vary from one another not merely in the features of their formal and decorative styles but also in technical characteristics. It is therefore important to consider also the development of the material, its manufacture and the techniques employed in working it. With this in mind we must pay redoubled attention to the achievements of the past.

If we compare what has survived with the vast quantity of glass that must have been made continuously and with diligence, skill and ever-increasing productivity during the five thousand years of the material's history, we cannot but recognise that these survivals represent a mere fraction of all that has been made. This awareness should enable us to value them more highly. They are the past's gift to the present.

The pictures in this book — which not only show typical pieces of glass, but it is hoped will also awaken pleasure in the objects — have been brought together with the assistance of the following, to whom special thanks are due:

Dr Wilhelm Angeli, Naturhistorisches Museum, Vienna

Dr Binsfeld, Rheinisches Landesmuseum, Trier

Dr H. Biehn, Verwaltung der Staatlichen Schlösser und Gärten, Bad Homburg

Fräulein Dr von Bock, Kunstgewerbemuseum, Cologne

Robert J. Charleston, Victoria and Albert Museum, London

Dr Kurt Degen, Hessisches Landesmuseum, Darmstadt

Dr Otto Doppelfeld, Römisch-Germanisches Museum, Cologne

Dr Hans Eckstein, Cochham, near Munich

Dr Carl Graepler, Universitätsmuseum für Kunst und Kulturgeschichte, Marburg

Dr Hanns-Ulrich Haedecke, Kunstgewerbemuseum, Cologne

Dr Max Hasse, Museen für Kunst und Kulturgeschichte der Hansestadt Lübeck

Dr D. E. L. Haynes, British Museum, London

Wilhelm Henrich, Antiques, Frankfurt am Main

M. A. Heukensfeld Jansen, Rijksmuseum, Amsterdam

James Humphry, Metropolitan Museum of Art, New York

Dr Friedrich M. Illert, Stiftung Kunsthaus Heylshof, Worms

Dr Hermann Jedding, Museum für Kunst und Gewerbe, Hamburg

Dr Niels Jessen, De Danske Kongers Kronologiske Samling, Rosenborg

Dr W. von Kalnein, Kunstmuseum, Düsseldorf

Herrn Helfried Krug, Mulheim (Ruhr)

Professor Giovanni Mariacher, Civici Musei Veneziani d'Arte e di Storia, Venice

Dr Heino Maedebach, Kunstsammlungen der Veste, Coburg

Dr Peter Wilhelm Meister, Museum für Kunsthandwerk, Frankfurt am Main

Frau Dr Christel Mosel, Kestner Museum, Hanover

Dr Paul Perrot, Corning Museum of Glass, New York

Dr Ernst Petrasch, Badisches Landesmuseum, Karlsruhe

Frau Dr E. Reiff, Rheinisches Bildarchiv, Cologne

Dr Alfred Schadler, Bayerisches Nationalmuseum, Munich

Dr Gunther Schiedlausky, Germanisches Nationalmuseum, Nuremberg

Dr Christian Theuerkauff, Kunstmuseum, Düsseldorf

Professor Wilhelm Wagenfeld, Stuttgart

August Warnecke, Hamburg

Dr Friedrich Wielandt, Badisches Landesmuseum, Karlsruhe

Frau Eva Wipplinger, Staatliche Galerie Moritzburg, Halle

Frau Dr Johanna Zick-Nissen, Staatliche Museen, Berlin

Glass in history

At first one might think that the development of glass began in Egypt and Mesopotamia, increasing steadily in perfection until it reached the nineteenth century, when its character changed and glassmaking, from being a craft, suddenly became an industrial procedure. This is a simplification and fails to render a true account of the history of glass, if only because at all times and in all places glassmakers have existed who had their own ideas, their own opportunities and their own objectives. As each method in turn prevailed, so a rival method grew up to take its place, as each style dominated the artistic field, so a counter-movement emerged, as each centre became the focus of activity, so it was supplanted by another. When one period gave way to another this change never entailed a clean crossing of a dividing line; there was always a period of transition, with the result that it is often extremely difficult to decide when one era ceased and a new one began.

The earliest glass was an element in a world informed by ideas of magic; dialogues with the environment on the reality of metallurgy — the art involved in the making of weapons — compelled men to give thought to technical usefulness. No artificial glass is known before the Late Bronze Age. The earliest finds in Egypt and Mesopotamia closely resemble one another and we still do not know in which country glass was first made. Centuries after glass had ceased to be made in ancient Egypt, glass vessels reappeared in the Mediterranean area; their origins remain unknown. Independently of these, another technique of glassmaking developed on the banks of the Tigris at the time when the Assyrian empire was at its apogee and this gained a high standing during the Hellenistic period.

A few decades before the birth of Christ — probably in Syria — the practice of blowing glass came into use and blown glass became an important element in the cultural and economic life of the Roman world. Glassmaking spread and as it did so Cologne in the second century became a new centre, maintaining a high artistic level until the fall of the western Roman Empire. The Frankish glasses of the Merovingian period (486–751) are the final products of this era.

As glassmaking spread, so new centres were formed. At the time of the Roman *imperium* the frontiers of the Empire and the area over which glass was made coincided. Only in the east had it — by the third century BC — passed beyond these frontiers, to India. There had been glass in China too since the Han Dynasty (206 BC—AD 220). During the following centuries glassmaking developed in three areas and followed a separate course in each: China, with its engraved glass; Islam, with engraved glass and splendid polychrome decoration; and the Christian west with stained-glass windows. This situation lasted throughout the Middle Ages, when the most important centre of production of glass vessels was the area occupied by Syria, Mesopotamia and Persia, whence glass found its way to Europe and China.

By the end of the thirteenth century glassmaking had reached an advanced stage in Venice too. Because of its favoured position as the focal trading port in the world commerce of the day, Venice became and remained for more than a hundred years — from the fifteenth to the early seventeenth century — the world centre of glassmaking. The later course of development was marked by increasing differentiation and quicker changes. By the seventeenth century there were already more than a dozen centres of glassmaking: China with its typical carving in high relief; India, with its delightful miniature-like style and rich gold decoration; Persia, with its elegant undecorated coloured glass; Venice, where a Mannerist tendency debased the Renaissance forms; Spain, where Venetian influence had a part in the exotic hybrid style; France, with its mirror glass; the Netherlands, with their diamond-engraved glasses; England, whose flint glass contained lead; Bohemia, where the glass contained chalk; Potsdam, where Kunckel made his ruby glass; Nüremberg, with its intaglio glasses; the Tirol, with its diamond-engraved, cold-painted glass; Sweden, whose glasses were à la façon de Venise; the German countries, with their enamelled Humpen; Denmark, with its Waldglas; Russia, whose first glasshouses were near Voskresensk and Moscow. America, too, had by this time a glass manufacture of her own. The seventeenth century was a particularly fruitful period. With the introduction of new kinds of glass from Bohemia and England, new decorative techniques — diamond-engraving, cutting and engraving — began to flourish. Painted decoration, modelling itself on porcelain-painting, became more delicate.

The triumph of glass over rock-crystal became complete with the deep engraving of the Baroque period. And while, with the dawn of Neo-Classicism, engraved glass lost some of its popularity, it was replaced by the sparkling brilliant-cut English lead-glass, which has lasted almost to our own day.

The nineteenth century presents every conceivable technique and style. The years of the Biedermeier were quietly productive. Thereafter industrialisation supervened and changed everything; development was accelerated by ambitious demands at one world exhibition after another for new, larger and more resplendent show-pieces. Although at the end of the century Art Nouveau put an end to the manufacture of reproductions of earlier styles, it was a luxury art and was unable to fulfil the social mission which technicians regarded as their justification. The 'Neue Sachlichkeit' (Functionalism) movement banished all decoration and approved only of pure functional form. Once this process of purification was over, 'humanisation' became the catchword.

From the earliest beginnings
to the Carolingian period

Glass: a product of the Bronze Age

In the later Stone Age, eight thousand years before our era, before man had begun to make pottery and, of course, before artificial glass had been invented, jewellery, cutting tools and stone utensils were made of natural volcanic glass, especially obsidian, as witness certain finds at Jericho. Most of the surviving pieces of volcanic glass were found in the area corresponding to present-day Hungary and on the Greek islands.

Glass in antiquity never equalled the importance of, say, bronze, which dominated the economy of all early civilisations, even those which were unconnected with one another. For Egypt the Bronze Age was the period of world power. And here lie the origins of artificial glass. Although glass was considered the equal of the most valuable of the semi-precious stones — lapis lazuli, for example — it still had something in common with bronze, a substance much less rare. Both were synthetic materials, both had earlier counterparts in natural products in which some of the later working techniques were anticipated. Copper was the forerunner of bronze and — since it often occurs in a pure state — was even in the early Stone Age often straightforwardly hammered. And before artificial glass had been invented, obsidian, jasper, chalcedony, rock-crystal and other quartz derivatives and semi-precious stones were polished, bored and cut and made into beads, amulets, seals and vessels in just the same way as glass was later worked. The Egyptian word *mefkat* means emerald and malachite, as well as artificial green glass. And the word *chesbet* used in ancient Egypt, Assyria and Greece to designate a deep blue glaze (azurite) stood equally for true lapis lazuli and blue glass.

The fact that copper or bronze and glass so often appear together suggests that there may be technical links between metallurgy and glassmaking. Copper is easily extracted from its ore; all that is required to reduce malachite to copper is — as R. H. Rastall has shown — a fire made of dung, Egypt's principal fuel. Under favourable conditions copper can be smelted pure from sulphidic ores even without a furnace. If the composition of the matrix is suitable and cooling takes place quickly, the dross can itself harden to a glassy state; it is in any case possible for it to be crushed and used as powdered frit or as a flux.

As a metallurgical procedure, glassmaking in its early days must surely also have benefited from the potters, whose experiences of firing had been handed down to them from a period as remote as the eighth millenium BC. Excavations of sites at El Badari in Upper Egypt dating from the fourth millenium have yielded steatite beads covered with a glaze composed of powdered malachite and alkali. The earliest glazed frit — known as 'faience' — does not occur until the beginning of historical times, at the end of the fourth millenium in the Nagada II civilisation in Egypt and in the Djemet-Nasr civilisation in Babylonia and Mesopotamia. It forms as it were an intermediate state in the discovery of glass, which first occurs as an independent material, distinct from ceramic substances, in the middle of the sixteenth century B C.

The first artificial glasses, entirely independent of any ceramic basis, are beads and amulets which, it must be noted, occur within a very small area. They are followed by glass vessels, of which the earliest known fragments are from the tomb of Thotmes I (1508–1493 B C). The earliest Egyptian glass vessel to have survived intact is from the tomb of Thotmes III and has been dated to 1470 B C. It is possible that it was brought to Egypt from Mesopotamia as a gift for the pharaoh, for it resembles Mesopotamian glasses. All the early glass vessels are opaque like stone. The colours were derived from compounds of cobalt or copper. Those coloured by copper may vary between pale sky-blue with a faint green streak and dark blue; those for which cobalt was used are deep blue.

We are still unable to date the discovery of glass any more exactly. We must be content to view the evolution of this material not as an act but as a process and to regard the entry of glass into the arena of history not as a point but as a span of time. This span extends from the first use of alkali as a flux to be added to the hot powdered minerals, to the time when glass became an independent material, that is, when it became clearly distinguishable from ceramic substances. This development took from about 3500 to 1500 B C, or some 2000 years. In terms of technique, the divorce of glass from its ceramic basis took place when it ceased to be shaped cold and began to be worked in a heated state. This was the beginning of a process of development in which, within a further fifteen hundred years, every technique of glassmaking — casting, drawing, pressing and blowing — was prefigured. In the way of working techniques nothing fundamentally new emerged during the following millenia.

We cannot, however, regard the pre-Christian millenia simply as a period of preparation. They form rather a sequence of eras of independent cultural character with autonomous movements and climaxes. Bronze and iron were correlated with these movements, while ceramics and glass, being less important materials, were dependent upon them. If we examine the early syntheses of the glass material and compare them with contemporary metallurgical developments, the first thing that strikes us is that colour was obviously sought as a means of producing an optical impression. Thus, for example, bronze was regarded in antiquity as copper which had been coloured yellow by having tin added to it. Most ancient languages, Egyptian included, make no distinction between copper and bronze. It is clear from the fact that powdered malachite and lapis lazuli were used as pigments for paint in ancient

Pedigree of Egyptian glass

The natural incidence of natron and calcareous sands in Egypt and the Near East as well as the experience of the potters, stone-workers and copper-workers favoured the emergence of glass. The earliest traces of synthetic glass are found in the glazes of steatite beads. These are similarly the forerunners of the alkali and sand frits ('Egytian faiences'). Glass had become distinct from ceramic substances by the middle of the sixteenth century B C. Sand-core glasses can be shown to have existed in Egypt only during the period between the reign of Thotmes I (1508–1493 B C) and 970 B C.

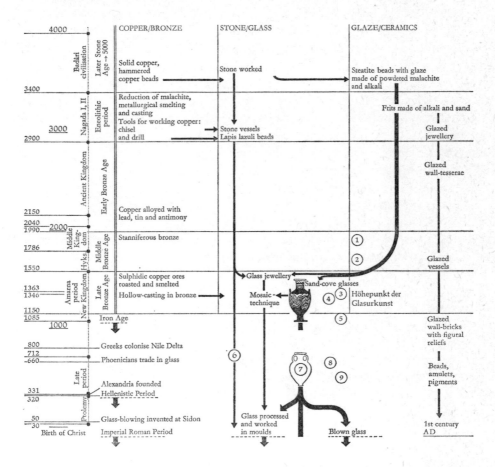

The following dates will enable the reader to compare development in Egypt with that of other countries: ① Kameras vases of the Middle Minoan Period (2000–1600 B C) ② Recipe for glazes from Seleucia on the Tigris (1700 B C) ③ Mycenaean plaque beads (before 1300 B C) ④ Sand-core glass from Ur in Mesopotamia (1300 B C) ⑤ North Tirolean copper-smelters' glass ring-beads of the Late Bronze Age in Europe (1200–950 B C) ⑥ Vase of Sargon II (722–705 B C) at Nimrud, Assyria. ⑦ Blue and polychrome Mediterranean sand-core glasses of unknown provenance. ⑧ Clay tablets giving account of glassmaking in cuneiform script from the royal library of Ashurbanipal (668–631 B C) ⑨ Little cups from Hallstatt and cup with handles from Santa Lucia on the Adriatic (c. 500 B C). Comparisons show that the discovery of glass in the Late Bronze Age was 'in the air'. The designation 'Late Bronze Age' must here be understood as a relative term.

architecture that the desire for colour played a part in the origin of glazes and glass. Malachite was also used in Egypt — at least from 4000 B C onwards — as a cosmetic for the eyes.

Behind the desire for colour there certainly lay the urge to transmit the magical powers colour was reputed to possess. By fusing an alkali with powdered malachite a green glaze was obtained, which, like malachite, enabled men to hear the language of the beasts and rendered them invisible to the eyes of other men. The blue of lapis lazuli warded off evil — as did cobalt glass; it radiated good. In Babylon none but the ruler had the right to engrave his mark in blue lapis lazuli, while in Egypt lapis lazuli was regarded as the stone of heaven — blue, embedded in cloudlike white marble and sprinkled with yellow-gold pyrites: nature had made it in heaven's image.

The inadequate fusing techniques in use at the time made it impossible to develop glassmaking further. The only means of obtaining a stonelike glass — although this was not entirely free of bubbles — was by fritting the glass-mixture. This phase in the development of glassmaking corresponds to the period in metallurgy during which low pit-furnaces and bellows were used. It was not until the period between 500 and 50 B C that taller and more efficient pit-furnaces began to be used. At about this time the technique of fusing glass must have been improved so as to enable the glassmakers to keep a larger quantity of glass in a suitably fluid condition. This may have been a factor in the invention of glassblowing, for the blowing-tube was already in use for other purposes in the ancient Egyptian period.

Nature, by preparing materials containing impurities — some of them beneficial — became the instructor from whom the early glassmakers learned the processes of synthesis. This applies, for example, to the calcareous Egyptian desert sand near Thebes, near Tel el Amarna, by the Belus and on the Red Sea. Until the seventeenth century the glassmakers continued automatically to add chalk to the mixture.

Whereas it was possible for glaze, technically the earliest artificial glass, to develop independently of copper — although not before it (natural copper is thought to have been first used in about 5000 B C) — the working of glass depended upon the availability of tools which would withstand the heat of the viscous glass mass. Copper and bronze may not have been indispensable to the independent evolution of glass, but they contributed powerfully to the possibility of something new and different from the polished stones and frit emerging. The basis of the innovation was the fact that the material was worked in a heated state and was dependent upon it being viscous — viscosity being, indeed, the typical property which makes it possible for glass to be worked at all.

Just as bronze was 'invented' in the Near East, in China and in South America — despite the fact that it has proved impossible to discover any connection

The earliest centres of glassmaking

Many factors favoured Egypt, the country which has provided the greatest number of finds and the only one in which waste from glasshouses has so far been discovered. The only written records of glassmaking in the pre-Roman period, however, relate to Mesopotamia. Mycenae, Hallstatt (Celts, Illyrians) and China can all claim to have discovered glass independently of Egypt and Mesopotamia.

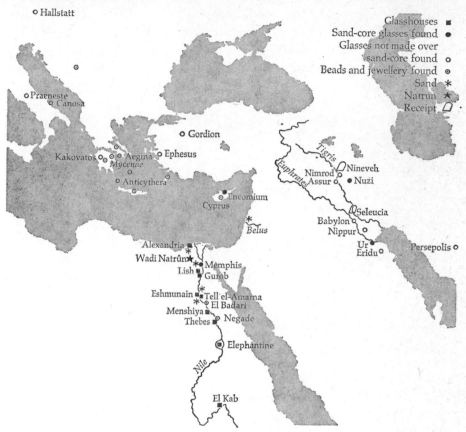

This map shows a few important sites where glass has been found and thereby indicates the area over which glass was made until approximately the last century before the present era and before the glassmaker's tube had permitted production to spread across the whole of the Roman Empire (page 29). The map also shows all the places which have so far — some rightly and some wrongly — been discussed as possible centres of glassmaking.

Two geographically distinct groups may be clearly recognised: the sand-core glasses in Egypt and in the eastern part of Mesopotamia from Ur to Nuzi and those glasses which were not made over sand-cores, which extend from Assyria in the east as far as Hallstatt in the north-west. As a result of the trading activities of the Phoenicians, the post-Egyptian sand-core glasses spread right across the whole Mediterranean zone.

Glasses not made over the sand-core are by no means homogeneous. Mycenaean glass is blue, glass beads made by the north Tirolean copper-smelters are red or blue, fragments of Assyrian glass which are drilled and cut and are an early form of 'luxury glasses' of a later date are sea-green and transparent. It is impossible to establish any connection between them — a fact which warrants the assumption that the inventions were made independently of one another.

between these areas — so it is known that glass was produced during the Bronze Age in different parts of the world, although it has not been possible to point to any way in which the knowledge might have been conveyed from one to the other. Thus Gero von Merhart has found that at about the turn of the first and second millenia BC — that is, during the Late Bronze Age in Europe — the copper-smelters of the North Tirol were producing not only raw copper and utensils but also numerous little ring-beads which they exported to many parts of Europe. The combination of concomitant substances is the same in the Tirolean Bronze-Age deposits of copper ore as in the glass beads found in the graves of cremated persons dating from the time of the Urnfield Culture. Impurities which can be identified by chemical analysis afford important indications of the origin and spread of glasses. We may suppose from this that the dross released when copper-ore was smelted was used to make glass.

A further indication that glass was discovered independently in the Late Bronze Age is afforded by the cast flat blue beads which have been found in the Pelopennese, in Attica and on Melos, Rhodes, Crete and Cyprus. Since the steatite moulds in which they were made have also survived they must be regarded as products of the Mycenaean civilisation. Other glass objects, however — a bowl from Kakovatos or tesserae for wall-decorations at Mycenae — might equally well be of Greek origin. The Mycenaean beads must be dated somewhere between the sixteenth and the thirteenth century BC, that is, during the time when the Egyptians were producing sand-core glasses. Later, in the third century BC, the Chinese independently discovered the process of glassmaking.

Most of the glasses of the early period have until now been found in Egypt. Favourable climatic conditions and the circumstances of the finds have undoubtedly contributed to the fact that the glass has come down to us in undamaged state. But the last word has not been spoken on the question of whether or not glass of an earlier date can be shown to have occurred in the countries north-west of Mesopotamia. Indeed the earliest known complete Egyptian glass vessel of the time of Queen Hatshepsut is exactly similar to glass from Mesopotamia and Nuzi.

Pottery, sculpture and copper-working had in both countries reached a sufficiently advanced stage of technical development to provide the conditions necessary for glassmaking. Mesopotamia had in many respects progressed further than Egypt: she had the earliest stanniferous bronzes, the earliest stamp-seals, and she produced glazes and frits containing silicic acid at the same time as Egypt, both countries making them of alkali and sand. But comparisons between the two civilisations are rendered extremely difficult by the fact that Mesopotamian datings are in many cases still uncertain.

It also remains far from proven that the Egyptians were the first to make glass jewellery. Nor can it be confirmed that they exported glass beads to Europe — as is often stated in the literature of the subject.

Sand-core glasses

We may gain some idea of the beauty of the earliest glasses — which were used either for jewellery or as inlays — from the wonderful glass jewellery found in the tomb of Tutankhamun (1344—35 B C). Although this work comes at the end of two hundred years' experience of making glass jewellery we can imagine how powerful the desire must have been, even at the outset of this period, to use 'precious stones' that could be made artificially for works of art of this kind. The inexhaustible scope that glass — and glass alone — already offered the craftsman was more likely to paralyse than to accelerate the urge to find new uses for the material.

If such complacency did exist among the Egyptians, it was shattered when it was confronted by oriental handcraft during the campaigns of Thotmes III (1490—36 B C). Even on the first campaign, after 1469 B C, undertaken to secure the Egyptian empire in the north-east, the enemy's display of magnificence must have made a deep impression on the Egyptians, for the tradition has lasted to this day. This contact with the exterior world acted as a spur to all the arts. Glass amulets, jewellery, inlays and glass vessels now began to be made in greater numbers.

During the cosmopolitan era initiated by Thotmes III, by the end of which the Egyptian empire stretched from the fourth cataract of the Nile as far as the Euphrates and took in the Aegean islands as well, Egypt was open to many foreign influences and was visited by many people from foreign lands. The prosperity of the country offered craftsmen abundant scope to develop. There is a whole series of glasses bearing the seal of Thotmes III, as well as glazed and painted faiences.

The earliest glass vessels are sand-core glasses and may have been made in one of two ways. By one method a core of sandy clay was dipped into the molten glass. When it was cold the sand was scraped out and the vessel was then cut and polished to give it its final form. The shapes were copied from stone vessels. The glass substance itself also had a stone-like appearance.

Besides this technique, which called for an extremely firm core, there was in all probability a second. By this process, the glass when hot and plastic was wound round the already shaped sand or clay core and then manipulated over the fire with polishing tools, spread, the rim bent outwards, the foot pressed out and threads of glass applied to form a pattern, these being then rolled into the body on a stone slab. In order to wind the basic 'gathering' of glass upon the core, more and more glass was probably pulled out of the molten mass with tongs — as Flinders Petrie has shown was the case with testing — so that as the work progressed several layers were added, one on top of the other. This winding process proves to be analagous with the procedure whereby glass is wound round a core in bead-making. Sand-core glasses 40 cm high were found in the tomb of Amenhotep II (c. 1437—11 BC); they are thought to have been imported from Mesopotamia, for no other Egyptian glasses of this period exceed 20 cm in height.

The colours of the sand-core glasses before Amenhotep III (c. 1401—63 BC) varied between light and dark blue, with occasional purple and white ones. They were decorated with threads running in curved or straight lines to form feather-patterns or festoons — also, very rarely, in zigzags.

There is no evidence of any break in glass-production between the reigns of Amenhotep III and Amenhotep IV. The glasses are identical.

The Egyptian glass-trade reached its greatest expansion during the Amarna period, thanks to the encouragement of Amenhotep IV (1363—46 BC), who called himself Akhnaton and built a new capital, Tell el-Amarna, on the banks of the Nile in Middle Egypt. In the sixth year of his reign he dedicated the city to the sun-god Aton and, with his wife Nefertite and his daughters, withdrew thither from Thebes. He abandoned his belief in Ammon, who had until then been revered as the sovereign deity of the Theban empire, and lived in monotheistic fanaticism, in pursuit of which he neglected the affairs of state. His mother and his wife left him. His third daughter's husband, Tutankhatun, became his heir, returned to Thebes, called himself Tutankhamun and died at the age of nineteen. Splendid examples of Egyptian glass were preserved for posterity in his tomb in the Valley of the Kings. Besides a vast quantity of glass jewellery, the Pharaoh's glass head-rest deserves special mention for its technical brilliance.

Despite the fact that General Harmahib, one of the subsequent pharaohs, had Tell el-Amarna systematically destroyed, examples of glass of the Amarna period were still found there during excavations in 1887—88, 1911—14 and 1923—29. Flinders Petrie says that there were three or four glasshouses and two large faience workshops in the city. They were situated between the great temple and the artisans' settlement. In addition to the base-walls of a kiln for glazed 'faience', quantities of glasscullet and faience moulds, there was also a hearth with flat bowls on inverted cylindrical pots. Flinders Petrie gives the following account of how the glass was made: the glass was melted in crucibles and then cooled. When the block of glass had hardened, the crucible, the scum on top and the sediment were knocked off. In this way an ingot of refined glass was obtained which was then crushed and re-fused. It is not impossible that the flat bowls found by Flinders Petrie were used for this second fusing process for they afforded a larger working surface (they measured 25 cm in diameter). The drops of glass which were found on the bottoms of the upturned pots also suggest that these flat bowls — which would be suitable for de-gassing the mixture — were used, not, as Flinders Petrie thought, for fritting, but for working glass-paste gems. The radiant heat given off by the larger surface of glass must also have been useful for the work of smoothing sand-core glasses held over the heat on bronze rods and for shaping their surfaces.

The nuances of colour in the glasses varied greatly. One of the causes of this lay in the inconsistencies — unrecognisable to the glassmaker of the period — of the raw material. Opaque fusions were used for vessels and beads; for inlays transparent ones were used as well. Blue was the commonest colour. Green, brown and yellow used as ground-colours were rare. Red was not used at all. Colourless transparent inlays were rare. The usual forms were those of the amphora and the krater with feet. Vessels without feet were rare.

As in the case of the earliest glasses, the commonest form of decoration was the festoon motif familiar since the Kamares vases of the Middle Minoan period. The existence of reciprocal influences in matters of art between the Minoan civilisation of Crete and Egypt is beyond dispute. Ludwig F. Fuchs goes so far as to conclude from this that Cretan craftsmen who had settled in Egypt were responsible for the early Egyptian glasses. In his chemical analysis of a Cretan glass, W. E. S. Turner found its composition to be the same as that of Egyptian glasses.

The occurence on these glasses of the wavy pattern composed of inlaid threads is probably not fortuitous. It may be symbolically connected with water. For the Greeks, from whom — if this supposition is true — the Egyptians borrowed it, water had a two-fold symbolic significance: it might be either the oblivion-bringing element of Lethe or the water of Mnemosyne, which both purified and evoked memories of the divine. There may be a connection here with the use of glasses in the cult of the dead and their employment as receptacles for consecrated oils. Mnemosyne was, however, not merely the goddess of memory but was also the mother of the Muses, which again may indicate that special store was set upon wares decorated in this way.

The Amarna period (1363–46 BC) is regarded as the apogee of the art of Egyptian glass and glazes. As regards the intensification and the spread of glassmaking this is certainly true. From the point of view of artistic quality, however, the glasses found in the tomb of Amenhotep II were equally fine and showed, indeed, greater variety than the wares of the Amarna period.

Apart from Tell el-Amarna there were glasshouses in Thebes, at Lish and at Menshiya. Suggestions that there were other workshops at Eshmunain, El Kab, Gurob and on Elephantine have so far proved impossible to confirm. Six glassmaking areas can, however, be clearly distinguished from the various colours and patterns of the Egyptian glass vessels.

No glasshouse of this early period is known outside Egypt. There are, however, vessels dating from the second millenium BC in Nuzi and Mesopotamia, for example, and dating from the period of the Second Assyrian Empire (eighth to seventh century BC) in Kish, for example (Iraq Museum, Bagdad).

Glasses of the pre-Christian era

The majority of early glasses are Egyptian sand-core vessels of closed form. Bowls have been found in the tomb of Amenhotep II, that is, as early as c. 1437—11 B C. It is not known how they were made.

The sand-core glasses were stone-like and opaque, but Sargon's vase from Assyria (second row right, 722—507 B C) is sea-green and transparent. Ancient recipes inscribed on clay-tablets record that arsenic was used as a refining alloy in the fusing of glass. Since the later Hellenistic luxury glasses (bottom row right) found in Asia Minor (Ephesus, Gordion) and Apulia (Canosa) as well as the glasses blown with the tube (page 31) were all transparent, it can be taken as certain that knowledge was passed from Assyria to Syria and Alexandria.
The first row shows glasses of the period 1500—970 B C: Egyptian krater and lenticular bottle, Mesopotamian bottle from Ur. The second row illustrates glasses of the period of the Phoenician traders between 750 and 300 B C: alabastron, pointed amphora, aryballos and, right, the vase of Sargon, King of Assyria, the first glass vessel not to be made over a core. The third row shows glasses of the Hellenistic period (300—30 B C); right, the bowl from Ephesus and above it a bowl from Canosa.

Egypt became impoverished by internal struggles under the successors of Rameses III (1182—51 BC). She lost the provinces of Palestine and Nubia. With the Dynasty (1200—1085 BC) the New Kingdom came to an end. About a hundred years later, in 970 BC, glassmaking in Egypt also came to a standstill. The only known find of the XXIst Dynasty (1085—950 BC) dates from the reign of Pinozem II; this is the glass found in the tomb of Nesikhonsu.

Egypt's economic influence ended as the Bronze Age gave way to the Iron Age. Egypt possessed no iron, so the focal point of world events moved to the eastern Mediterranean where the maritime peoples had already been using iron for some time (cf. page 316).

Centuries after the Egyptian period of glassmaking, sand-core glasses reappeared in the Mediterranean area. They came neither from Egypt nor from Alexandria. Their origins are still unknown. They continued to be made until the first century AD, when production finally ceased.

The general geographical and economic movements of the first century BC were towards the eastern Mediterranean area and the focal centre of glassmaking seems also to have become concentrated in this area. Glassmaking here and at this period is closely bound up with the trading activities of the Phoenicians. The centre of production may even have lain in Phoenicia. At all events, Phoenician glass was so much the most common that Pliny with absolute assurance attributed the discovery of glass to the Phoenicians.

While the glasses which the Phoenicians carried to so many parts have continued for thousands of years — indeed, until the present day — to arouse the interest of the world at large, a glass manufacture developed independently and almost unnoticed in the northern part of Mesopotamia and produced wares, which, although far fewer in number, are highly deserving of notice.

Hellenistic luxury glasses

At the turn of one period, as it begins to be superseded by the next and the two run parallel for a while before finally separating, when the old is moribund and the new is beginning to assert itself, tensions which are most interesting to observe usually become evident. In the first period of glassmaking, the sand-core glasses — having reached their artistic apogee at an early stage — were not simply supplanted by the sudden invention of the glass-blower's tube; instead, a transparent glass which was not made over a core developed in Assyria at the beginning of the first millenium BC. From these beginnings grew a manufacture of luxury glasses which reached its zenith in the Hellenistic period.

At Nimrod, not far from Nineveh on the Tigris, a clumsy, thick-sided alabastron dating from the eighth century BC was found; it has a cylindrically bored opening and carries the seal of Sargon II (722 —705), King of Assyria. This vase was obviously not made over a sand core. The glass substance is also quite different from the usual, being sea-green and at this thickness quite transparent. This glass together with a series of similar finds may be regarded as a coherent group. They are Assyrian glasses of the period between the late eighth and the late seventh century BC. It is assumed that Sargon II fostered the art of glassmaking.

A glass bowl was found at Gordion dating from the same period and made of the same type of material. It is believed to have been made by slowly heating crushed glass-powder between an outer and an inner mould. There is another hypothesis according to which it is suggested that a 'lost model' may have been used, which would correspond to the process of *fonte à cire perdue*.

The bowl from Gordion is ribbed and has a navel-like boss (omphalos) on the bottom. The glass was found lying in a bronze omphalos bowl and was shaped from it. Bronze bowls of this type have been found both in Assyria and at Hallstatt. Strangely enough, however, there were glass vessels not made over a sand core in the first millenium BC not only in Assyria but also at Hallstatt. Those at Hallstatt were the '*Hallstätter Tässchen*', or small cups.

The tradition of the Nimrod glasses persisted in Asia Minor. A series of widely separated finds dating from the seventh to the sixth centuries BC (cf. page 44) makes it seem probable that Assyria also had a glass industry under Ashurbanipal — evidence for this is afforded by the collection of glass recipes of the seventh century found at Nineveh. And the earliest written record of glassmaking — the Babylonian clay-tablet of the seventeenth century BC deciphered by Gadd and Thompson — also shows that the tradition of glassmaking in Mesopotamia goes back to very early times. It persisted in Achsemenid Persia and into the Hellenistic period. One of these finds, made at Ephesus in the fourth century BC, is particularly remarkable for being the earliest known glass with engraved decoration. It is a bowl with a central petal-motif.

During the Hellenistic period Alexandria and its sphere of influence inherited the tradition of the luxury glasses not made over a sand core, while, as a result of the introduction of blown glass, Syria became the centre of mass-production. A number of outstanding luxury glasses dating from the second half of the first millenium BC have been attributed to Alexandria, which, in the third century BC, became a centre of late Hellenistic Roman civilisation. The celebrated Alexandrian library, founded by Ptolemy II (283—46 BC), was of paramount importance in furthering the spread of the Hellenistic genius. In the sphere of art, between the third century BC and the fourth century

A D Alexandria, besides producing new literary works and new themes, subject-matter and motifs in painting and sculpture, produced fresh creations in glass as well. It becomes obvious time and again how strongly glassmaking is influenced by the general cultural life of a period.

Ever aspiring to the highest, Alexandria borrowed the experiences of the Egyptian, Syrian and Assyrian glassmakers and developed them to unsurpassed perfection. Mosaic glasses — which have become celebrated under the name of 'Murrhine bowls' or *millefiori* glasses — are of Egyptian origin. Already at Tell el-Amarna experiments with glass threads, tubes and beads had resulted in the first application of this technique. It consisted in laying different coloured threads next to one another to form a rod with a patterned section. The pattern might be geometric, floral or figural (heads and grotesques). The rods could be cut to make *millefiori* beads, or the resulting little discs with geometric or floral patterns could be fused together to make *millefiori* glasses; these were mostly bowls — certainly no closed forms were made. In many of them the rim was surrounded by a band of twisted threads of different colours (later known as *reticelli*). Rim surrounds like this in fact occurred on the earliest Egyptian glasses of the middle of the second millenium B C. Coloured bands, sometimes combined with flat pieces of *millefiori* glass, were made into vessels in the same way as true *millefiori* glasses. The bands could also be plaited from *reticelli* cords. Gold too was sometimes enclosed in these mosaic glasses.

Onyx glasses may be regarded as a further development of the mosaic technique. They were made by fusing together glass threads or bands of different colours and were veined like onyx. In some pieces sharply drawn stripes run in a zigzag formation and these recall the thread-decoration of the sand-core glasses, whereas in most onyx glasses the stripes merge more softly into the ground-colour.

Engraved glasses — the forerunner of which we encountered in the bowl from Ephesus — are of Assyrian origin. Cameo glasses with figural scenes appeared for the first time in Alexandria during the first century B C. Here the dark ground is overlaid with a pale, opaque glass. These glasses owe their fame rather to the glass-engravers than to the glassmakers themselves, although the impeccable combination of two different glass-fusions which was achieved in these layered, or 'flashed', glasses ranks among the most astonishing accomplishments of ancient glass technique. The glasses (bottles, jugs, amphorae, urns) enjoyed a high reputation and in the first century A D were also engraved in Rome. It is in fact the most celebrated pieces of this type — to which the Portland Vase belongs — which have been attributed to Roman cameo-engravers.

Finally, these Hellenistic luxury glasses, early though they were, also included glasses with gold inserts. They consist of two bowls which fit into one another and are fused together, the inner one having had gold leaf attached to it for decoration. There are only very few gold glass bowls of this period in existence. The most important and the best preserved are two that were found at Canosa. A more recent find, made at Gordion in 1955, is important — despite the fact that it consists of only a few fragments of a bowl — because it makes a more exact dating possible. It comes from a Hellenistic stratum of the period before the Roman victory over Antiochos III near Magnesia (189 BC). It is mere supposition that these glasses were made in Alexandria; they may equally well have been made at Antioch, at that time the capital of Syria.

Hallstätter Tässchen — which we have already mentioned — are vertically ribbed Celtic bowls dating from the sixth to the fifth century BC. Similar bowls, except that they have high curved handles and threads in contrasting colours applied in a zigzag line, were found at Santa Lucia, near Trieste, a district inhabited by Illyrian tribes. Beads and ornamental clasps and the like with similar thread decoration were made in the sixth century BC in Aquileia, not far away. And further south-east, within the Illyrian region — that is, in present-day Yugoslavia — glass hoop-shaped fibulae with bronze pins were made of fragments of Celtic glass bracelets. These Celtic and Illyrian finds of the La Tène period and the Tirolean ring-beads of the Bronze Age (page 18) show that from the Alps to the Adriatic coast a tradition existed which extended far back into pre-Roman times.

Imperial Rome

Not surprisingly, the golden age foretold by Virgil in the Fourth Eclogue of the *Bucolica* never dawned; yet the Augustan Age, regarded by the Romans as the good old days, became in retrospect so far transfigured that it may almost be called a golden age. It was a period of achievement in glassmaking, during which both technique and artistry developed to the full. Glass-blowing was invented at the beginning of the period, just at the right moment — as is so often the case with inventions — to accommodate itself to the cultural and civilising needs and the economic receptiveness of this golden age. Just as the use of utilitarian glass spread to an unprecedented extent because it not only provided the material for drinking vessels but also served certain purposes connected with those essential pillars of Roman civilisation, baths and games, so, because it fitted in with the cultural needs of the time, the manufacture of luxury glass attained great heights of artistry. The effects of Roman civilisation, culture and technique long remained active and continued to bear fruit during a period which could really no longer be considered a golden age. Glass-blowing is thought to have been invented in the Syrian city of Sidon. The earliest blown glasses to have been found date from the middle of the first century BC. By the year AD 50 technical methods had reached a degree of maturity at which they could be made economically viable. This technical maturity consisted partly in the development and use of tools and moulds and partly in the improvement of the glass-substance. The original stone-like glasses of previous centuries had given way to those transparent, fragile structures which are, indeed, the only ones which fit our latter-day idea of glass.

The first blown wares were made of deliberately coloured glass-fusions. The main colours are blue, green, honey-colour and dark amber and purple. There is also milky white glass. The 'natural' colour of glass — which always contains impurities of a ferrous nature — is bluish-green. It can be seen in certain small *balsamaria*, which appear at first to have been the only ones to have been made of uncoloured glass. Shapes were formed by negative moulds in two or more sections made of fired clay, wood or metal; when the pieces had cooled and been removed from the moulds, the body was reheated and handles, threads and feet were attached. As early as the first century AD *entrepreneurs* with an eye to business were putting moulded inscriptions giving the name of their firm on the vessels. The best-known was called Ennion; others were Ariston, Artas, Hirenaios, Frontinus, Iason, Menes and Neikon. All were probably Syrians. Their names might be found anywhere in the Roman Empire, for they opened branches in Italy, in the Rhineland, in Britain and on the Black Sea. They naturally set up their glasshouses in places where suitable raw materials were available.

Apart from the sand of the Belus, one of the best-known glassmaking sands in antiquity was that which occurred in Campania at the mouth of the Volturnus, mentioned by Pliny. Here, between Cumae and Liternum, the glass-industry settled; the workers were Alexandrians and there was even a glass-makers' quarter in Puteoli. By AD 14 Rome also possessed a glasshouse; it was situated at the Porta Cassena and later on Mons Coelius. Strabo (63 BC–AD 20) wrote of clear glass made in Rome.

We can tell the extent to which glassmaking spread through the Roman Empire once blowing had been invented, from the striking number of finds dating from as long ago as the first century AD which have been made in the east, in Italy and in the west. 350 glasses dating from the first century were found in the burial-places of Locarno alone; among them was a facet-cut beaker and a painted bowl. This shows that by that time glass was already in general use in the Alpine regions. The glasses found in central and southern Italy have been no less numerous; only here — in Rome and Pompeii, for example — more pieces of the Alexandrian type than of the Syrian, blown kind have been found. This suggests that the Roman upper classes and the pensioners at Pompeii liked the luxury glass; but it does not preclude the fact that engraved glasses were also made — as Ulpian records — at Aquileia in northern Italy. The Syrians, however, seem to have penetrated further north. In Europe to the north of the Alps glassmaking spread to the valleys of the Rhône, the Saône, the Moselle and the Rhine. During the second century the industry became established in Trier and Cologne. It then spread north-west to present-day Belgium and to the wooded country on both sides of the modern frontier between France and Belgium, to the valleys of the Meuse, the Sambre and the Oise, and even as far as Britain.

Glasshouses seem to have existed in Spain even before the coming of the Romans — as is indicated by the curious glass-moulds which have been found there in addition to glasses of the Roman period.

Glassmaking did not spread only in a westerly direction, although the west certainly exerted the strongest attraction. Blown glasses dating from the second century have also been found in Mesopotamia and southern Russia. The individuality of the forms and decorations suggests that these are not mere imported glasses from Syria. Such glasses were certainly found in all parts, even beyond the Limes and other boundaries, in Scotland, Denmark, the north Germanic countries, Scandinavia, Afghanistan and in the Sahara. They reached these places by way of trade or plunder.

It can hardly be a matter of surprise that in the Roman Empire, in which, with its remarkably dense network of roads and good shipping services, men came into contact with one another through trade and military service, often being relegated to some remote corner far from their homes, the glasses show similarities from which it is always inferred that the new glasshouses maintained links with the parent factories in Syria and Alexandria. Similarities of style and fashion — in details of borders, for example — persisting over a long period cannot be explained in any other way. Wares in all parts of the Empire so greatly resembled one another that it is almost impossible to attribute them to any one factory. The available glass analyses even suggest that the newly established glasshouses continued for centuries to receive supplies of soda from the Near East.

Alexandria and Syria had specialised — though not exclusively — in a few groups of glasses. The emphasis in Egypt during the early Imperial period was on cut and polished glass, a trend which was probably influenced by the artistic metal-work then flourishing in Alexandria. It is not impossible that this influence extended even to methods of glass-working, the processes of casting and pressing being adapted to the special nature of the ductile glass-fusion. For the forms of metal to be imitated in glass is a familiar 'sin of youth' and should be regarded as a symptom of the beginning of a trend. Thus prototypes in metal-work are recognisable in these forms. This is particularly true of the so-called Pterotos types of the first and second centuries. These are bowls with

The spread of glassmaking

A fortunate conjunction of political, economic and technical circumstances — the annexation of Syria (64 BC), Octavius's victory at Actinum (31 BC) and the addition of Egypt to the Empire, flourishing trade, increasing prosperity and the invention of glass-blowing — all these resulted in a swift spread of glassmaking at the beginning of the Roman Empire. As early as the first decades after the birth of Christ glasshouses appeared in Italy and in the Iberian Peninsular. The main movement was towards Rome, the metropolis, where the Alexandrian luxury glasses were in the greatest demand. By AD 14 glass was already being fused in Rome and in Puteoli. The fame of Italy, however, resided rather in the art of cameo-engraving, which was carried on both in Rome and Aquileia. Glass-blowing, executed by Syrians, became established in Gaul and, during the first century AD, spread north of the Alps. In the second century it reached Cologne and Trier, where glass-blowers and glass-cutters found themselves side by side once more. Knowledge of glassmaking spread north-west from here to reach Britain. The present map shows the area over which glassmaking had spread by the fall of the Western Roman Empire (AD 493). For greater intelligibility modern names have been given, as well as the names for places and rivers.

* Sand
⊞ Natrun

Knowledge of the method of glassmaking reached eastwards as far as India as early as the third century BC. At the same period there was glass in China which had been evolved indigenously. During the Han (206 BC–AD 220) and the T'ang (AD 618–906) periods, nevertheless, the Chinese imported glass from the west by the Silk Road.

The most important sources of raw materials for glassmaking in the Roman Empire were the sands of the Belus, the Volturnus and the Rhine, while soda continued until the Middle Ages to come from Egypt and Syria. The ashes of the plant *Salicornia* are named as far back as the recipes in Assurbanipal's library of clay-tablets of the seventh century BC as a source of alkali. The natural soda from the salt-lakes of the Wadi Natrun were also used as an alkali raw material. Egypt and Syria (and later Spain) continued into the eighteenth century to supply the glasshouses of Europe with soda. Only the glasshouses north of the Alps where *Waldglas* was made (from the tenth century) were independent of these sources of raw materials.

Astonishingly enough, despite their remoteness, the glasshouses of the Rhine must for four centuries have maintained their links with the parent-houses in Syria, for it is impossible to explain in any other way the fact that the two developments were identical, down to technical details of production.

two projecting handles above the loops of which are horizontal mouldings. It is possible that enamel-painting on glass, which is found in Alexandria from the second to the fourth century, also derives from metal prototypes. Glass having in its early days been modelled on the forms of metal-work, and on those of ceramics, was later — when silver became scarce under Septimius Severus (193—211) — used as a substitute.

Behind the technique of cutting and engraving glass certainly lay a tradition of stone-carving in the Near East which reached back over at least 4000 years. Its greatest days, however, were seen in Rome and in Cologne. As regards precious stones, deeply incised (intaglio) gems were largely used as the stones in the rings with which the owner impressed his seal in wax; while cameos, with their high-relief carving, were used to decorate cups. As regards glasses, engraving and facetting are found on first-rate glass-material in the second to the third century. Intaglio work is also found in Cologne during the third century but not relief carving; this was cultivated in Alexandria and particularly in Rome. Of the few known glasses with relief carving, most have an opaque white outer layer out of which the relief is cut. The basic glass is blown, measures some 3 mm in thickness and is usually dark blue; these glasses show marks of the cutting wheel both inside and out. Mythological scenes were the favourite themes for the reliefs: Bacchus and amoretti appear most often, but sometimes there are only grapes and leafy tendrils.

The Portland Vase is undoubtedly the most celebrated of these pieces. It owes its fame to a number of circumstances: the scene portrayed has not been identified and this fact has led to repeated discussions among art historians. But the activities surrounding the vase have done more than art-historical or scholarly issues to bring it before the public eye. The vase is thought originally to have been a pointed amphora, the point having been later replaced by a flat bottom, on which Paris is portrayed wearing the Phrygian cap. It stood in the Palazzo Barberini, that celebrated masterpiece of Roman Baroque on the Quirinal in Rome, and had, according to tradition, been found in a sarcophagus, where it held the ashes of a Roman emperor. But this later proved to be untrue. It was bought from the Barberini family by a Scot, who resold it for £1000 to Sir William Hamilton, the British ambassador in Naples — not, however, before he had taken a mould of it, made sixty copies and disposed profitably of the reproductions as well. The Duchess of Portland bought the vase from Hamilton for £1800 and put it in her cabinet of curiosities. Soon afterwards the Duchess of Gordon broke the vase — and the chronicle records the fact that this temperamental lady had caused a sensation when she was still a child by riding through the streets of Edinburgh on a pig. The vase was then placed on loan at the British Museum, where in 1845 a young scene-painter unaccountably smashed it to smithereens — in fact into more than 200 pieces which were glued together again by a skilled restorer named John Doubleday. Fortunately

Roman domestic glass

The discovery of glass-blowing in the first century BC in Syria made it possible to produce glasses in great quantity to meet the demand created by Roman civilisation. These included drinking-vessels and wine-bottles, *balsamaria* for the baths and beakers with circus scenes. Syrian glass manufacturers with an eye to business set up branch-establishments in many parts of the Roman Empire. Many of the glasses carry their names, which were incised in the moulds used as part of the process of blowing.

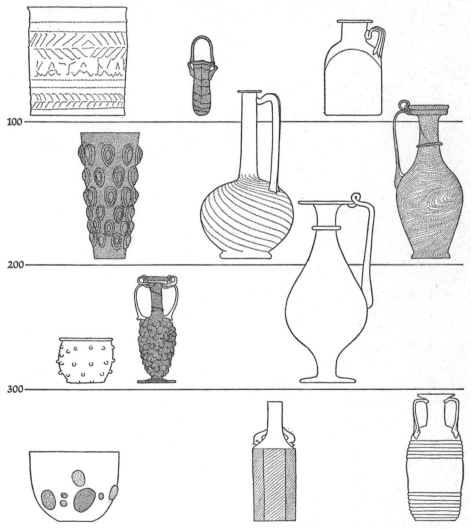

The first row shows examples of the three ways in which blown glass could be made: a Syrian beaker made in a mould throughout the whole process; a free-blown Syrian *balsamarium*; a jug with a celery-handle first blown in a mould and then finished freely. Second-century specimens: lotus-bud beaker; 'optically blown' bottle; lekythos. Third-century specimens: beaker with fused glass drops; bottle with grape-like bosses; jug with handle. Fourth-century specimens: beaker with coloured drops in the German taste; bottle with handles in the form of dolphins; jug with hoops, signed 'Fron' (Frontinus).

our smart Scot had already had copies made, of which one now did service as a model. The scandal was completed when the scene-painter was fined a mere three pounds for damaging the glass case, while for some far-fetched legal reason the basic action went unpunished. The vase again became a topic of conversation when in 1790 Josiah Wedgwood copied it in stoneware. The copy was successful, was favourably regarded everywhere and so became an advertisement for the Wedgwood factory — which it has remained to the present day. In 1876 John Northwood copied the Portland Vase in glass.

What, in fact, are the scenes portrayed on this famed and mysterious Portland Vase? The subject has been discussed times without number and two interpretations have emerged which seem most probable: the scenes may be from either the legend of Peleus and Thetis or that of Theseus and Ariadne. The protagonist may thus be Peleus seeking his wife, the goddess Thetis, in the kingdom of his father-in-law, the sea-god Nereus, and his consort Doris, and finding her in the company of Hermes and Aphrodite — marriage with the sea-princess must have been very cold (this is how Haynes, of London, interprets the scene): or, if the second hypothesis were true, the youth would be Theseus as he approaches Poseidon in his search for Minos's ring, while the second scene would show him with Ariadne on Naxos in the presence of Aphrodite the goddess of love (such is the interpretation of Möbius, of Bad Homburg).

The Portland Vase is thought to be the work of Roman glass-cutters of the first century AD. It is not impossible that the glass itself came from Alexandria, especially as the writings of Ulpian inform us that the *diatretarii* obtained raw glasses from the glasshouses. Confidence in the quality of the Alexandrian glass may have been matched by the desire not to waste the laborious work of cutting and engraving on poor material. Although Ulpian, the lawyer, stresses the liability of the glasshouse vis-à-vis the *diatretarius* in matters of damaged material, it was surely wiser to avoid endangering the work because of the material.

This passage in Ulpian has provided a powerful argument in the controversy over the way in which the glasses of the *diatretarii* were made and has been used by Otto Doppelfeld to support the theory that they were cut, against the hypothesis that they were plastically shaped. If it is accepted that the *diatretarii* also made the glasses which go by their name, this instance of liability means that the raw glasses they used were obtained from one glasshouse. If this is so, they could only have been worked cold and could not have been shaped while in the hot plastic state, although K. Wiedemann's plastically made copies have led to surprising results. Indeed, the last and most important *vasa diatreta* to have been found — it was excavated in Cologne in 1960 — shows extremely clearly that this glass was made from different-coloured pre-blown raw glass and then cut. Doppelfeld, who published the find, rightly pointed out that, as in other fields, so with glass, reticulated work forms the pinnacle of the technical achievement of the art-historical period in question.

So far nineteen *vasae diatretae* have been found, three in Cologne, one each in Trier, Strasbourg, Bonn and Budapest, in Italy and Austria, but the majority on the northern frontier of the Empire. They all consist of a network surrounding a beaker which has no foot but sometimes carries an inscription in raised letters. The Situla Pagana, which entered the Treasury of San Marco when Venice conquered Byzantium in the year 1204, is an exception. It is a glass bucket *(situla)* 20 cm high with a hooped handle and a stand; the network is at the sides only. It consists of a chequered pattern surmounted by a hunting scene including two riders, dogs and a panther. The method by which another famous example of ancient glass was made has also remained totally unexplained; this is Lycurgus's beaker, which has been dated to about AD 300. It shows Lycurgus, King of Thrace, fatally entwined in the tendrils of a vine. Dionysus had in fact changed the nymph Ambrosia, whom Lycurgus had assaulted, into a vine. A shepherd, Pan, Ambrosia herself, and a panther complete the group. What is unusual is that the beaker appears olive-green or ruby-red according to how the light strikes it. Analysis of a splinter taken from it has shown that it contains three to five *per cent* gold, which explains why the colours change. Eberhard Schenk zu Schweinsberg has conjectured that this property might make the beaker a magic vessel, in which water could be changed into wine.

In the case of pseudo-*vasae diatretae* ornaments and figures are not cut out of the complete piece but are applied at a later stage to the glass after it has been reheated. Such pieces include the beaker decorated with shell-fish motifs (page 58).

Among early Christian wares from catacombs and graves of the third to the fourth centuries, the gold glasses are the best known. The majority of these were glasses with gold inserts like those of the Hellenistic period which have already been mentioned as having been found at Canosa. Although they are mere fragments, the early Christian glasses show greater variety in the use of this technique, most noteworthy being the combinations of gold with coloured glass, and gold medallions etched with a needle which were cemented into the tombs or to the catacomb-walls. They portrayed biblical scenes.

Enamel-painting also became popular in Alexandria in the period between the second and the fourth century. Only one example dating from an earlier period is known, the jug of Thotmes III of c. 1500 BC. But many painted glasses of the Roman period have been preserved, including some specimens of cold-painting. One of the most remarkable pieces was found in southern Russia. This is an opaque-white jug on which Apollo and Daphne are shown between scattered flowers and a gold rim. It is preserved in the Corning Museum of Glass in New York and is dated to the second-third century.

One final method of decoration employed during the Roman Imperial period remains to be mentioned; this is the practice of engraving the surface with flint, rock-crystal or other minerals. Having closely examined a dish decorated with circus scenes (page 51), La Baume came to the conclusion that a fine cutting technique using a small wheel, sand and water had been employed. The diamond was still unknown as a specific type of mineral.

The shaping of the viscous glass — or working the glass — was also perfected as development went forward. W. E. S. Turner has drawn attention, for example, to a large blown-glass bottle which was found in the royal tombs of the third century at Balana in Nubia and is preserved in the Museum of Antiquities in Cairo. The bottle, which resembles a modern acid container, is made of dark olive-green glass, stands 55 cm high and 45 cm wide and weighs 7.72 kilograms. A glass-fusion of at least 9 kilograms would have to have been prepared in order to make this bottle.

An old decorative technique already used on sand-core glasses consisted of applying hot threads of glass straight from the fire. This technique is found again later on Frankish and early Islamic glasses. It was used in Roman times for making handles, among other purposes; in some of these several threads were laid side by side to form a broad ribbon-like 'celery handle'.

An unusual form of thread decoration came into fashion at the end of the second century in Syria and in Cologne; this is known as snake-thread decoration. Patterns are made of white and coloured threads in whorls so exact that R. Penkert even suggested that they were pre-shaped on a hot iron-plate. Snake-thread glasses have never been made elsewhere or at any other period.

It was different with the optical blowing which began in the third century. Here the glass was first blown in a cylindrical mould with grooves running lengthways and then blown freely, the grooves corresponding to those of the mould; it could also, for example, be turned and the grooves made to run spirally round the vessel — as was, in fact, often done. If the glass were blown against a flat plate, the raised pattern occurred only on the inside; but it looked as though it had been 'optically' patterned. This technique was well suited to the material and long continued to be employed.

A cup decorated with shells dating from the fourth century and found in Cologne represents a pinnacle of fine workmanship in glassmaking. It is a straight-sided cup on a fairly low foot and is surrounded by four vertical bands of three shells each and by twisted threads, all springing from a network circle. The shell-shapes and supporting structure were pressed on to the glass while it was still ductile with a special pair of tongs (page 54).

Nuppengläser came into use in the fourth century, originally in imitation of precious stones in precious-metal settings. Drops of coloured glass or threads rolled out to form button-like shapes were applied to transparent glasses.

The variety of Roman glass, of which all this is evidence, is further proof of

Luxury glasses of the Roman Imperial period

Precious glasses, masterpieces of the glass-blower *(vitrearius)* or the glass-cutter *(diatretarius)*, were made in Alexandria, Rome, Aquileia and Cologne. Some of them are famous pieces whose fortunes are of interest. They were made, among other purposes, for burial rites and as prizes for the victors at the circus games or gladiatorial combats. For important commissions Alexandrian glass was preferred — at any rate in the form of raw glass which would be finished by the *diatretarii*. At the time of Severus Alexander (AD 222—235), Egypt, which was bound to pay tribute to Rome, was still obliged to settle part of her 'income-tax' in glasses.

The medallion-shaped glasses with gold inserts *(fondi d'oro)* found in the Roman catacombs must also be counted among the distinctive glasses of the Roman Imperial period.

Specimens of the first century AD: bowl of the pterotos type; vase with cameo-engraved decoration; vase and cover. Specimens of the second century: facet-cut beaker; cup with snake-thread decoration; kantharos (forerunner of the glass cup). Specimens of the third century: beaker decorated with shell-fish motifs; Lycurgus's beaker; bottle (forerunner of the *Kuttrolf*). Specimens of the fourth century: 'Situla Pagana'; cup decorated with shells; diatreton.

the great inventiveness and technical talent of the Romans, whose technical achievements in so many spheres astonish us. As regards glass technique, they fully exhausted every possibility known to the age in which they lived. They reached a level of craftsmanship which has remained basically unchanged to the present day. They prepared the way experimentally for many processes which became more important later on. Glass mirrors coated with silver amalgam were known to them and they made window-panes as well. Glass panes can be shown to have been used as early as the first half of the first century AD in the baths at Pompeii and Herculaneum. The use of glass panes must have become extremely widespread after this, for an inscription of the third century on a gravestone in Carnuntum shows that among the troops stationed there, there was a 'window-glass master of the fourteenth legion'.

Whereas the technique of blowing hollow glasses can be considered to have been similar throughout the Empire, various regions seem to have developed their own methods of making glass panes. At all events, the panes must have been made in many different places, for both the forms and the materials vary greatly. It had long been assumed from the marks left by tools that window-panes were at that period always made by pouring the molten glass and then pulling it out with metal tools to increase its width. In 1959, however, D. B. Harden published research which led him to conclude that in the western part of the Roman Empire window-panes were made from glass cylinders which were cut and stretched in a furnace; while broad, discus-shaped glass balloons were found in the east — evidence of a process similar to that used in making crown-glass and employed many centuries later in the manufacture of bull's-eye panes. The use of cylinders has until recently always been dated to the period of Theophilus (tenth century) because he was the first to describe it. Now, according to Harden, it too should be attributed to the Romans. This exploration of every technical possibility naturally from time to time produced results which cannot exactly be counted among the great classical works of art. This is particularly true of the great quantities of vessels in the form of heads, gladiators' helmets and other shapes which were blown in negative moulds, and of the whole category of glasses which were made in a mould from first to last, thus removing all opportunity for free hand-work, imagination or inspiration. Their shaping and decoration were basically the business not of the glass-blower but of the mould-maker. Nevertheless, all the wares of the Roman glassmakers — particularly the Gallic beakers with scenes from the circus — are much sought after by collectors — and rightly so, for the passage of centuries has made them valuable more than anything else as products of a period in which the foundations of our life and civilisation were laid and which has thus the power to inspire later generations.

Frankish glasses

The Hun assault of AD 375 set the Ostrogoths moving and unleashed the Barbarian Invasions, which ended in 568 when the Langobardi settled in Italy. During this period of nearly two hundred years Christianity became the state religion (AD 380), the Roman Empire was divided (AD 395) and the Merovingians founded the Frankish kingdom (AD 486). In AD 493 Dietrich of Berne, otherwise known as Theodoric the Great, murdered Odoacer and the Western Roman Empire fell.

The term 'Frankish glasses' used by historians of glass embraces a group of glass vessels found in the period from about 400 to about 700 over an area which extends from Lake Constance to southern Norway and from Bohemia to Britain. Most of the finds have, however, been made in Belgium, from which it may be assumed that the centres of production were there. The fact that they spread eastwards is due to the bartering which took place between the Franks and the Slavs, who settled in Bohemia in the second half of the sixth century. So Frankish glasses even spread north-eastwards across the Vistula. Johann Knobloch's etymological studies have led him to the discovery that *stoklo*, the Slav word for glass, dates back to these trade connections.

The influence of the Teutons on the outward form of the glasses had been obvious in the Rhineland and in Gaul even before the actual period of the Barbarian Invasions, when Teutonic tribes settled on the northern frontier of the Roman Empire, becoming confederates and undertaking the defence of the frontier in return for annual allowances. There are, for example, a number of *Nuppenschalen* dating from the early fourth century. From one to three rows of round green, red, purple or brown 'eyes' were applied in the form of drops of hot glass to the pale green glass bowl. This colourfulness was to the taste of the Goths, whose brightly hued style derived from southern Russia. The eyes served to ward off demons, as did the 'wolf's tooth' which ran round the bowl in the form of a zigzag coloured thread or pinched band (page 57).

Belief in demons, drinking customs and burial rites certainly influenced the form, decoration and use of glasses. According to Nordic saga, the tribal mother proffered the love-drink in the drinking horn, which was then passed round. The libation in this case is not, of course, a love-potion but a gesture of respect to a god or of remembrance of a dead person. Glass drinking horns, which are found as early as the third century, derive from the horn of the aurochs, whose strength the huntsman took upon himself as he drank from its horn. This rite and the drinking horns themselves occurred among almost every people, but only the Teutons had drinking horns of glass. Thirty have so far been found, in pairs. Most were found in women's graves. Traces of liquid in a pair of ox-horns discovered in a bog in Jutland have been analysed and one horn was found to contain wheaten beer while the other held honey mead. These findings may also perhaps derive from some particular rite. The custom of placing objects in graves in pairs was carried over to the cone-beakers (*Spitzbecher*), which did not come into existence before the fourth century.

Four types of glass drinking horns may be distinguished, the earliest of which faithfully imitates the form and curvature of the natural horn. These drinking horns, which were exported as far as Sweden and Finland, are decorated with threads, some of them with snake-threads, and were therefore made in Cologne. Those of the second group have a flattened end and are thought to have originated at Namur in the fourth century. It is from this form that the cone-beaker derives; it has plain thread-decoration. The drinking horns of the third and fourth groups both belong to the fifth and sixth centuries, although one is Frankish while the other has been found in Lombardic graves in Italy. The Lombardic group carries white threads in wide spirals on vividly coloured glass. These horns are less elegant in shape than those of the north. 'Eyes' and 'wolves' teeth' are also found on drinking horns.

The earliest cone-beakers had a stunted foot but they were later made without this foot, like most Frankish beakers which the drinker had to empty before he could stand them on the lip. This lack of a foot and the colour — which varies between a greenish and a brownish hue — is characteristic of Frankish glasses. The metal is always full of flaws and bubbles.

If the 'natural-coloured' Frankish glasses — which are coloured only by the impurities of the raw materials — be compared with the colourless, transparent or clear-coloured glasses of the Roman period, it will be found that the art of glassmaking in the refined and highly cultivated form practised by the Romans had come to an abrupt halt. The cause of this may have been the march of the Vandals through the Rhineland and Gaul in the year 406. Perhaps also, when Cologne passed into the possession of the Teutons, the surviving glass-makers moved across the Meuse towards Belgium, where the centres of the glassmaking industry now lay, while for a time the glasshouses of Cologne lost their importance. (Raimond Chambon in 1952 found traces of two Merovingian glass-furnaces at Macquenoise.) This does not, however, explain the sudden change in style. Moreover, the failure of imports of raw materials could account only for the deterioration in quality of the metal and the lack of certain colours. Lack of reinforcements of specialist workers from the east might have had the same effect. Clearly, however, there is no trace of any intention to carry on the Roman tradition with inadequate means and man-power; on the contrary, new habits are now in the ascendant and new men with different aesthetic ideals and needs which glass now has to meet. Thus the majority of Frankish glasses are drinking vessels in the shape of bells, horns or bags, without handles, without foot and with rounded lips — except for the

Teutonic glasses

The customs and the sense of form of the Teutons was the determining factor in glassmaking north of the Alps during the period 400–700 BC. These 'Frankish glasses' are for the most part drinking beakers blown from greenish-brownish glass and later also from blue and amber-coloured glass, without handle or foot and neither cut nor painted. The only decoration is grooving or threading. The Teutonic custom was for the drinker, when he had emptied his glass, to stand it on its rim in order to ward off the evil eye. The rims are rounded, except for the drinking horns, in which they are sharp. Frankish glasses extended mainly over what is now Belgium, the Rhine-Main region, Britain, southern Norway and the island of Gothland. Teutonic influence had been apparent as early as the third century (cf. page 31) in the coloured 'eyes' and 'wolf teeth', which were supposed to afford protection against demons.

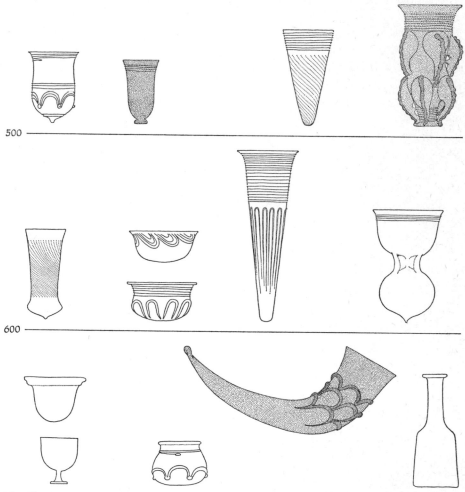

The illustrations show the following examples dating from the fifth century: *Sturzbecher* with inlaid white threads, a bell-cup, a small grooved *Spitzbecher* after the Roman pattern, a *Rüsselbecher*. Sixth-century pieces: grooved *Sturzbecher*, two bowls, large *Spitzbecher* with applied threads, *Kuttrolf*. Seventh-century pieces: tumbler, stem-glass, *Kugelbecher* beaker with inlaid threads, drinking horn with applied threads and a bottle.

drinking horns which have a sharp rim. The only remaining decoration is the grooving which the vessel acquired from the mould, and the threads which were applied later. These consisted either of opaque-white threads which were fused into the body in the form of a garland or feather pattern — these were employed in the fifth century particularly — or of applied threads made of the same glass as the body. The most usual are delicate spirals applied to the rim; less common is an elaborate form of decoration composed of thick threads rising in slender arches from the point — these are already luxury glasses of a kind. The *Rüsselbecher* or claw-beaker with its hollow, plastic projections resembling elephants' trunks *(Rüssel)* is an exception among decorative techniques.

Neither the method of manufacture nor the purpose of these demonic *Rüsselbecher* has been explained. There were shell-fish beakers with applied hollow projections as early as the fourth century. They were shallow, as the illustration on page 58 shows, and carried two rows of these projections. True *Rüsselbecher* begin in the fifth century and are squat in shape, measuring about 15 cm in height, and finish in the eighth century, having extended to a height of about 25 cm, with the projections occupying an ever smaller area and looking increasingly limp. The upper rim and the area below the projections are decorated with thin, spiralling threads and in later specimens the upper limit of the area occupied by the projections is bounded by one or two thick grooved cords. The basic form is represented by the cone-beaker or *Spitzbecher*, which also evolved from the squat form of the fifth century, when the beakers measured 10 cm in height, to a height of 30 cm in the eighth century. Since similar forms have been discovered on metal fibulae of the same period, the projections have been interpreted as stylised birds' heads. Technically they evolved from the 'eyes' of the *Nuppengläser*. The round shape of the projections of the fifth century has led to the supposition that the wall of the beaker was first pierced with a specially shaped blowing-tube and that drops of hot glass were then applied and blown into shape from inside. *Rüsselbecher* have been found at widely scattered sites north of the Alps as far afield as Scandinavia, where later specimens especially have been found. These finds have shown that the vessels were still being made in the eighth century and, indeed, from blue glass. Not until the fifteenth century did a related form of decoration reappear; this time the beakers were encircled by a single row of glass drops of trunk-like shape which reach down to the foot. Applied to the drops are ribs of blue glass.

Whereas *Rüsselbecher* occur relatively frequently, another form, that of the *Kuttrolf*, is very rarely met with. Only two *Kuttrolfe* of the Frankish period

Right: double *Balsamarium* with thread-decoration, iridescent. Syria, 4th century AD. Height 12 cm.

The earliest glass vessels. *Left:* Cup in turquoise blue opaque glass. Lip and foot-ring gilt (gilding restored). Seal of Thotmes III. Egypt, between 1501 and 1447 BC. Height 13 cm. *Right:* Jug in blue opaque glass with yellow painted decoration. Seal of Thotmes II. Egypt, between 1501 and 1447 BC. Height 8.2 cm.

Sand-core glasses. *Left: Alabastron* in blue opaque glass with white combed threads. Syria, 2nd century BC. Height 13.5 cm. *Right:* Amphora in white opaque glass with dark brown combed threads. Egypt, 5th century BC. Height 11.6 cm.

Glasses not made over a sand-core. *Top:* Bowl in sea-green glass with foliate decoration. Assyria 7th–6th century BC. Diameter 17.5 cm. This is the earliest glass with engraved decoration. *Bottom left:* Small cup from Santa Lucia di Tolmino, c 500 BC. Height 5 cm. *Right:* Hallstatt cup, Hallstatt, Upper Austria, c 500 BC. Height 5 cm.

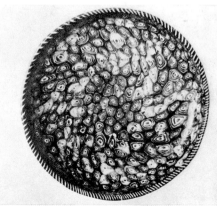

Millefiori glasses (mosaic glasses, *vasae murrinae*). Probably Alexandria, 1st century AD. The bowls in the lower illustrations have their edges decorated with a rope pattern. The sections of glass rods are placed lengthways in the upper bowl and cross-ways in the two lower ones.

45

Top: Flecked bowl. Alexandria, 1st century AD. Height 6.5 cm. *Bottom:* Box with gold marking. Alexandria or Syria, 1st century AD. Height 5.6 cm.

The Portland Vase. Dark blue glass with white upper layer. Probably made by Roman cameo-engravers of the 1st century AD. 35 cm.

Syrian glasses. *Top left:* Jug with decoration blown in a mould. Sidon, 2nd century AD.
Height 15 cm. *Top right:* Vase with fourteen thread handles in pale green glass. Syria, 2nd–
3rd century AD. Height 8.5 cm. *Bottom left:* Glass in the shape of a head, blown in the

mould. Syria or Palestine, 2nd century AD. Height 9 cm. *Bottom right:* Small bowl with folded rim in pale bluish-green glass. Syria 3rd–4th century AD. Height 4.1 cm.
Two *balsamaria* in greenish glass. Rhineland, 3rd–4th century AD. Height 18 and 14.5 cm.

Circus glasses. *Bottom left:* Glass blown in the mould with four gladiators and their horses. *Top:* The decoration spread out to its full extent. The names of the gladiators are: Hyrax, Pyram, Cocas and Cruscus. The horses: Ihcit, Hirpin, Ciao and Sacha. North Italy, 1st century AD. Height 9.2 cm. *Bottom right:* Bottle with incised decoration, probably a kind of challenge cup since it carried four place names, two of which are wreathed with the laurels of victory. Height 15.5 cm.

Right: Circus beaker, blown in the mould. Gaul, 2nd century AD. Height 6.4 cm. *Bottom:* Shallow bowl with fine wheel-engraved (small wheel, sand and water) representation of a chariot-race in the Circus Maximus in Rome at the time of the Emperor Constantine the Great (306–337). It shows the sun-god *(sol)* in the centre surrounded by four

charioteers *(aurigae)* in two-wheeled chariots and outside them at the top left and bottom right the three winning-posts *(metae)* which stood at the end of the dividing wall *(spina)*. Competitors had to go seven times round the winning-posts (they counted the laps by impaling or removing eggs). At the top left is the obelisk erected by Augustus; there is no sign of the second one put up by Constantine II, which means that the piece is to be dated before that period (according to La Baume). Diameter 24.9 cm.

Glasses from the Rhineland. *Left:* Jug with applied threads and blue spots. Rhineland, 2nd century AD. Height 42.8 cm. *Above:* Snake-thread glass with colourless threads (rare). Cologne, 2nd century AD. Height 10.5 cm.

Left: Cup decorated with shells in colourless glass. Cologne, early 4th century AD. Height 21 cm. *Right:* Gallo-Roman *Kuttrolf.* Colourless glass with applied shells and coloured threads. Cologne, 3rd century AD. Height 22.5 cm.

Vasa diatreta (network beaker). Pale green beaker with network which is dark green at the bottom becoming yellow at the top; inscription in red: 'Drink, live fair for evermore!' Found at Köln-Braunsfeld, early 4th century AD. Height 12.1 cm.

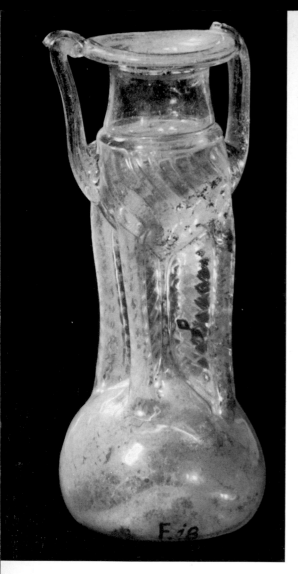 

Top left: Kuttrolf, Rhineland, 4th century AD. Height 16.5 cm. *Top right:* Ribbed beaker, Rhineland, 2nd century AD. Height 12 cm. *Opposite:* Frankish glasses. *Top left:* Beaker with foot and thread decoration. Rhineland, 5th century AD. Height 12.5 cm. *Top right: Spitz-becher* with threated decoration. Rhineland, 6th century AD. Height 27 cm.

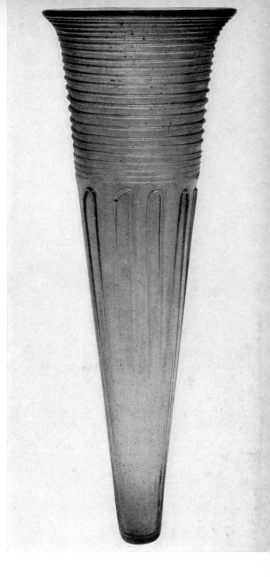

Right: bowl in green glass with pinched band and three purple mask-seals. Roman, in the Teutonic taste, 4th century AD. Height 13.3 cm.

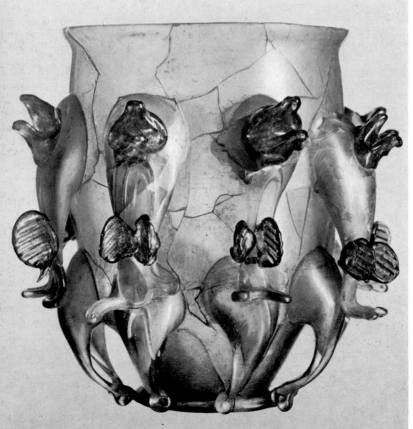

Two beakers with
shell-fish motifs. *Top:*
attached figures of
sea-creatures and blue
threads. Found in
Cologne, 4th century
AD. Height 11.5 cm.
Bottom: Trunk-shap-
ed 'dolphin forms'
with blue wings
pinched with tongs.
Height 11.6 cm. *Op-
posite: Rüsselbecher.*
Frankish, c 500 AD.
Height 19 cm.

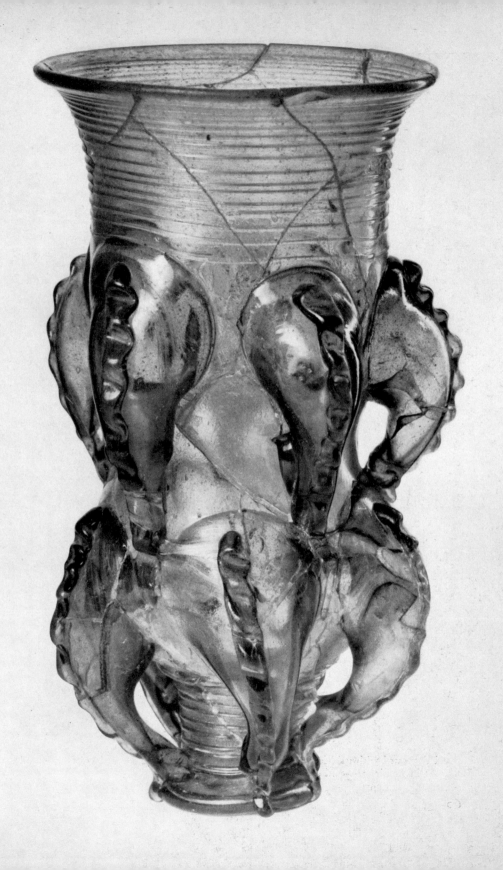

Bowl decorated with gold-leaf enclosed between double walls *(Zwischengoldglas)*. Found at Canosa in Apulia. 3rd–2nd century BC. Diameter 21.2 cm.

have so far been found. These too had precursors among Roman glasses, as may be seen from the specimens illustrated on pages 54 and 56. In the fourth century there were in Syria as well as in Gaul and the Rhineland beakers and 'gurgling bottles' in the form of *Kuttrolfe*. The principle is the same in both cases: two containers placed one above the other are joined by five tubes, so that when the liquid is poured out it flows only drop by drop (*Kuttrolf = Guttrolf* from *guttes* = drop) out of the lower into the upper container. The whole vessel was made from one blown gathering by a technique of blowing and sucking which has since been lost. The theory has gained credibility from the copies which Hans Löber of Wertheim has recently made. If the theory is correct, the middle tube of the *Kuttrolf* illustrated on page 56 would have been removed with a blowpipe. *Kuttrolfe* in the form of beakers and bottles became more widespread in the fourteenth and fifteenth centuries.

The majority of Frankish glasses were beakers of various kinds; in addition to the *Sturzbecher* (a beaker having no foot, which had to be emptied and then placed upside-down) and *Spitzbecher*, there were both bag-shaped beakers and globular beakers *(Kugelbecher)*. The bag-shaped beakers were presumably made in Britain, since that is almost the only place where they have been found. Traces of glasshouses have, in fact, been found at Glastonbury.

The so-called *Tummler* or tumblers are also curious. They are ribbed beakers without a foot which appear for the first time in the sixth century and widen out in the seventh century into flat, bell-shaped bowls with a thick rim. There are a whole series of bowls and a smaller number of bottles and stem-glasses. But these are important because they last beyond the Merovingian period. The prohibition passed during the Carolingian period on using glass cups — derived from the Roman kantharos — as chalices for the Mass temporarily put an end to their production; but bottles continued to be used, especially for medicines.

Finds of Frankish glasses of even the seventh and eighth centuries become more meagre. With the conversion of the Teutons, Celts and Slavs to Christianity — endorsed in about 700, when Boniface felled the Oak of Donar, and continuing into the thirteenth century — the heathen custom of placing goods in the graves of the deceased was forbidden. As a consequence, finds extend furthest in places where paganism lasted longest: among the Vikings in Haithabu, near Schleswig, in Denmark, Scandinavia, southern England and on the Friesian islands. The latest grave-goods to have been found date from the tenth century. All the finds show that the output of hollow glasses fell continuously throughout the eighth century and reached its lowest level in the Carolingian period. The same is true of pottery.

Carolingian art lasted from the mid-eighth to the mid-tenth century and emanated from the imperial palace and the monasteries. Although only a small quantity of glass of this period has been found and what has been found indicates a low ebb in the development of hollow glasses, glassmaking did not

cease altogether. It is certain that broken glasses were constantly being re-
fused, so that in judging quantities we have to take into account a 'will to
destroy' which had a technical basis. But it is equally certain that western
glassmaking at this time stood at a low level of efficiency. No luxury glasses
were made, for an important purpose which they might have served was barred
to them when the use of glass chalices for the Mass was prohibited — as it was
in 803 by the Council of Rheims, again by Pope Leo IV (847–55) and by the
Council of Tribur in 895. But there was another important sacred use for
hollow glasses which dates back to an early medieval papal edict which laid
down that every altar must be provided with a relic. Glasses were often used
as reliquaries; they were sealed with wax, into which the abbot, during the
consecration of the altar, impressed his seal — a practice which provides an
exact dating. Unfortunately, however, this source of information was often
destroyed — particularly during the Reformation. There was a third sacred use,
in the making of little oil-dishes for the church lights. In addition, glass certainly continued to fulfil its purpose as a container of liquids, at least of
medicines.

Despite the fact that — because of the insignificance of their wares — the makers
of glass vessels enjoyed no great respect, the monasteries, being the economic
and cultural centres of the time, made efforts to attract glassworkers to make
stained-glass windows. The abbots of the English monastery of Wearmouth
turned to Gaul for skilled glassworkers as early as 674 and again in 758 to the
bishop at Mainz, while several monastic records (Reichenau, ninth century;
St Gall, tenth century) mentioned a 'Fra Vitrearius' who was concerned with
the monastery's glass. Certainly there were no more *diatretarii* after the fourth
century.

Art developed under the leadership of Church and Empire; the new stone
buildings gave it its foundations; and within this framework a monumental
task fell to the craftsmen of the monastic glasshouses. The earliest beginnings
of stained glass date from the Carolingian period, although it did not flower
until the day of the Romanesque church — perhaps not fully, even, until that
of the Gothic cathedral.

From the early Islamic period
to the present day

East and West

Despite all its variety, ancient glass had some features in common. Not only the wide distribution of soda-glass and the technique of blowing, but also the general standard of civilisation, the prevailing view of life, military service, systems of trade and commerce — all contributed to the uniformity of the picture. As far as the history of glass is concerned, the Teutons played no distinctive part in the process of differentiation which followed the age of antiquity. They did, however, further the general development with their technical innovations in the sphere of agriculture. They introduced the wheeled plough, the three-field system, trousers in place of the toga, butter instead of olive-oil, rye, oats, hops and cooperage. They laid the foundations for the increase in production of foodstuffs which made it possible for business and trade to develop in the more inhospitable regions of the north. But they did nothing to breathe new life into the transmitted culture of antiquity.

The ancient tradition of glassmaking ran its slow course through the somewhat humble phase of Frankish glasses in the west and the Byzantine period in the east.

It was not until the seventh century that a sudden change came in both east and west. In the west, Christian religiosity became the formative power in history. A similar process — but under the sign of the half-moon — took place in Arabia. In both cases the newly awakened religious conviction inspired impressive efforts to bring about the rule of the one god in one kingdom. So that it was not until this period that the homogeneity of the ancient tradition was truly dissolved: the empire of Mahomet and the Christian empire of the Carolingians formed two self-contained units which placed history and civilisation in a new context.

The Muslim world was friendly to those within it and hostile to outsiders. The flowering oasis in the inhospitable desert symbolised its idea of paradise. The Muslims transformed their mosques, houses and cities into centres of rich decoration. In this atmosphere a special mission fell to the lot of glass: together with faience, it was required to replace the gold and silver vessels excluded on grounds of faith.

It was otherwise in the world of the Christian west: in contrast to gold, silver and rock-crystal with their precious, symbolic properties, glass was not noble enough for its use to be permitted at divine service. Glass therefore acquired a different mission and became the bible picture book by which the faith was spread; its nature was such that, in fulfilling this function, it also bathed the devotional shrines in a supernatural light. Such remained the mission of glass as long as the west remained undivided under emperor and pope. Then in the thirteenth century a new and more relentless process of differentiation set in. It began, most notably in France, with the emergence of national differences; classes and guilds soon became distinct from one another. 'Divinely willed order' took the place of unity and, finally, the individual stood alone confronting this order.

In the new secularised world which had emerged, glass, too, was a worldly thing. The Gothic sense of form, emanating originally from France, spread across Europe and brought to the field of glassmaking forms that were new but were long to remain unchanged.

Comparison between the two spheres of civilisation (pages 68—69), the Christian and the Islamic, makes one of the most interesting chapters in the history of glass — despite the fact that complete anonymity is still the rule. It is illuminating to observe what became of the tradition of antiquity — the common point of departure — under conditions that differed both externally and internally. There was common ground at least in the fields of material and technique; and this proved to be sufficiently fertile to nourish many different offshoots.

The difference in quality between the extremely refined oriental glasses of the thirteenth century and the modest products of early Gothic hollow glassmaking left only one direction in which stimuli could pass. In this sphere the west had nothing to offer the east; but it had remained extremely backward in other technical matters too. When the Mongols invaded Europe they already had gunpowder and knew how to print on paper (playing-cards). They returned home from Europe with alcohol and eye-glasses.

It is not uninteresting to discover, despite the one-sided relationship in the field of hollow glass, which paths in later European glass lead back to the east. One instance is that of the Syrian beakers, which, in the European glasshouses making *Waldglas,* became *Krautstrunk* or cabbage-stem glasses (page 94); another is that of the bulging jugs with handles which originated in post-antique times in the east, were adopted by Islam and passed on to the Persian glasshouses, finally reappearing north of the Alps. When tracing antecedents in this way it is, of course, impossible always to take account of every influence at work in a given case, for there were almost always vessels in other materials — especially precious metals — offering themselves as examples to be copied in a new field. And its use of such models is almost a measure of the youthful freshness of a movement.

The crusaders lent a certain air of adventure to the intercourse between the two medieval spheres of civilisation. The peaceful trading connections which existed between the Moorish Hafsides in Tunis (1228—1534) and the Italian republics are less well known. But the advanced scientific knowledge of Islam made its strongest impact upon the Christian west via Spain and Sicily after the conquest of Toledo in 1085 and of Sicily in 1091. Islam proved to be the guardian, promoter and transmitter of ancient Greek, Indian and Chinese science and culture. Medical, mathematical, alchemical and optical research was carried on in Islamic 'houses of wisdom', observatories and libraries. The Muslims followed the Chinese in making paper long before this technical achievement became known in the west. And, finally, the question of the development of oriental glass through the encouragement it received from the splendour-loving oriental princes in this atmosphere of vigorous intellectual and artistic life is in itself an extremely interesting one.

Glassmaking in antiquity spread east as well as west and the distinguished wares made in Persia and India and even as far away as China show a maturity which could only have arisen from a broad cultural base. The glass-maker's art in the east rose to new heights in lustre-painting, cameo-engraved and enamelled glass. Of these, Venice in the fifteenth century took over only the enamel-painting. Glass-engraving ceased entirely; only in China did it remain, now as earlier, a dominant type. Otherwise, throughout the world, from the twelfth century when glass-engraving ceased in Egypt, until the seventeenth century when glasses from Nuremberg and Bohemia appeared, nothing but blown glass with no engraved decoration was to be found; in the western glasshouses where *Waldglas* was made, in the Spanish Mudejar glass-houses, in Venice, Persia and India. Engraved glasses were in many places regarded as works in precious stones, but in Europe, as far as interest in glass was concerned, enamel-painting commanded most admiration.

It is interesting to trace the course (pages 68–69) by which in the fifteenth century the art of the Islamic glassmaker declined, while the position of Venice became increasingly secure. Venice had been in contact with Near Eastern glassmaking since the eleventh century. The fame of the enamelled glass of Syria took Venetians to Damascus in the thirteenth century to learn methods of production and especially to launch trading enterprises. By about 1400, when Tamerlane's conquests, devastations and deportations brought glass-making in Syria to a standstill, the Venetians had made such progress that they were able in their turn to supply glass-wares to Damascus. The great days of Syria and Egypt had gone for good. Not until the seventeenth century does the position of Turkish glassmaking in Istanbul improve again; and, as though the tide had turned — and the distances were shorter — this development too was preceded by the establishment of trading connections, in the form of im-ports of glass from Venice. By 1479, the state of war with the Ottomans had ended, and there were already cultural contacts and a Venetian ambassador in Istanbul. In 1502 Leonardo da Vinci submitted to the sultan, Beyazid II, four projects for building a bridge across the Golden Horn; in 1569 mosque-lamps made of threaded glass and glass windows for the villa of the Aga of the Janis-saries near Istanbul were ordered from Murano.

707 Great Mosque at Damascus with glass mosaic

836—883 Samarra the residence of the Abbasids: lustre-painting

190—1170 Works in rock-crystal and engraved glass in the Fatimid style ① in Cairo

1

5

10th—11th cent. lustre-painting in Cairo at its peak

13th cent. Enamel-painting on glass at its peak in Aleppo, Damascus, Raqqa and under Mamluk rule ②

2

3

1258 Hulago Khan conquers Baghdad. ③ Art forms subject to Mongol influence

c 1280 Aldrevandinus of Venice (?) and other 'Frankish' glassmakers employed in Syrian glasshouses: export glasses with Christian motifs and arms

1317 and 1370 Syrian enamelled glasses and coloured glass exported to Venice, gilt glass-ware to Asia Minor (Antalya)

1402 Tamerlane conquers Damascus. Glassmaking declines

1474 Sultan Kaitbai, Damascus, imports glass (mosque lamps) from Venice

1517 Aleppo and Damascus cease production

1569 The Grand Vizir Mohammed Pasha orders 900 mosque lamps, of threaded glass, from the Venetian ambassador in Istanbul

1587—1629 Shah Abbas in Isfahan, patron of glassmaking, glass-industry set up in Shiraz (maintained its importance into the 18th cent. ④)

1644—1667 Chardin, a Venetian, gives account of glassmaking in Persia

1062 Treasure of the Caliph Mustansir plundered in Cairo

1095 Pope Urban II preaches the Crusade

1099 Conquest of Jerusalem

1102 Cup of Holy Grail taken from Caesarea to Genoa

1187 Sultan Saladin reconquers Jerusalem

1204 Enrico Dandolo conquers Constantinople, which is occupied until 1261. Byzantine glasses ⑤ to San Marco

1229 Jerusalem becomes Christian by treaty

1244 Ayyubids finally re-conquer Jerusalem

1277 Treaty between Venice and Antioch

Enamelled glasses with Christian inscriptions from Syria. The 'Luck of Edenhall' reaches England ⑥

1291 Acre, Tyre, Sidon and Beirut, the last Christian strongholds conquered by the Mamluks

Christian pilgrimages ⑦ to Jerusalem continue until 1400 (beaker of St Eigberg c 1400)

6

4

7

... and the Christian west

800 Ornamental window with *Schwarzlot* painting at Séry-les-Mezières

9th—13th cent. Glass made in monastic glasshouses ⑧

803, 850, 895 Ecclesiastical prohibition on the use of glass chalices for the Mass

900 Mattheus Vitrearius, the monk and artist in stained glass, at Reichenau

c 950 Theophilus: *Schedula diversarum artium*

1066 Abbot Didier brings glassmakers from the east to Monte Cassino

1085 Archbishop Raymond sets up in Toledo an institute for translating Islamic works of learning

1090 Endowment for stained glass of Chartres cathedral

1091 Michael Scotus in Sicily translates Aristotle's works and works on alchemy from the Arabic

1100 Five windows portraying prophets in the cathedral at Augsburg⑨

1134 Bernard de Clairvaux prohibits the use of stained glass windows by the Cistercian Order

13th cent. Glassmaking becomes independent of the church, glasshouses making *Waldglas* grow up north of the Alps

13th cent. Glass-cullet imported from Venice to make alchemical apparatus in Germany ⑩

1270 Gothic nave in Strasbourg Minster

1275, 1282, 1295 Venice prohibits the export of glass-cullet, alum and sand; emigration forbidden

1279 Venetian guild of glassmakers founded

1282 Duty on German pedlars of glass in Venice ⑪

1317 First Venetian trading-vessels in Bruges, Antwerp and Middelburg

1406 Charter of the guild of glassmakers of the Spessart under Count Ludwig von Rieneck

1453 Greek (Byzantine) glassmakers driven out by the Turks flee to Venice

1454 and 1547 Families of Venetian deserters liable to arrest

1486 Niclas Walch of Vienna receives a licence for a glasshouse in the Veneto

1490 Venetian armorial glass for King of Hungary

1508—1524 Peter Månson, a Swedish priest, writes *Glaskonst*

1518 Merchant families of Augsburg, Nuremberg and Ulm order armorial glass (Fugger ⑫) from Venice

1540 Biringuccio, Venice, writes *Pirotechnica*

1550 Glasshouse at Antwerp on the Venetian pattern

1556 Agricola, Chemnitz, writes *De re metallica*

1562 *Bergpostille* by a Lutheran Mathesius, in Joachimstal

1612 Antonio Neri, Florence, writes *L'arte vetraria*

The main influence of Venetian glassmaking was, of course, directed towards the rest of Europe, where the making of hollow wares was still in its infancy. There was no escaping the fact, however, that — just as had happened earlier in the field of Islamic civilisation — Venice's commerce with the northern glasshouses contained the seeds of the extinction of its own highly refined glass. There was no prohibition by which the Venetians could protect themselves. By the eighteenth century Venetian glass was merely eking out a scanty livelihood. The mechanics of this supersession, wilful though it may have been in individual cases, contained certain recurrent characteristics: a spontaneous urge led the glassmakers to distribute their wares in the way of trade, as a result of which their methods of manufacture also became common knowledge. At this stage in history such transmissions still took place from region to region; later, in an age when techniques were to ignore national frontiers, the regional question would become unimportant in comparison with the social.

Islam, the East and Spanish glass

The theory that the glass of modern times may be traced to a new origin in the Near East is supported by internal and external contingencies which recall the development in antiquity.
Closely associated with bronze and ceramics, glassmaking is here again involved in the early phase of an empire, flourishing and declining with it, while its products are taken up by the west, continued and spread. New advances consolidate the importance of the classic homes of glassmaking. With the advent of Islam, glassmaking spread eastwards beyond Persia to India, while for a time communication by means of the Silk Road reached as far as China. In the west the territory dominated by Islam spread across the southern Mediterranean as far as Spain.
Like all Islamic art, the glass of Islam contains common features in the rich ornamental decoration with its copious use of writing-characters and in the distinctive, elegant forms which remind the observer of graceful minarets. The Turks and Mongolians who poured in from the east brought radical changes in the appearance of Islamic art. The period to be considered here begins with the conquest of Syria, Egypt, Mesopotamia and Persia by the great Caliphs in the middle of the seventh century and ends with the stagnation of the art of glassmaking in the Ottoman Empire and the decline of the arts in Persia and India in the eighteenth century. Following the great hist-

orical changes of this period, the centre of the Islamic world was continually shifting eastwards: from Damascus to Baghdad, then to Isfahan and Samarkand. Some glassmakers remained in their ancestral lands and attained new peaks of achievement under the Abbasids in Samarra, the Samanids in Nishapur, the Fatimids in Cairo and under the Seljuks and Mamluks in Aleppo, Damascus, Raqqa and Baghdad. Some of them, however, following the favour and patronage of the mighty, moved from Mesopotamia to Egypt and thence to Persia and India, spreading forms and techniques as they went. Only Tamerlane is reputed to have failed to uproot the glass-workers from Aleppo and to move them to Samarkand, despite the fact that craftsmen of all kinds and from all parts of the world were domiciled there.

The table on page 73 will, it is hoped, give a clearer picture of the temporal and regional development of Islamic glasses. Lustre-painting between the eighth and the eleventh centuries, cut and engraved glasses between the ninth and the twelfth centuries and enamel-painting between the twelfth and the fifteenth centuries represent the peaks of achievement.

The early Islamic period at first brought no change in the appearance of the glasses. The ancient Syrian style continued to be cultivated under Byzantine rule and was retained in Syria and Egypt; while east of the Euphrates the Sassanian style — itself continuing certain forms and techniques (e. g. gold glasses) of the Parthian-Hellenistic tradition — persisted for a considerable time. The new ideas were only gradually accepted. Their stylistic models were the great mosques and palaces of Syrian Omayyad and Iraqi Abbasid. The Dome of the Rock in Jerusalem, the Omayyad mosques in Damascus and Cordoba and other great trend-setting buildings of the early period were decorated with precious mosaics.

It is interesting to note the emergence of symbolic circles — they might be cut, engraved or incised — on the glasses of the pre-Islamic and early Islamic periods (page 81). This ornament is of Hellenistic origin; in its later, simplified form it became the *Kugelschliff* or circular cut motif. The circles with a dot in the centre are regarded as characteristic of the Byzantine style and they possess, in a metaphorical sense, a significance similar to that of icons. The circle is a symbol of order and, in the various religions, of knowledge, redemption and ultimate wisdom as well — as in the case of the Indian wheel or the Buddhist mandala. A similar symbolism undoubtedly underlies the circular ornament on Coptic, Iraqi and Iranian vessels too, for even at a later date in the west, with its progressive rationality, Christian art was full of symbolic elements. It is, however, noteworthy that this symbol of spiritual composure should have been widespread just at a time when, after a stormy period during which old orders had been collapsing, the Christian religion was being consolidated and Mohammedanism was emerging as a new religion.

The Islamic style became more distinctive under the Abbasids; the arabesque came into being, as did decoration based on writing-characters and, especially, lustre-painting on faience and glass. The best-known of the Abbasid Caliphs was Harun el Rashid (786—809), who resided in Baghdad and Raqqa. Harun el Rashid was the contemporary of Charlemagne and his ally against Byzantium. His reputation is based on the tales of the *Thousand and One Nights*. But more important for the history of glass is the period between 836 and 883, when the residence of the Abbasid Caliphs was at Samarra. Here Herzfeld and Sarre found fragments of flat pieces of *millefiori* glass, which had been used for wall-decoration, fragments of cut and engraved glasses and cullets carrying lustre-painting — all evidence of the high level of glassmaking; they also found shards of Chinese porcelain and celadon stoneware, which prove the existence of trading contacts with the Far East. The popularity of Chinese celadon ware may even have inspired the potters of Samarra to experiment with ceramics fired in a reducing kiln and so have led to the invention of lustre-painting on faience and glass. This invention has, however, always been associated with the denunciation of luxury contained in the Koran which compelled the Muslims to use other materials in place of gold and silver. It is known, however, that the Islamic courts possessed gold and silver table-ware which they used to display their magnificence. The situation was the same with the prohibition on portraying living creatures: this was another restriction which, particularly in Persia and India, but also under the Fatimids in Egypt, was not strictly observed. Purely ornamental possibilities were, nevertheless, explored to the full — as can be seen in the case of that classic example, the arabesque.

Lustre-painting on glass, which originated in Mesopotamia and reached its peak under the Fatimids in Cairo, is closely connected with the lustre faiences of the same period. These became the symbols of Islamic craftsmanship in its highly evolved form. After the twelfth century pre-eminence in this technique passed to Persia and Spain.

Between the ninth and the twelfth centuries Persia and Mesopotamia produced cameo-engraved glasses with animal motifs and simple, often symmetrical, ornament in the shape of hearts, palmettes and spirals, which represent the final flowering of the cut and engraved glasses of these countries (page 81). After this date we find nothing but blown glasses throughout the whole of the Near East. The style of this low relief in its early days recalls the Sassanian metal vessels; later only the outlines were left in the form of fillets and the animals were represented in a more stylised manner. The metal is transparent and clear; the low reliefs are sometimes cut out of an upper layer of pale green, blue or brown transparent glass. At the same period there were also rock-crystal beakers, bottles and water-jugs, the similarity of which suggests that the same artist worked in both materials. These cameo-engraved glasses probably originated in Nishapur, where the style differed slightly from that

Islamic glasses

|| EGYPT, SYRIA | MESOPOTAMIA, PERSIA ||

Early Islamic

Blown glasses
in all possible techniques
and decorative cutting
(*Kugelschliff*)
as in the Byzantine period.
Modification of forms ①.
Coloured glasses
with patterns made in
one with the body,
impressed or applied.
Cut glasses ②,
also coloured facet-cut glasses.

969

Fatimid

Blown glasses, with
extremely thin walls,
also coloured glasses,
with impressed or
applied patterns.
Lustre-painting ⑤.
Engraved glasses copied from
rock-crystal prototypes:
Hedwigsgläser.

1250

Mamluk

Enamelled glasses, with
red
out-
lines ⑦,
also gilt,
in Syria. In
Egypt: glass
made in
imitation of
porce-
lain.

1517

Ottoman

Decline in
the art of
glass-making
in the 16th century.

Early Islamic

Blown glasses in all
possible techniques
and decorative cutting
(*Kugelschliff*)
as in the Sassanian period.
Modification of forms ③.
Lustre-painting.
Cameo-engraved glasses

3

with animal
motifs ④
and ornaments, also
incised decoration.

1055, 1037

Seljuk

Blown glasses,
Cameo-cut glasses and
glasses cut in intaglio as before.

Enamelled ⑥
glasses, also
cold-painted
and gilt glasses
in Seljuk Syria.

1227, 1256

Mongolian

Enamelled glasses,
with red outlines,
also gilt.
Painting shows
Chinese influence,
also in Syria ⑧.

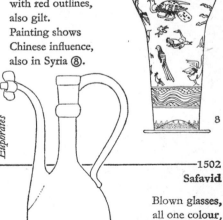

Euphrates

1502

Safavid

Blown glasses,
all one colour,
in elegant shapes ⑨.
Stagnation sets in at the
end of the 18th century.

73

at Samarra. At a later date, *intaglio* engraving came into use too. From the ninth to the eleventh century similar works are found in Cairo, first little facetted bottles, later *intaglio*-engraved glasses — and once again similar to work being done in rock-crystal as well. The most usual supposition has been that they originated in Egypt, for legend had it (cf page 95) that in the year 1062 the treasures of the Fatimid Caliph Mustansir (1035—94) had been plundered in Cairo and many pieces of rock-crystal and cut glass had found their way to Europe.

The best-known group comprise thick-walled glasses engraved in cameo relief; they are not, however, according to W. A. Shelkovnikov, of Egyptian origin — as has hitherto been supposed — but are the work of a twelfth-century White Russian workshop in Novo Grudok which belonged for a time to Poles and was presumably under Byzantine influence. They are known as 'Hedwig glasses' because two of them belonged to St Hedwig (1174—1243), wife of the Duke of Silesia, Henry I (the Bearded), who witnessed the miracle of water turning into wine in a glass of this type. The beaker illustrated on page 79, however, belonged to her niece, St Elizabeth (1207—31), wife of the Landgrave of Thuringia. It is told of this saint that she was surprised by her husband while carrying a basket of food for the poor down from the Wartburg. He compelled her to open the basket and behold: it was full of roses. The beaker later came into the possession of Martin Luther; it was credited with miraculous powers at childbirth and was lent to friendly royal houses.

Between 1099 and 1244 the crusading countries conquered the Syrian coast. From 1094 until 1174 the hinterland remained under Seljuk rule. It was at this period that the ancient techniques of gilding and enamel-painting were revived in Syria. It was followed until 1260 by the Ayyubid era.

Enamel-painting on glass was practised not only in the Syrian cities of Aleppo and Damascus but also in the nearby Iraqi city of Raqqa on the other bank of the Euphrates, in Baghdad and in Persia. Mesopotamia had been since 1055 and Persia since as early as 1037 under the rule of the Seljuks, in whose empire enamel-painting and the damascening of bronze reached a high level. These techniques were carried further under the Mamluks and reached their highest perfection in the thirteenth and fourteenth centuries. The typical mosque-lamp form also originated in Syria at the time of the Seljuks.

The development of enamel-painted glasses in the twelfth century is matched by the ceramics known as 'Minai wares' which emerged at the same period in Persia and Asia Minor. But the damascened bronzes which reached their high-water mark at about the same time as the enamelled glasses, that is, during the thirteenth and fourteenth centuries, in Syria, Persia and, above all, in Mesopotamia, appear also to be not only stylistically, in form and decoration, but also technically related to the glasses; the red pre-drawn contours on the glasses are paralleled by the roughly incised contours on the bronzes. At the end of the

Forms of Spanish glasses

Oriental and Islamic influences and the use of Venetian techniques are recognisable in the popular glasses which remained characteristic of Spain until the eighteenth century and some of which are still being made today. In the eighteenth century Spanish glassmaking merged with the general European development.

Top row: Southern Spanish glasses of the 16th–17th century: Funnelbeaker or *jarrita;* rose-water-sprinkler or *almorratxes;* vase. Second row: Venetian-influenced Catalonian glasses of the 17th century: Vase with applied flowers; wine-glass with *latticino* threads; enamel-painted bottle. Third row: Catalonian glasses of the 18th century: Vase; jug or *cántaro;* drinking-bottle or *porròn;* small bottle.

fifteenth century this manner of filling in with paint previously drawn outlines was also adopted by the Chinese on their blue and white porcelain.

Many enamel-painted glasses were brought to Europe by the crusaders and
pilgrims to Jerusalem. They were described in Charles V's inventories as
glasses *à la faience de Damas,* for Damascus was the main trading-centre at the
time. The British Museum possesses a celebrated piece of enamel-painted glass
in the shape of the 'Luck of Edenhall'; it was once in the possession of the Lords
of Edenhall and dates from the thirteenth century. It has survived undamaged.
Coloured enamelling and gilding influenced the art of glass in the east as well
as in the west. At their beginnings in the Seljuk period we find not only arabes-
ques and a strange mixture of stylised plant ornaments and figural representations in the form of scrolls with animals' heads (page 73) but miniature-
painting as well — this form of painting having just begun in Islamic art as a
whole with the founding of the Baghdad school of miniaturists. The later
Mongolian influence is revealed in the dragon, the phoenix, the peony and the
cloud-band. In the fifteenth century, under the influence of contemporary
miniature-painting, enamel-painting in Venice, Persia and India changed and
began to show delightful figural representations with narrative themes. But
whereas in India — the extreme south-east of this continuous territory — as in
the countries north of the Alps — the extreme north-west — enamel-painting
retained its position until the eighteenth century, in Venice and Persia it had
by the sixteenth century already been ousted by unpainted glass vessels whose
form is their distinctive feature. Indeed, the technical appearance of these
coloured jugs with handles, vases and sprinkler bottles which continued to be
made in Persia into the eighteenth century, is monotonous by comparison with
the technical inventiveness of Venetian glass, which was pursued to the point
where technique became an end in itself.

The glass of the Iberian Peninsular shows unusual features. Islamic influence
was strongest here in the southern glasshouses of the former kingdom of Gra-
nada, which remained under Moorish dominion until 1492. The most celebrated centre of glassmaking in this southern province of Andalusia is Almeria,
mentioned as early as the thirteenth century. The Moors, however, are reputed
to have set up a number of glasshouses in southern Spain as early as the ninth
century. The glass-forms which were still coming from the south in the eighteenth century — some of which are still being made today — are exotic in
appearance. Barcelona, the more northerly centre of Spanish glassmaking
— which was already known at the time of the Romans — did not come to the
forefront again until the fifteenth century as a result of contact with Italian
glass. The same applies to Valencia, Lisbon, Toledo and many other centres in
Catalonia and Castile, where emigré Venetians and Altarists, as well as Neth-
erlanders and native glass-workers, practised the Venetian techniques of

Beaker with enamel-painting showing a griffin and an eagle and the inscription 'Ave Maria gracia plena'. Syrian, to European order c 1300. Height 11.2 cm.

Glass situla with applied and impressed bands and drops. Probably Byzantine c 500. Height 25.5 cm.

Hedwig glass. Cameo and intaglio technique. Originating from Novo Grudok, White Russia, under Byzantine influence. 12th century. Height 10.3 cm.

Left: Sassanian beaker in
green blown glass. Persia
c 500 AD. Height 7.6 cm.

Page 80: *Top left:* Green glass bottle with out decoration (traces of the lapidary's wheel). Nishapur, Persia, 9th–10th century. Height 14.5 cm. *Top right:* Yellowish-coloured glass, blown in the mould, with scroll-decoration in cameo-relief. Baghdad, 9th century. Height 7.5 cm.

Page 81: *Top left:* Beaker with animal motif (three birds with scrolls) and Kufic script in cameo-relief. Persia 10th century, Height 10.2 cm. *Top right:* Bottle with cut neck and circular motifs cut in intaglio. Nishapur, Persia 9th-10th century. Height 18.5 cm.

81

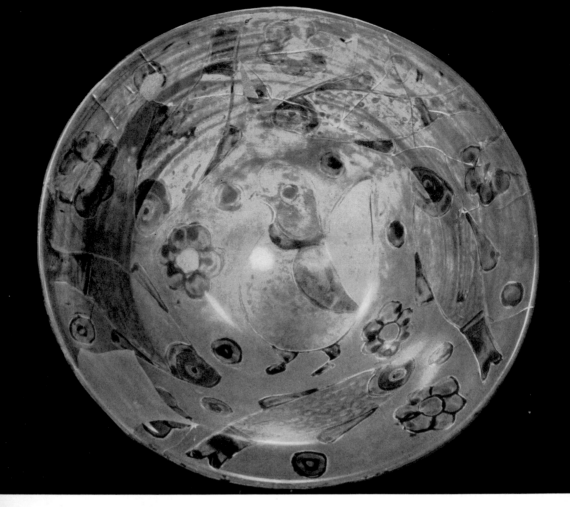

Top: Lustre-painted bowl. Egypt, 10th–11th century. Diameter 14.5 cm. *Left:* Lustre-painted bottle. Egypt, 10th–11th century. Height 20 cm. At the right can be seen the opening of a glass blister turned inwards into the bottle, which was used as a cooling-vessel.

Top left: Enamel-painted beaker. Syria, 13th century. Height 18.9 cm. *Top right:* Enamel-painted beaker with Frankish lettering. Syria, 13th century. Height 9.3 cm. *Right:* Enamel-painted bowl. Islamic decoration on the outside, Chinese figures on the inside. Syria, early 14th century, from the Imperial Treasury at Peking. Diameter 22.1 cm.

Jug, lustre-painted and gilt. Persia, 13th century. Height 23 cm.

Left: Jug of pale blue glass. Shiraz, Persia, 18th century. Height 18.8 cm. *Right:* Bottle of cobalt-blue glass twisted, with white thread-decoration. Persia, 19th century. Height 31.8 cm.

Enamel-painted bottle. Barcelona, end of the 15th century. Height 32 cm.
Opposite: Vase with dragon-decoration. Thick-walled agate glass in grey, yellow and orange
with red and agate-coloured flashing. Cut in high relief. China, 18th century. Height 18.2 cm.

Bottles made of thick colourless glass with applied relief, gilding and polychrome enamel-painting. Indian motifs, flowering scroll decoration. India, 18th century. Height 13.5 cm. and 10 cm.

glass-working. So coloured glasses, white thread-decoration in the technique known as *latticino*, ice-glasses, enamel-painting with gilding applied cold and even diamond-engraving after the Venetian fashion are found here. Some of the forms are based on native tradition, some show Moorish or Venetian influence, while the enamel-painting is preponderantly Moorish in influence (page 86). Just as in earlier times there had been Christians who had become assimilated to the Muslims (Mozarabs), so after the Reconquista there were Muslims who worked for Christian employers (Mudejars). The Mudejar style, a special form of the Moorish style with Gothic and Renaissance influences, is named after them. Under the art-loving Bourbons and in consequence of the commercial activity of the Bohemian glass-merchants, Spanish glass of the eighteenth century became increasingly assimilated to the general European development. With the founding of the royal glass-factory at La Granja de San Ildefonso in the year 1728 the Bohemian style of cut-glass superseded the Venetian age here as well. It was Lorenz Eder, a Swede, who brought about the breakthrough of the new trend. Nor did Spanish glass remain untouched by the fashion of making enamel-painted milk-glass in imitation of porcelain.

The position of Chinese glass is that of an outsider. Despite its links with the Near East, China has always preserved its own character. The first Chinese glasses — they were limited solely to small, jade-like engraved figures — date from the Han period (220 BC—AD 206). It was the fact that, as analysis showed, they contained barium that enabled them to be identified as Chinese wares, for at that time glass containing barium occurred nowhere else in the world. In addition to jewellery and figures, glass vessels were also produced in the T'ang period and in the later Ming period. Except for a short period under K'ang hsi, during which the Jesuits under the Dutchman Verbiest (1622—1688) were making fine blown glass in Peking, Chinese glasses were always thick-sided, opaque and engraved like jade. Cameo-engraved glasses were the most numerous; the motifs were sometimes cut out of several layers of coloured flashes (page 87). This Far-Eastern type of glass exerted a very strong influence in the nineteenth century on Art Nouveau, especially in France.

Romanesque glass

In the west by the period of the Romanesque, which lasted from the mid-tenth into the thirteenth century, Byzantine, oriental and indigenous elements were already combining. Favoured by political events, a flood of influences — imperceptible at first but continually increasing in volume — flowed into the stream of western art. Although Christianity was at first little inclined to make use of the advances made by the heathen, precious objects found their way into Europe earlier than did the fruits of knowledge, some arriving via the Italian ports — then the centres of world trade — some coming as military booty or as gifts. In the aftermath of the Cluniac reforms and thanks to the might of the papacy and the opposition to Islam, Europe at that time was in a state of high religious hopefulness. This was reflected in the swift development of stained glass and the priority given to the manufacture of polychrome window-glass in the monastic glasshouses.

In their role of guardians of the tradition of antiquity, the monasteries, especially those of the Benedictine Order, preserved and added to the received literature of glassmaking. The works on this subject by the Bishops of Seville (seventh century) and Mainz (Hrabanus Maurus, *De universo*, c 845) derive from Pliny, the outstanding technical encyclopaedist of antiquity. The *Codex Luccensis* (c 800), however, on which the collection of recipes of the tenth century known as *Mappae clavicula* is based, was the product of Byzantine experience. And the two streams finally united in the collection of recipes by Heraclius, whose first two books date from the tenth and the third from the twelfth to the thirteenth centuries. But the most important work is the *Schedula diversarum artium* of Theophilus Presbyter written in the tenth century. These writings have been much criticised on the grounds that they plagiarised one another or were full of fantasies. But it should not be forgotten that they did, after all, bridge a period of a thousand years, during which they kept alive a branch of artistic technique which would otherwise have died, so that, once offered new impulses, it could flower again.

A few slight observations have come down to us which indicate that glass was again gradually increasing in estimation. Barbarossa bequeathed to his chancellor, Gottfried von Spitzberg (1184–90), a glass beaker bearing his arms; Henry II in 1388 gave the Abbot of Cluny an Alexandrian glass; a miniature in the manuscript of Manesse of the beginning of the fourteenth century shows Minnesänger of Buchheim holding up a Syrian glass (of the type of glass which later became the model for the *Krautstrunk* and the *Römer);* troubadours and Minnesänger, influenced perhaps by the love-lyrics of the Arabian courts, used glass as a symbol of purity and miraculous incarnation: Reinmar von Zweter wonders at the pure glass which emerges from the dull ashes, while in his allegorical verse epic, *Le Roman de la Rose* (1277), Guillaume de Lorris has other experiences to record. In Normandy, where he comes from, glass is made of plants which grow on the sea-shore. Thus both *Waldglas* and soda-glass are mentioned in medieval literature.

Despite these records of glass in the Romanesque period, only a few pieces dating from that time have survived. Literature records a spherical bottle with a long neck dating from the eleventh century which was found in France and a few little medicine-bottles of the twelfth to the fourteenth century found on German soil. Since, however, Theophilus in his *Schedula* mentions large and small *vasas* (= vessels) and bottles with long necks, we must assume that these three categories of hollow glasses were, in fact, in use. The *Schedula*, however, mades no mention of drinking vessels.

Gothic glass

In the thirteenth century — which saw the end of the Crusades and the beginnings of trade with the east and in which an Albertus Magnus could renounce his bishopric in order to live for science rather than for the persecution of heretics—the bourgeoisie began to dominate economic life, because its members represented trade and commerce. Glass manufacture broke free of the monasteries and began to face the newly emerging demand. The new glasshouses were moved into the wooded valleys because, owing to the risk of fire, the craft was not tolerated in the towns. These forest glasshouses were moveable establishments which were transferred to fresh parts when one area had become deforested. The forest was the basis of their existence: it provided wood, sand and ash for the *Waldglas* and clay for the pots in which the glass was fused. Among the products of the glasshouses, the greatest demand at first was for window-glass, for the monks in the monastic glasshouses had until this time made little or none for private persons. It was not until the fifteenth century that every prosperous citizen in Germany possessed glazed windows in his living-rooms.

While the glass industry was spreading in the Spessart district, in Hesse, Lorraine, Thuringia and the Böhmerwald, the first Venetian trading vessels landed in Flanders in 1317 and opened up the exportation of Venetian glass to countries north of the Alps.

The assertion that the greenish colour of the glass from the forest glasshouses

Gothic glasses of northern and southern Europe

The Gothic which first emerged in the thirteenth century in the buildings of northern France also produced the earliest evidence of glass on French soil. These extremely scarce early Gothic glasses are forerunners of the populer green *Waldglas* decorated with dropped-on spots, which greatly increased in numbers in the course of the fourteenth century.

13th century: *Kopf* from Schwäbisch Hall, c 1280; goblet found at Liège; standing bowl found at Rouen; bottle found in Poitou. 14th century: *Nuppenbecher* from Normandy; wine-glass from Rouen; two early Gothic forms of the *Angster* or *Kuttrolf*. First half of the 15th century: *Maigelein*, tall glass with dropped-on spots; double-cone bottle; Venetian bottle. Second half of the 15th century: jug; *Scheuer;* club-shaped glass; *Krautstrunk;* Venetian goblet made of blue glass with enamel-painting; bowl. First half of the 16th century: beaker; jug; *Nuppenbecher* with foot; Venetian goblet and cover, gilt, with enamel-painting; blue jug; beaker.

— which first began to flourish in about 1350 — was due only to backwoods ineptitude is quite untrue. It was — and rightly — regarded as beautiful. It is rare to find blue glasses of this period.

Thick-walled coloured glass was extremely popular in Venice too. Syrian enamel-painting was also taken up in Venice as early as the fifteenth century, whereas it did not come in north of the Alps until about 1550, with the Renaissance. Thus the dematerialisation peculiar to the Gothic was achieved in different ways in north and south: in the north the natural-coloured green glass made of potash was enlivened by plastic means, while the Venetian natron glass was coloured and painted. North and south each influenced the other. Thus Venice borrowed the network of the *Maigelein* and other beakers and a few *Nuppengläser* are found south of the Alps too. The *Waldhütten* for their part later adopted Venetian enamel-painting.

The only elements in the decoration of Gothic *Waldglas* are fluted and twisted patterning, applied threads, drops melted on to the surface and *Nuppen* or large drops drawn out to a point. The *Angster*, the *Kuttrolf*, the double-cone bottle, the jug with handle and, especially, drinking vessels — the *Maigelein*, *Krautstrunk*, *Römer*, *Stangenglas* and *Scheuer* — are all part of the formal repertoire of *Waldglashütten*.

That characteristic feature of the Gothic, the upward, aspiring movement, is apparent in the tall *Nuppengläser*, the *Stangengläser*, the club-shaped glasses and in the long-necked bottles. During the Late Gothic period the beaker was placed on a foot, as also, in Venice, were flat bowls. The foot and the beaker and, often, the knop of the stem, are vertically fluted. The cover, which makes its appearance at this period, increases the height of the cup even more. This emphasis on upward movement is apparent even in the arrangement of the drops in vertical rows. Not until the Renaissance did they begin to run diagonally. Another feature typical of this period is the tall 'kick' of the beakers and bottles and the finely toothed foot-ring.

Many of the formal prototypes came from Syria, but contemporary metal vessels were even more important. The glass vessels we use today may be traced back to this period of new beginnings.

Page 94 shows the pedigree of the stem-glass, the goblet, the *Römer* and the ordinary beaker. The Gothic period lasted until about 1530—50. During this period the beaker of Syrian origin with its small drops evolved to become the *Krautstrunk;* this type remained in use only until the seventeenth century, having assumed gigantic dimensions during the Renaissance. The *Krautstrunk* led on to the 'Roman glass', later known as the *Römer*. (Anna Elisabeth Liederwald-Theuerkauf has recently been investigating the history of the *Römer*. The *Krautstrunk* was also the source of the *Stangenglas* and the *Humpen*. The line of development of the club-shaped glasses runs parallel with that of the *Krautstrunk* with the flared lip. Besides decoration in the form of

Genealogy of the drinking glasses of today

The forms of drinking glasses may be traced back to the fourteenth century. Models drawn from the ancient world and from the orient were elaborated in an original manner during the Gothic and Renaissance periods. The green *Waldglas* is printed grey in the diagram below. Colourless glass took its place in the 17th century. The only exception is the *Römer* which today still shows traces of its green origins.

The diagram begins with antiquity, the period from which the first vessel dates (top left). The tradition of antiquity lived on in Syrian and Venetian glass. Northern Europe was influenced by the Syrian beakers brought back by the Crusaders, while to some extent the Venetians went straight back to ancient prototypes.

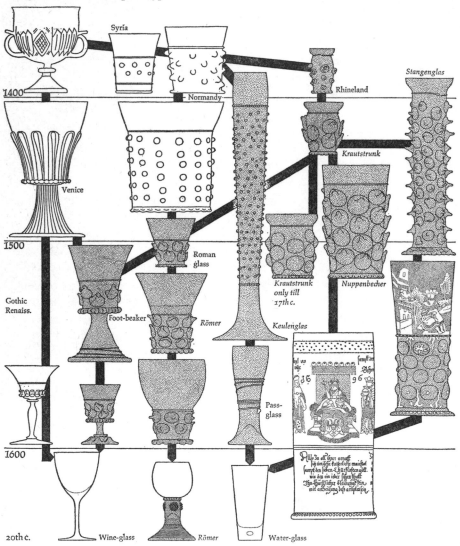

The above diagram illustrates the development up to the late Renaissance only, when the basic features of the present-day forms were already clearly apparent. Later stylistic variations are shown in diagrams further on in the book.

drops, applied threads are often found. From those are derived the 'passes' which are markings on pass-glasses and *Passhumpen* showing the amount which the drinker had to swallow at a draft. Club-shaped glasses and *Humpen* are forerunners of the beakers of the present day. The drop, that form of decoration beloved of the makers of *Waldgläser*, is found even in the ancient world, as is the foot-beaker, from which goblets and stem-glasses have evolved.

Venetian glass and its spread to other centres

It is impossible to establish the exact date at which the glass began to be made in Venice. The country round Venice — that is, the northern coast of the Adriatic — had already played an important part in the earlier history of glass. Venice itself was a settlement created by tribes fleeing to the lagoons before the advancing Huns and did not come into being before AD 452.

The earliest records of glassmaking date from the eleventh century and are concerned with Venice's relations with the Near East — from which we may assume that glassmaking had already reached a stage of some importance.

The cities of Pisa and Genoa had in the eleventh century successfully resisted the Saracen pirates and their plunderings and had tipped to their advantage the balance of power in the Mediterranean — a determining factor in trade and navigation. The Italians now adopted the role of aggressive pirates and plagued the coasts of north Africa and Egypt with their despoliations. Piracy, booty, privateering, the slave-trade, commerce in oriental wares, revenue from the Crusades, for which they furnished transport and supplies — these were the sources from which the capital accrued and made the north Italian cities powerful economic centres. During the Fourth Crusade, after Byzantium had been conquered in 1204, not only did numerous glasses find their way into the Treasury of St Mark's but many Byzantine glassmakers also moved to Venice. There exists a contract with Antioch of the year 1277 on the subject of exporting glass-cullet to Venice. By the thirteenth century glassmaking was flourishing and in 1291 the glasshouses were moved to the island of Murano. The bead-makers were the only ones permitted to continue manufacturing their wares in the city itself. In 1376 marriages between nobles and the daughters of glassmakers were declared socially acceptable. Venice's star was now in the ascendant. Following her victory in 1381 in the maritime war against Genoa, she became mistress of the Mediterranean and her most important possession was her monopoly of the Levantine trade. From the Levant spices, perfumes, alum and articles of luxury flowed into Europe. This brisk trade also caused industry to flourish. The Levant was the only bridge which avoided Islamic territory and led to China and India. This was the route by which Marco Polo, the Venetian, travelled to China. The Levant also afforded sole access to the regions of the Black Sea where slaves were captured. The Italians remained until the fifteenth century the leading protagonists in the slave-trade. It was not until 1453 when the Ottoman Sultan Mohammed II conquered Constantinople — and many glassmakers are reputed to have fled to Venice — that the Levantine trade, and with it the supply of slaves, was blocked. By this time the Portuguese under Henry the Navigator had begun to explore the Atlantic coasts of Africa and to undertake slave-hunting expeditions to the Canary Islands and West Africa. The trade with negro slaves of the Guinea coast began in 1470. The Venetian glass-bead industry played a small part in this. Pazaurek states that slaves were traded against glass beads, among other things, and a black slave is alleged to have cost four pounds of beads, which could be bought in Marseille for thirty-two sols. Following the discovery of America the output of Venetian glass beads rose steeply, for they were extremely popular with the Indians.

The glass fused in Venice was made of the ashes of marsh-plants and crushed pebbles from river-beds. During the first third of the fourteenth century enamelled glass and coloured glass for stained-glass windows were still imported from Syria. The improved glass known as *cristallo* did not make its appearance until the fifteenth century. It is either of a pale yellowish straw-colour or is grey, like smoke-glass. It was made from ashes of plants containing lime and natron imported from the Levant and from Alicante.

Relations between Venice and the kingdom of Aragon, to which Alicante belonged, were of the best. Indeed, when Charles VIII of France invaded Italy in 1494 and captured Naples, Venice joined the forces of resistance against the French and after they had been repulsed in 1495, Frederick II of Aragon rewarded her with the ports of La Puille.

Venetian glass, in the ascendant during the period between 1450 and 1500, reached its peak during the first half of the sixteenth century. Characteristic features of this age of brilliance are the hollow stems of the goblets and *tazze* with moulded lion-mask reliefs. The winged glasses which were regarded in the rest of Europe as typically Venetian were not particularly common in Venice itself; indeed, many of them come from the Netherlands and elsewhere. The period between 1550 and the seventeenth century saw the spread of Venetian glass. Venetian power was suffering under the Italian wars and in the Cinquecento it was already undermined. The city was also losing its economic importance. Trade with the East Indies and with America was transforming the Atlantic coasts into the centre of world commerce.

Bizarre winged glasses and open-work wares of the seventeenth century already proclaim the decline of Renaissance glass. Glass ships and goblets with stems in the form of animals or plants embodying a technique so heightened as to have become virtuosity are common. The forms become Mannerist, luxuriant and restless. Among drinking glasses, the slender flute-glasses — which came originally from the Netherlands — reached a height of over two metres, like the giant flute-glasses in the Zwinger in Dresden. These excessively slender Mannerist forms were spread by Venetian glassmakers in northern Europe and were partially reflected in the vertically stacked double goblets and the clusters of goblets (page 139) made by the *Waldglashütten.*

The enamel-painting practised in Venice between about 1460 and 1530 was until the fifteenth century usually applied to green, Burgundy red or dark blue glasses and the style of representation contains no suggestion of oriental prototypes. The adoption of the Syrian technique must therefore be regarded merely as the initial impulse, a seed which fell upon fertile ground because painted decoration satisfied the expressional needs of the age. According to Astone Gasparetto, during the fifteenth century certain artists were summoned to the firing kilns on Murano, where they painted chalices, goblets, dishes and fruit-bowls in enamel colours on commission for rich customers desirous of possessing show-pieces. This was the earliest case of non-professionals collaborating in the manufacture of glasses.

The Venetian enamel, unlike that used in Syria, was not transparent; Venetian enamel-colours were opaque. Native knowledge of faience provided a basis for producing them. Enamel decorations with figural scenes, processions (page 105) and representations of weddings on a dark ground were supplanted after 1490 by coats-of-arms and other rather more sparing decoration on colourless glass (page 106). By about 1530 enamel-painting had ceased to be fashionable in Venice, although it continued to be made for export, especially to Germany. Orders from German merchants, most of them from Augsburg and Nuremberg, were numerous. Their example was followed by the princes. Matthias Corvinus, King of Hungary, at the end of the fifteenth century, was probably the first to commission armorial glasses in Venice. There is a beaker of Ferdinand I of Hungary, with portraits, dated 1529 (illustrated on page 109). During the sixteenth century the Fugger and many other families commissioned armorial glasses in Venice just as, at the same period, people ordered majolica plates decorated with their coats-of-arms to be made for them in Italy. In the collections of the Veste Coburg there is a tall glass dating from the end of the sixteenth century which belonged to the Praun, a family of Nuremberg merchants, despite the fact that enamel-painting was already practised on a large scale in Germany itself. The reason why these commissions went to Murano must therefore be sought in the first instance in the public's preference for the quality of Venetian glass. Furthermore, the green in the palette of the German enamel-painters is less bright than the Venetian

Renaissance forms . . .

Venetian glasses in the Renaissance style date from the second half of the fifteenth century. Gothic influence remains apparent until 1525; there are no more monochrome coloured glasses after the end of the Gothic period. Venetian awareness of antiquity produced highly distinguished forms, while delight in experimentation created numerous variations; both of which mark the new Venetian *cristallo*.

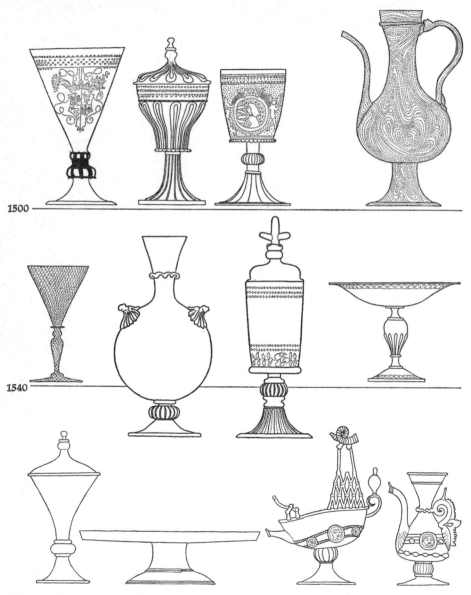

1500

1540

Distinguishing features of Renaissance glasses include the blown stems (hollow balusters and hollow knobs) and the folded foot-ring. The Venetian *cristallo* is of a pale straw-colour. Enamel-painting between c 1460 and 1530 only.

. . . Venetian glasses and glasses in the *façon de Venise*

Towards the end of the sixteenth century Mannerist features begin to appear; these become more obvious in the glasses of the seventeenth century and are apparent in northern wares in the *façon de Venise* as well. The twisted thread-decoration of the winged stems and the wings in the shape of the double eagle are found outside Venice only.

1600

Glasses from Venetian glasshouses
in northern Europe

green, and yellow usually replaces gold. At this time Venice also received orders for mosque-lamps from Damascus (c 1550) and Byzantium (1569). From about 1530 the Venetians, for their own use, began to go in for cold-painting on flat vessels, often after woodcuts and engravings. Decorations in oil-colours at first continued to be combined with bead-like dots of enamel. Gold decoration was now also applied with the brush, not, as previously, engraved on gold-leaf. The gilt stucco ornamentation on colourless (page 118) or coloured glasses of the seventeenth century are the forerunners of the glasses with gold relief decoration on an enamel foundation so popular later in Saxony (second quarter of the eighteenth century) and Bohemia (mid-nineteenth century, page 260).

Venice's most felicitous period lay between 1500 and 1550. The Gothic continued to make its presence felt until 1525, its vigorous upward surge being transformed into a noble elegance. This development towards Renaissance forms leant heavily upon metal prototypes. According to Gasparetto, many glasses of this period can be related to designs for the use of goldsmiths executed by Pierin del Vaga, Agostino Veneziano, Francesco Salviati and Albrecht Dürer. Designs by the Veronese painter, Ligozzi (in the Uffizi, Florence) and the monogrammist CAP (in the British Museum) and the *Libro del Principe d'Este* (the book of the Prince of Este), with its bizarre forms, were received into the Venetian State Archive between the mid-sixteenth century and the seventeenth century. These formal designs by outside artists brought to the outward form of the glasses of the Renaissance that underlying air which, as in the fine arts, seems to reflect the intellectual situation of the period. The new age was to bring with it the liberation of the individual from the anonymity of the community, an efflorescence of humanity and learning and a great flowering of science and art. During the first half of the sixteenth century, at the time when the High Renaissance was exerting so strong an influence on the intelligentsia of Europe, glassmaking as an art also attained one of its zeniths.

Renaissance delight in experimentation and scientific method is revealed in a wealth of new types of glass and techniques of production. Besides *cristallo*, there are coloured glasses, and glasses made to resemble chalcedony, malachite and agate, aventurine glasses shimmering with copper spangles (page 108) — they were made in China during the eighteenth century as well as in Venice — and porcelain-like white milk-glass; Medici porcelain made its appearance in Florence in about 1557. These glasses remained popular until the eighteenth century.

During the sixteenth century the transparent, pale straw-coloured glass known as *cristallo* usually remained without painted ornamentation. When a true colour was used besides the oil-colours, this was as a rule blue glass made into plastic decoration, particularly of the stems. Gilding too — which, indeed, in Venice is older than enamel-painting — was often concentrated on the stems.

It was the bead industry — which used semi-manufactured articles in the form of glass rods and tubes of all colours — which gave the Venetian glassmakers the idea of employing the ancient Alexandrian technique of *millefiori* glass. The manufacture of glass rods and tubes led on to another innovation which quickly gained ground and was one of the factors which in about 1550 brought Venetian glass to its high-water mark: this innovation took the forms of *latticino* and *vetro di trina* (pages 110, 111). These effects are obtained by enclosing white or coloured threads (*latticini*) in the glass. They could be arranged in parallel lines, spirally or in a network pattern. Because, due to the technique by which they are made, there is an air-bubble in every mesh of the more intricate patterns, they are often likened to lace (*vetro di trina* or lace-glass). Besides these thread decorations the Venetian glassmakers of the sixteenth century also revived the early Egyptian technique of combed threads.

Other new types of glass were ice-glass (page 112) — made at Liège and elsewhere — and mould-blown glass with a structured surface or squared pattern. From the second half of the sixteenth century until the eighteenth century light engraving with a diamond-point (page 107) was also used as a means of decorating glass; this technique found imitators in Venice, in the Tirol (pages 122, 123), in the Netherlands (page 121), in Germany and in England.

The manufacture of glass for spectacles constituted an important branch of the glass industry; nor, finally, was the making of glass for mirrors a negligible factor. It originated in Venice in the early sixteenth century. The celebrated Venetian mirrors were so expensive, however, that when at the end of the seventeenth century Colbert was ordered to install the Salle des Glaces at Versailles he felt constrained to set up a native French mirror factory.

After the end of the sixteenth century the Venetian glasses are barely distinguishable from those made in the Netherlands and Germany *à la façon de Venise*. Winged glasses were the most popular in northern Europe, where the wings were made in the shape of the double eagle (page 118), a type which did not occur in Venice itself. The heads are pinched and are often made of blue glass; while the snake-threads (*verres à serpent*) which decorate the stems are of different colours. Massive stems or quadrilobe knobs also denote a provenance outside Venice.

Work similar to the Venetian was done in many other north Italian towns, as well as in Naples and Rome. By the thirteenth century Venetian makers had already set up glasshouses in north Italy. It was thereupon made a punishable offence for glass-workers to move away from Venice. The prohibition was renewed in the fifteenth and sixteenth centuries and it was decreed that if the deserter failed to return when ordered to do so his nearest relatives would be thrown into prison. Deserters who still did not return were to be killed by hired assassins. A number of Venetians fell victim to this decree, which remained in force until the middle of the eighteenth century. The attitude of Altare was quite different. Glass-workers from France — indeed, from the region which later became Normandy — had settled there in the ninth century as the Normans invaded their home. They formed a guild which was led by an elected 'consul'. Unlike the Venetians, their practice was to move to distant parts and afterwards to return home. They spread the knowledge of Italian glassmaking, particularly in France, their former homeland, which had now become a sovereign state. Their major foundation was the glasshouse at Nevers, set up in 1585; it continued to flourish into the eighteenth century when the Italian style had elsewhere already given place to the *verres de Bohème* or to the English *verres cristaux*. Nevers was founded by Saroldi and was subsequently directed by other Altarists. The best-known and most celebrated wares of this glasshouse are its figures (page 118), which included groups of the comedy characters so popular during the eighteenth century. We encounter the Saroldi family in Lyons, Paris, Melun, Cologne and in Poitou as well. Another of the best known of the Altarists was Jean Castellani, who took over the Nevers glasshouse from the Saroldi in 1647. His nephew, Bernard Perrot, set up the glasshouse at Orleans in 1662. He is credited with the invention of the casting process for sheet glass. The most important manufacture of mirror-glass is, however, that of Saint-Gobain, which dates back to the establishment founded in 1665 by Colbert in the Faubourg Saint-Antoine, Paris. Colbert engaged two Venetian mirror-makers for the purpose but both are alleged to have met mysterious deaths within the first fortnight.

Before he went to Nevers, Saroldi was in Lyons, where Italian experience had been utilised since 1511 in the making of enamelled glass. Thus, with enamel-painting still flourishing in Venice itself, Venetian influence found extremely early expression in Lyons. The later foreign foundations set out to make only undecorated *cristallo*, despite the fact that other types of glass figured in their production-programmes.

The favourite destinations for deserting Venetian glassmakers were Flanders and Holland. The first glasshouse was set up in 1531 at Middelburg in the county of Zeeland. Another followed in Antwerp in 1549. At these factories, as in Amsterdam and Haarlem, Altarists and Venetians worked side by side under native factory-owners. The most enterprising employers in Brabant and Liège were the Bonhomme family who in 1658 took over a glasshouse in Brussels which had been set up by the Venetian Antonio Miotto. Through them Liège, where Altarists had set up a glasshouse, became the centre of the glass industry of the Netherlands. In their three factories at Liège from 1638 onwards they produced Venetian and — with the assistance of workers from Hesse — German glass. In 1680 they began to add flint-glass *à l'anglaise* to

The spread of Venetian glass

Severe penalties threatened the glassmakers of Murano — an island in the Lagoon to the north of Venice — if they betrayed the secret of glassmaking. Despite this, many of them allowed themselves to be lured into seeking their fortunes abroad. In contrast to the Venetians, the glassmakers of the little town of Altare were free to change their place of work without danger. During the period 1550—1680 Muranese deserters and Altarists emigrating freely, spread the Italian glassmakers' art throughout Europe.

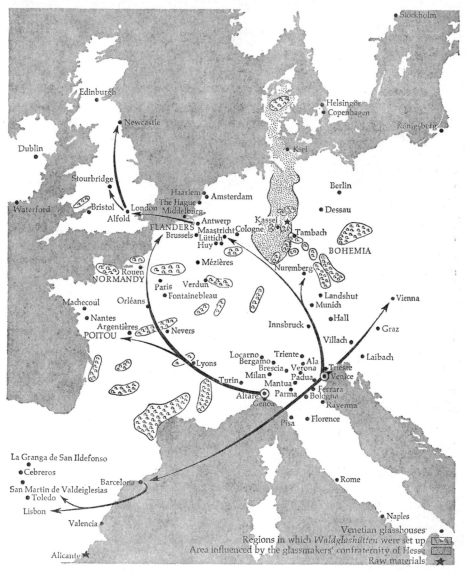

With the co-operation of native craftsmanship glassmaking *à la façon de Venise* succeeded in establishing itself in France, the Netherlands and England. In Germany, however, the Venetian glasshouses were everywhere short-lived. They were completely supplanted by indigenous glasshouses when Bohemian chalk-glass made its appearance in c 1680.

these. Besides those in Brussels and Liège, the Bonhommes possessed glasshouses in Bois-le-Duc, Huy, Maastricht, Neuville and Verdun.

In France, too, glassmakers from Murano as well as Altarists are found. Most of these were in Lyons, but there were others in Paris, in Lorraine and in Poitou. Glassmakers were known in France as *gentilshommes verriers* and counted as members of the nobility.

The production of Venetian *cristallo* began in England about the middle of the sixteenth century, when Protestant glassmakers from Lorraine settled in Surrey. Jean Carré, their master glassmaker, obtained a licence in 1567 and set up a furnace at Alfold in Sussex and another later in London. Soda was imported from Alicante in Spain. Differences soon arose, however, with the native glassmakers on the issue of wood for fuel. Wood had become so scarce in England at that time that prices had increased eightfold whereas other prices had only trebled. The Lorrainers then moved to the Forest of Dean and subsequently to Blore Park in Staffordshire; a few even reached Newcastle-on-Tyne. In so doing they were following the movement universal among industries dependent upon firing, away from the south to the coal-fields of the midlands. Then in 1615 there was a general prohibition in England on the use of wood for glass-furnaces, primarily so that ship-building should not be jeopardised by the shortage of wood. By this time people had already gone over to a large extent to firing by pit-coal. There was in consequence a vast increase in the demand for coal and the mine-owners recognised the need to solve their technical problems more quickly. The most pressing problem was that of how to keep down ground-water, for which an efficient pumping system was needed. Certain English mines required five hundred horses simply to work their pumps. In 1698 the first steam pump was tried out in an English mine. It was a forerunner of the atmospheric steam-engine invented by Thomas Newcomen, a blacksmith, which in 1712 was installed in all the coal-mines in the British Isles. It was while trying to improve the efficiency of this machine that James Watt invented the true steam-engine. Although the part played by the glasshouses in this development was very small, they did at least contribute to the initial impulse.

The first Venetians are reputed to have reached London by 1549. Nothing, however, is known of their fate. Giacomo Verzelini, who came to England from Amsterdam, is the first, of whom we know that he was in 1573, on the strength of a licence granted by Queen Elizabeth I, running a glasshouse in Crutched Friars in London — probably the one set up by Jean Carré (d 1572) — which was followed by a second in Austin Friars. The Anglo-Venetian glass

Right: Coblet made of dark green glass with gilding and coloured enamel-painting. Venice, last quarter of the 15th century. Shows a wedding-procession with a ceremonial float led by a horn-blowing putto on horseback. Retinue in contemporary dress. Inscription: ASAI DI-MANDA CHI SERVENDO TACE. Height 15.6 cm.

Opposite: Water bottle with gilding (partly rubbed off) and polychrome enamel decoration. Arms of a bishop. Venice, before 1530. Height 28 cm. *Right:* Colourless *Stangenglas* with cover. Diamond engraved arms of EBERHART SEVITER VENEDIG. Venice, dated 1596. Height 32.5 cm. *Left:* Pale straw-coloured goblet. *Cristallo* with enamel-painting and gilding. Scale-pattern and foliate ornament. Venice, beginning of the 16th century. Height 32.5 cm.

Top: Small bowl with inserted hollow body. Venice, 17th century. Height 6 cm. *Bottom:* Bowl-made of agate-glass with flecks of aventurine. Venetian, 18th century. Height 5.8 cm.

Top: Blue beaker with polychrome painting and gilding. The portraits probably represent Ferdinand I, his consort Anna of Hungary and Frederick III. Venice, dated 1529. Height 9 cm.
Bottom: Bowl with foot. Venice, 17th century. Height 12 cm.

Top: Basilisk (a fabulous creature, half cock and half dragon, whose glance was alleged to be lethal) in *latticino* glass. *Façon de Venise,* 17th century. Length 22 cm. *Bottom:* Tall container and plate made of *vetro di trina.* Venice, 16th–17th century. Height 14 cm., diameter of plate 14 cm. *Opposite:* Bottle in the shape of an *Angster* made of *latticino* glass. Venice, 16th century. Height 25.5 cm.

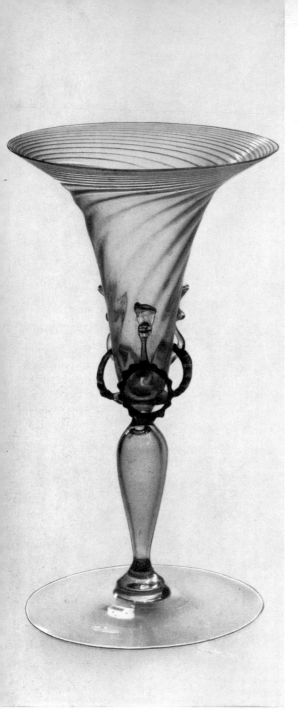

Left: Goblet made of colourless glass with blue pendant rings. Venice, second third of the 17th century. Height 16 cm. *Right:* Goblet and cover made of smoke-coloured ice-glass. Traces of turquoise-blue cold-painting and gilding. Venice, first half of the 16th century. Height 28.3 cm.

Top: Small jug with lion-mask and mask of Neptune. Venice, c 1600. Height 15 cm. *Left:* Cup in *vetro di trina* on blue foot. Venice, 16th century. Height 18.7 cm. *Right:* Table-bell made of *vetro di trina* with silver mount. Venice, c 1600. Height 20.5 cm.

Tazza made of straw-coloured *cristallo*, with lion-head knop gilt. Venice, mid-16th century. Height 15.2 cm.

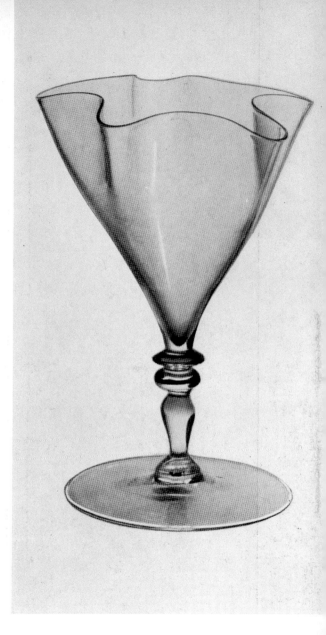

Left: Goblet with stem in the shape of an animal made of dark blue glass with white and paler blue spots. Venice, 17th century. Height 28.2 cm. *Right:* Goblet of colourless glass. Venice, 16th–17th century. Height 14 cm.

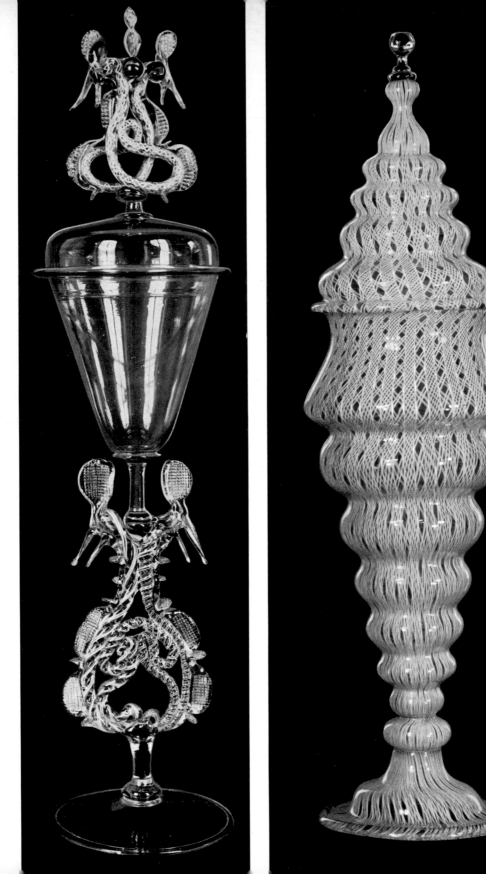

Opposite left: Goblet and cover from the Venetian glasshouse at Cassel 1583—1585. Height 46 cm. *Opposite right.* Vase and cover of *latticino* glass. South Netherlands c 1600. Height 45.5 cm. *Right:* Goblet and cover with the monogram of Charles XI and Eleonore. Stockholm-Kungsholmen before 1697. Height 32 cm.

Left: Scent-bottle of straw-coloured glass with stucco decoration gilt. Venice, 17th century. Height 15 cm. *Right:* Wing-glass. Blue wings and white, red, blue and yellow threads. Netherlands, 17th century. Height 24.8 cm.

Figures of the Kings made at Novers. Flesh in white glass, clothing blue with polychrome (mostly yellow) threads and spots. 16th–17th century. Height 5.8 cm. and 8.4 cm. *Opposite:* Wing-glass. Netherlands, first half of the 17th century.

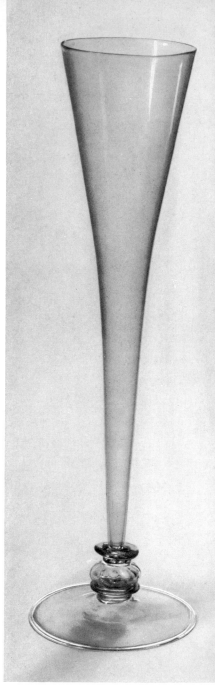

Left: Goblet with hollow baluster-stem in colourless glass. Belgium, 17th century. Height 21.8 cm. *Right:* Flute in colourless glass. Netherlands, mid-17th century. Height 28.5 cm. *Opposite:* Wing-glass made of yellowish and blue glass with diamond-point engraving. Netherlands or Germany, second half of the 17th century. Height 26 cm.

Top: Goblet with blue beads. Hall in Tirol, 16th century. Height 18 cm. *Bottom:* Diamond-engraved tazza. Innsbruck Court Glasshouse 1572—1580. Height 15.5 cm.

Left: Diamond-engraved vase. Innsbruck Court Glasshouse 1572—1580. Height 21.4 cm.
Right: Bottle-green glass with cover with diamond-point engraving and gilding. Hall in Tirol, c 1620. Height 27.5 cm.

made by Verzelini was decorated by diamond-engraving or painting in gold. An example dating from 1577 may be seen in the Victoria and Albert Museum, London. Another glass with gold decoration and dating from 1590 created a sensation in 1966 when it was sold at auction. Churchill, a London dealer, bought it at a sale held by Sotheby & Co in London for £ 9,500, the highest price that had ever been paid for an object made of glass. It is a coverless cup somewhat resembling the cup in lace-glass illustrated on page 113 and was formerly in the possession of the Duke of Northumberland. Verzelini died in 1606. He had sold his concession to Sir Jerome Bowes in 1592. Bowes sold it to Vice-Admiral Sir Robert Mansell, who by degrees bought up all the licences for glassmaking in England and so became the most influential *entrepreneur* in the English glass industry of the seventeenth century — until the Civil War broke out and destroyed his life's work. He died in 1656. During the last third of the seventeenth century the lead-glass first made by Ravenscroft in 1676 began to gain ground.

In the German-speaking countries north of the Alps the history of the setting up of glasshouses for *Cristallynenglas auf Venedische Ahrtt* goes back to the year 1428, when there is mention in Vienna of a Venetian named Onossorius de Blondi. It remains unclear whether this relates simply to an import licence or to an attempt to set up a factory — which may possibly have been only for mirror-glass. The first of the Viennese glasshouses of which we have inform-ation is that of Niclas Walch, which is known to have existed between 1486 and 1563. Some Venetian glassworkers settled in the Austrian towns which lay nearer to Venice, much earlier: in Villach and Trento in 1468, in Laibach in 1526, in Ala on the Adige in 1552 and in Graz in 1650.

The glass manufacture at Hall in the Tirol is in a category of its own. In 1534 Wolfgang Vitl of Augsburg set up a workshop here, which derived its prestige between 1540 and 1569 from Sebastian Hochstetter. The glasshouse remained under Augsburg directorship until 1602. It employed only German workers, but used as models Venetian forms and styles of decoration, which were combined with native ones. This hybrid style incurred the displeasure of Archduke Ferdinand of the Tirol, who in 1570 founded the court glasshouse at Innsbruck with Venetian workers. The Glasshouse at Hall under Chrysos-tomos Hochstetter took the Innsbruck decorations as its models and trans-ferred them fairly faithfully to indigenous forms, usually *Stangengläser*. It had to contend with great difficulties. In 1635, after it had stood idle for some ten years, the glasshouse was given to the Franciscan Order. In about 1640 production ceased altogether. In all the Tirolean glasses there are decorative pieces in which diamond-engraved lines, lace-work or scroll-work occur to-

Opposite: Ewer made of agate-glass. Arabic writing-characters painted in gold. Venice, be-ginning of the 16th century.

gether with cold-painting (pages 122, 123). The typical colour-combination is gold, red and green. Diamond-engraved double eagles and polychrome arms are also frequently found. The Tiroleans supplied armorial glasses and raw glass to many parts of Europe. The glass metal is not always colourless but often varies between greenish and dark green. Our knowledge of the origins of these glasses is largely based on a fine collection which had been preserved at Schloss Ambras near Innsbruck and was transferred in 1806 to the Kunsthistorisches Museum in Vienna.

In the first half of the sixteenth century Venetian deserters who originally intended to go to Antwerp are said to have settled in Nuremberg. It is uncertain whether they can be associated with the glasses then being made in Nuremberg. The Nuremberg goblets differ both from the Venetian and from the *Waldgläser*. We do not know in which glasshouse they were made. What is certain is that the patricians of Nuremberg, whose taste governed the craftsmanship of the city, commanded wide-ranging trading connections, and that these included commissions for armorial glasses given by themselves in Venice.

More exact information comes from Munich, where in 1584 Duke Wilhelm V entrusted the Venetian Giovanni Scarpoggiato with setting up a glasshouse. It was not, however, a commercial success.

The glasshouse for making crystalline glass founded in 1583 in Cassel by the Landgrave Wilhelm IV with the assistance of Francesco Warisco of Venice was short-lived. Warisco brought other compatriots from the Netherlands, among them Tiberius Frizer, who later set up a glasshouse at Simmern for the Count Palatine Reichart. After a year and a half spent in unprofitable production, during which they made various 'treasures of ingenious work', the Venetians left Cassel. A copious selection of wing-glasses (page 116) as well as drinking 'pipes' and thread-glasses have survived. A master glassmaker from Bohemia, who from 1594 onwards ran a glasshouse in the 'Schörgründen' with glassmakers from Hesse, is reputed to have made more wing-glasses and other types of glass.

For about a year and a half, between 1607 and 1609, a Venetian glasshouse operated in Cologne. The citizens expressed their disapproval of this inflammable enterprise by armed attacks on the factory, and in the end it seems in fact to have been burnt down. One of the glasshouse owners came of the Saroldi family, whom we have already encountered as the founders of the glasshouse at Nevers.

In Thuringia Duke Bernhard von Sachsen-Weimar (1604–1639), well known as a general during the Thirty Years' War, had Venetian glass made at Tambach by Italian workers.

In 1679 Johann Georg II entrusted the Venetian Bernardo Marinetti, whom he had summoned from Vienna, with the founding and running of a glasshouse at Dessau; it continued until 1686 and records report a 'good success'. Having quarelled with Johann Kunckel and being disillusioned with the French master glassmaker, Simon de Tournay, Kurfürst Friedrich III of Brandenburg in 1696 sent for the Venetian Giovanni Pallada then in Haarlem to go to Berlin. A glasshouse was set up in the Molkenmarkt to make large round French sheets of glass and delicate drinking glasses. But Pallada was incapable of running the concern; he incurred debts and in 1698 secretly left Berlin 'with a considerable sum of gold'. He travelled to Nijmegen and thence to Nuremberg, on his way back to Venice. In Nuremberg he sent his Berlin coachman home. Attempts to seize Pallada failed.

Two Venetian glasshouses in Stockholm were more successful: one had been set up as early as 1640 by Melchior Jung, the second was founded by Giacomo Scapitta in 1676. Using Italian workers, they continued into the seventeenth and eighteenth centuries respectively to make glasses after Dutch, French and Italian models. The glass illustrated on page 117 comes from the factory set up by Scapitta on the Kungsholmen in Stockholm, which remained in production until 1815. Five similar glasses from Sweden with moulded initials on the stem are known. One of them — preserved in the Hamburg Museum für Kunst und Gewerbe — has a monogram within a circular frame.

During the second half of the seventeenth century still other Venetian glasshouses were set up in northern Europe — in Kiel, Copenhagen and Königsberg — but engraved glass was already making its appearance and the Venetian houses were soon superseded.

After its great successes, the Venetian glass industry was now in a serious position. We hear of one Giuseppe Briati who in about 1700 went to Bohemia to study the new style of glassmaking. But he was unable to restore Venice's fortunes.

Waldglas and its manufacture

The social position of the glassmakers varied. In Venice, Altare and France some rose to the ranks of the aristocracy. By contrast, the position of the glassmakers of the forest glasshouses was less fortunate: they were outsiders. During the summer sorties these men lived secluded lives in the forest and complaints of 'wrangles, brawls and blows' were not infrequent. They passed on their knowledge to none but their sons. In this way and by intermarrying, they became to an ever-increasing degree a single large family. The same names crop up again and again in the regions of the glasshouses: Gundelach and Kunckel in Hesse, Wenzel and Schürer in Bohemia, Preussler in Silesia, Greiner in Thuringia, to name only the best-known families. Glassmakers from the German forest glasshouses appear in Denmark, Sweden, the Netherlands and Lorraine as well.

The wares were sold by itinerant merchants; in the Black Forest there were organised companies of glass-carriers. The merchants were, however, permitted to sell the glasses inside the country only. Export was usually reserved for the glasshouses. The principal exporting country was Hesse, which in the sixteenth century occupied second place after Venice. Wares were exported both to north and east: to Holstein, Mecklenburg, Denmark, Sweden, Russia, as well as down the Rhine to Holland.

There are documents which record the existence of *Waldglashütten* in central Europe dating from the early fourteenth century. Thus there is, for example, a decree of the Emperor Ludwig IV, the Bavarian, dating from the year 1340, concerning the closure of the glasshouses in the imperial forest near Nuremberg. The region of the Fichtelgebirge, the Thuringian forest, Silesia and the Solling were also mentioned as early as the fourteenth century. Written records relating to Bohemia, Hesse and Lorraine date only from the fifteenth century, but we should not conclude from this that the glasshouses in these regions were more recent. All the sources show that production had already long been in progress.

The first area to achieve a position of considerable consequence was the Spessart, where 'on Friday before the day of St James, the holy Apostle, counting from the birth of our lord Christ fourteen hundred years and thereafter in the sixth year' forty glassmakers in and around the Spessart set out their conditions of work in an open letter. Nominating 'the noble gracious lord, Count Ludewick, Count of Rieneck', whom they appointed arbiter, they acknowledged the following regulations:

Glass was to be made only between Easter and 'St Martin's day' (11 November) each year.

No work was to be done on Monday (this decree must have referred to the final stages in the making of a glass and have been designed to prevent fusing being kept as part of Sunday's work).

A master and his journeyman were not to make more than two hundred *Kuttrolfe* 'or the equivalent of a *Kuttrolf*' or three hundred beakers in a day. The second journeyman, 'who stands in front of the small hole (the working opening in the pot furnace)', was to make one hundred *Kuttrolfe* or 'seven quarter beakers' (175 pieces) at the most per day.

A day's output of window-glass was not to exceed six hundredweight of small glass or four hundredweight of large glass.

No glasshouse was to possess more than one stretching furnace for window-glass.

Waldgläser and their descendants to the 18th century

The influence of the Renaissance was not felt in northern Europe before c 1530. The applied drops used in the decoration of *Nuppenbecher*, disposed vertically during the Gothic period, were now arranged diagonally and the drops themselves were flatter. The vast *Humpen*, the measure of the mighty thirst of the period, became the most usual form of drinking glass. In the Netherlands the *Römer* attained a gigantic size. *Waldglas* with enamel-decoration made its first appearance c 1530—1550 and remained popular until the 18th century.

The designation *Waldglashütte* or forest glasshouse is justified only until the time when the travelling glasshouses became established in one place or until the period when manufacture came under the protectorship of the prince. This happened in the 17th—18th centuries. The notion of *Waldglas*, however, remained in use until as late as the 18th century as the qualitative designation for 'green glass'.

First row: bowl, below it *Krautstrunk*, beaker, *Passglas*, *Igel* (hedgehog glass). Second row: glass of the Saxon court cellars, glass with pendant rings, *Kuttrolf*, bottle. Third row: *Humpen* with Imperial eagle, *Römer* from the Netherlands, glass with thumb-impressions.

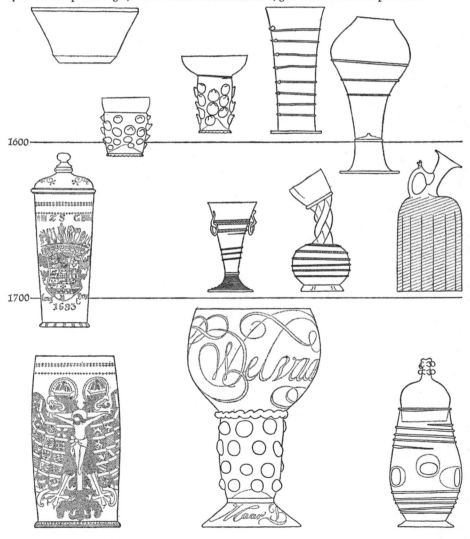

Trade-secrets were to be passed on to none but the sons of glassmakers and these were to adhere to the conditions of work.

No journeyman coming from 'other fields' was to be taken on unless he swore to abide by the conditions of work.

A beginner (apprentice) was to learn for three hours every day on one or two glasses; anything he made above and beyond this was to be destroyed or it would be deducted from the master's permitted total.

Each of the forty glassmakers commended these regulations to the Count 'and in person with outstretched hands took an oath to the saints'. Anyone who broke his oath was threatened with the penalty of being classed as 'dishonourable' and of having to pay twenty florins, of which five were to go to the Count or his heirs, five to the Spessart forest-warden and the remaining ten to the glassmakers. Everyone was placed under the obligation of informing: 'and one of us shall denounce the other by name on the grounds of the above-mentioned oath if he should see or hear that one or more fail to hold to this article, and whoever does not do so, as shall truthfully be discovered, shall also be fined. . . .' The document was sealed by Count Ludwig zu Rieneck and 'Junker Haman Echter, now vidame and forest-warden at Aschaffenburg'.

All controversies arising out of this charter were dealt with 'on the Spessart on the Bechless', where the glassmakers met anually on Whit Monday.

When the Peasants' Revolt broke out in Hegau in 1524, spread to become the Peasants' War and — condemned by Luther — was finally put down amid bloodshed, the glassmakers of the Spessart were on the side of the peasants. The Swabian League under Truchsess von Waldburg laid waste their furnaces and glasshouses, and the harsh punishments meted out by the princes, which cost the lives of Thomas Munzer, Florian Geyer and countless others, affected the glassmakers of the Spessart too. The Archbishop of Mainz, to whose see most of the Spessart belonged, withdrew the privilege from his glassmakers, who were thereby compelled to move elsewhere. They transferred to the neighbouring principality of Hesse, which had in the meantime become the most important of the glasshouse districts and whose glassmakers also belonged to the Spessart federation. Almerode in the Kaufunger Wald became a new guild-centre; it was here that the largest deposits of sand for glass and clay for the pots lay — deposits which are still being worked today. The federation was now — from 1537 onwards — called the 'Hessischer Gläsnerbund' because the glasshouses procure 'the earth for the pots, the ashes and the journeymen for glassmaking from the principality of Hesse'.

The *Hessischer Gläsnerbund* was the most important of the glassmakers' guilds of the fifteenth century. Its glasshouses were situated in those wooded areas from the Main to the Elbe which were favourable from the point of view of raw-materials and of commerce — they thus lay in different sovereign territories. These were joined in 1574 by Schleswig-Holstein — although it possessed only one glasshouse—and in 1585 by Denmark. The protector of the guild was Philipp, Landgrave of Hesse. He had six guild-masters who operated as jurors as well and whose duty it was to visit the glasshouses to see that guild regulations were observed. The most powerful was Franz Gundelach (page 145), known as Becker; he represented the glassmakers vis-à-vis the Landgrave. The strength of the guild lay in the fact that it could refuse both to allow the glasshouses the raw materials from the Kaufunger Wald which they needed and to send journeymen glassmakers from Hesse. It was empowered to request the journeymen of erring glasshouse masters to leave the glasshouse. Princes who did not, as did Philipp of Hesse, possess deposits of raw materials could only offer their glassmakers the wood they needed for fuel and ash. In case of need, pebbles from river-beds could be found everywhere. But the fire-resistant pot-clay of Almerode was almost irreplaceable. The demand for it remains high to this day.

The glassmakers set up their glasshouses by streams in areas allocated to them by the forest-warden. Here they worked from Easter until St Martin's day, while their families remained at home in the villages. Each master had from two to three journeymen: one made drinking glasses — he was the only one to work at the 'small hole' — one prepared the glass substance, and one, the stretcher, made window-glass. The statutes in force in the Hessian federation from 1537 onwards — which are in the main similar to those of the Spessart guild of 1406 — enable us to calculate approximately how many glasses were made in 1557 by the Hessian guild alone, assuming that its members comprised the two hundred glassmakers who met in this year at Almerode as required by the guild regulations. If there were between three and four glassmakers to each glasshouse, the number of glasshouses may have been in the region of fifty-five. Altogether they were permitted to make 16,500 beer-glasses (e.g. *Passgläser*, page 139) or 26,125 beakers, as well as 330 hundredweight of small or 220 hundredweight of large window-glass every day. That makes in the 148 working days between Easter and St Martin's day some 2,500,00 beer-glasses or four million beakers and either 2,400 or 1,600 tons of window-glass in a single year. The master received one florin for two hundred beer-glasses and the same amount for 225 *Steinbecher* (beakers with glass spots or small drops drawn out to a point). If the output of a glasshouse were equally divided between beer-glasses and *Steinbecher,* its gross annual takings for drinking glasses amounted to about 250 florins. We do not know at what prices window-glass was sold.

The taxes payable by the *Waldhütten* comprised tax on the glasshouse, forest dues, tax on clay, and tribute glass. Around 1557, tax on the glasshouse in Hesse amounted to thirty thalers, the forest dues to thirteen thalers, the tax on clay to five thalers, that is forty-eight thalers in all, or ninety-six florins. Besides this the prince exacted sixty beer-glasses and six lots of window-glass as so-called tribute glass. This brought the taxes up to about one hundred florins. Then there were the journeymen to pay; these too were paid in kind, presumably in glasses. Besides this, the man who made the drinking glasses received an initial payment — the amount of which was controlled by guild regulation — to prevent his being enticed elsewhere. Payment of the journeymen was not mentioned until the latest charter, of 1629. It amounted to sixty thalers for the first and fifty for the other journeymen and to seven and a half for crucible hands. By this time the tax on the glasshouse had also risen to one hundred and twenty thalers, the forest dues to sixty thalers and the tax on clay to five thalers. In compensation, it was open to the glasshouses to increase their income through gilding and enamel-painting. A price-list of Adam Götze's glasshouse dating from 1658 gives the price of gilt armorial glasses as one thaler each; while one hundred *Römer* cost only three florins (1 thaler = 2 florins). Economic conditions had, indeed, fundamentally changed by about this time, for the glasshouses now had to contend with difficulties in selling. The Thirty Years' War had brought business in general to a standstill. Even the *Hessischer Gläsnerbund* had long since lost its influence and had shrunk to a local guild of the Cassel district. The Harz with its rich endowment of raw materials had deserted as long ago as 1570. It was inevitable that the power which the federation had wielded over glasshouses belonging to foreign princes should in time lead to legal tensions. In particular, there were differences which persisted for some time between Hesse and Brunswick-Calenberg over territorial rights in that frontier district in the Kaufunger Wald favoured by glassmakers because of its nearness to sources of raw materials. Besides this, the limitation of production originally imposed by the glassmakers themselves in the interests of quality and marketability became more and more of an impediment from which the foreign glasshouses were the first to seek to free themselves. They increased their output and paid higher wages, had severe penalties imposed upon them; refused to acknowledge them and called upon the authorities to protect them; the federation withdrew supplies of raw materials and journeymen, and the final split came when new stocks of raw materials were discovered. The *Hessischer Gläsnerbund* lost its importance during the seventeenth century.

Many things now happened all at once: there was the war with its devastations, the territorial limitation of the principalities, the setting up of their own glasshouses by other princes in sales areas which had hitherto belonged to Hesse, and, not least, the recognition that the forest — unprofitable at first but so suitably turned to account by the glasshouses with their taxes and forest dues — was in fact being too drastically exploited.

Opposite: Goblet with enamel-painting. Foot supplied in silver gilt. Venice, c 1500. Height 28 cm.

Beaker with moveable rings in loops. Germany, beginning of the 17th century. Height 9.5 cm.

Kerzenbecher made of thick brownish-green glass. Germany, 17th century. Height 12 cm.

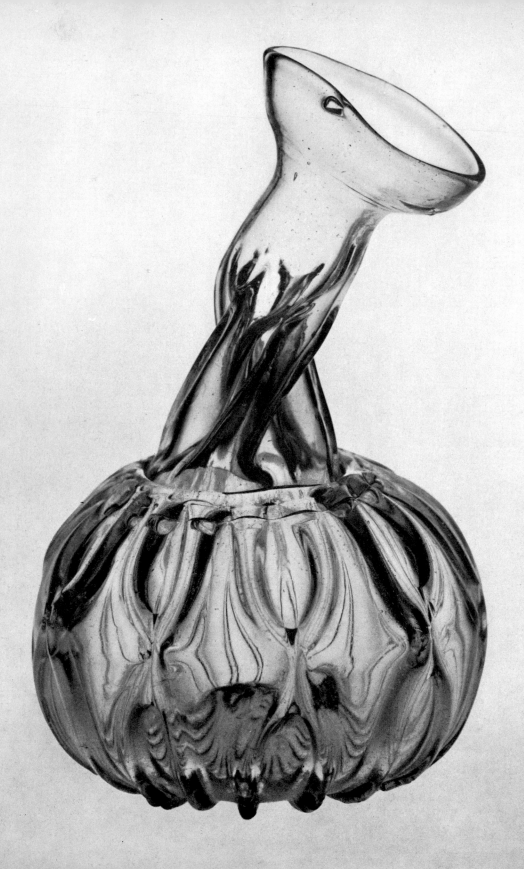

Opposite: Kuttrolf made of colourless glass. Neck consists of four intertwined tubes. Germany, end of the 16th century. Height 20.4 cm. *Top: Scheuer* made of dark bluish-green glass. Germany, c 1500. Height 6.4 cm. *Bottom: Nuppenglas.* Germany, c 1650. Height 21.5 cm.

Left: Double beaker in the shape of a woman carrying a basket. Glass with a purple glint, blue glass, white enamel painting, pincered thread decoration. Germany, 17th–18th century. Height 24 cm. *Right:* Bottle with ornamental stopper and glass chain. Germany or the Netherlands, 17th century. Height 21 cm.

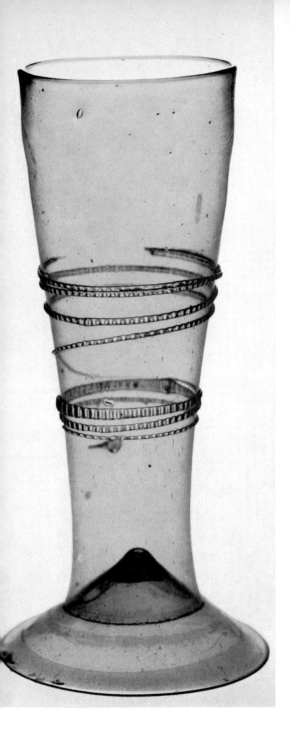

Left: Club-shaped glass. Light moss-green glass with applied and pincered thread. Germany, second half of the 17th century. Height 15.3 cm. *Right:* Group of glasses in bluish-green. There were originally eight small beakers hanging from the cover. Germany, 16th century. Height 53 cm.

Left: Humpen belonging to Joachimus Zoller. Bohemian-Silesian, dated 1669. Height 28.5 cm.
Right: Marriage glass, south Germany, dated 1596. Height 17 cm.

Left: Humpen with lines in praise of idleness. Bohemian-Silesian, dated 1621. Height 27 cm.
Right: Pastor's glass from Schmalenbuchen (Pastor Nicholas Schuttwolf in Neuhaus am Renn-steig). Thuringia, 1702—04. Height 19 cm.

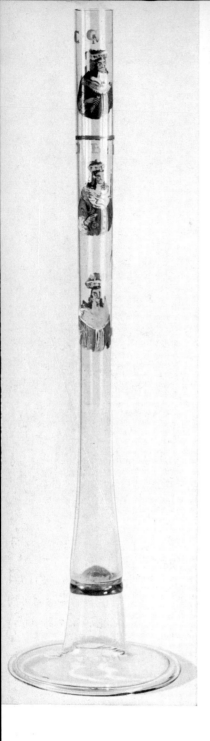

Left: Stangenglas with Electors in cold-painting. Central Germany, c 1650. Height 42 cm.
Right: Kurfürstenhumpen (Elector glass). Smoke-coloured glass with polychrome enamel-painting. German Emperor with the Seven Electors. Bohemia, dated 1596. Height 28.6 cm.

Left: Reichsadlerhumpen. Greenish glass. Double-eagle with portrait of Emperor Leopold I and his son, also arms arranged in the Quaternion system. Bohemia, dated 1685. Height 18.9 cm. *Right:* Elector glass. Central Germany, dated 1645. Height 31.4 cm.

143

Left: Willkommhumpen or greeting-glass of the Coburg bakers' guild. Olive-green glass. Lauscha, Thuringia, dated 1672. Height 23.5 cm. *Right: Hallorenglas.* Saxony, 1681. Height 42 cm. *Opposite: Humpen* showing Franz Gundelach and family. Hesse, dated 1602. Height 28 cm.

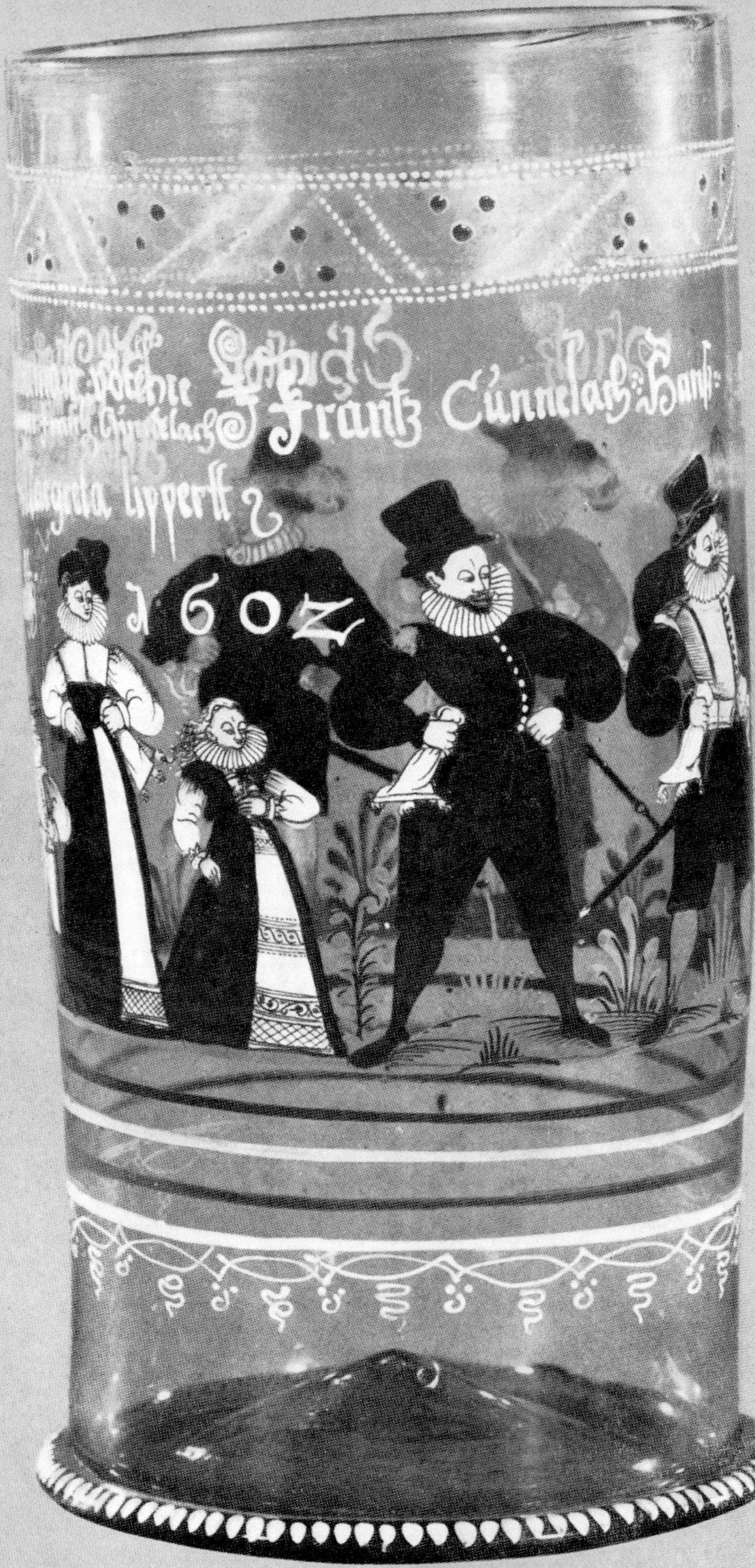
Frantz Cunnelach
1602

Left: Goblet and cover. Colourless glass. St George and the Dragon. Germany, dated 1677. Height 31 cm. *Right: Humpen* and cover showing the Peace of Westphalia. Franconia, dated 1652. Height without cover 27 cm.

Cup showing the *Ochsenkopf*, a mountain in the Fichtelgebirge. Bischofsgrün, dated 1717. Height 20.8 cm. (Back and front).

Left: Passglas with playing-card (King of Spades). Thuringia or Saxony, dated 1734. Height 24.5 cm. *Right:* Cylindrical *Humpen* showing shooting-contest. Bohemia or central Germany, dated 1607. Height 28.5 cm.

Left: Humpen showing animals playing musical instruments. Upper Franconia, dated 1683. Height 17.6 cm. *Right: Roemer* with cover showing a man on horseback, from a series of similar glasses. Property of the Von Schwertzell family of Hesse. Probably Hesse, dated 1665. Height 35 cm.

Passglas with white enamel-painting. Germany, 17th–18th century. Height 27 cm. *Top right:* beaker with *Schwarzlot* painting. Johann Schaper, Nuremberg, 1664. Height 7 cm. *Bottom right:* Beaker of horn-coloured glass with gold and coloured enamel-painting. Inscription 'An Gottes Segen ist alles gelegen' Anno 1679 (God's blessing gained, all is obtained). Germany, dated 1679. Height 8.9 cm.

Beaker. Colourless glass with battle-scene painted in *Schwarzlot*. Signed 'John Schaper, 1665'.
Nuremberg, dated 1665. Height 10 cm.

Left: Humpen with enamel-painted musicians. Bohemia, dated 1667. Height 18.7 cm. *Right: Humpen* with hunting scenes. Hesse, dated 1669. Height 29.2 cm.

Painting on glass

Enamel-painting is a technique which has been practised, with interruptions, since the time of Thotmes III in about 150 BC (page 42). It reached its high-water mark in Syria in the thirteenth century, whence it passed, by way of Venice, to Germany, enjoying there the greatest popularity during the sixteenth and seventeenth centuries, and even in the eighteenth. The earliest enamel-painted glasses in Germany were the armorial glasses which had previously been commissioned in Venice; later on, glasses made in Venice were painted in Germany and finally native glass vessels were painted there.

A special group dating from this early period comprises thread-glasses made in the forest glasshouses, most of which carried painted Saxon arms, though some bore hunting scenes; the glasses were *Humpen*, beakers, bottles and goblets, which were undoubtedly modelled on the technique of the Venetian thread-glasses although they did not match them in delicacy or regularity. During the late sixteenth century they were made in Bohemia and Silesia and in the seventeenth in Saxony.

Polychrome figural representations after engravings or woodcuts are far more numerous than the armorial glasses. They are pleasant, naive paintings which make no claim to be great art. Certain specific groups appear over and over again; of these the *Reichsadlerhumpen* or *Humpen* showing the imperial double eagle (page 143) deserve first mention, then the *Kurfürstenhumpen* or Elector *Humpen* (page 142) showing the Emperor and his seven Electors, the *Familienhumpen* (page 145), in which all the members of the family are arranged in their hierarchy, and the *Humpen* bearing hunting scenes, apostles, the ages and conditions of man, and portraits. The commonest form of vessel was the cylindrical *Humpen* with a projecting kick (page 145) — described by Luther as 'obscenely large' — which supplanted the *Stangenglas* with the high base (page 148, left). But beakers, jugs (especially in Bohemia at the end of the sixteenth century), *Römer*, goblets and even flutes were painted with similar motifs.

The great majority of enamel-painted glasses bear both dates and inscriptions. Dating therefore presents few difficulties. It is, however, almost impossible to localise them. There are, nevertheless, a few motifs which were favoured in particular districts. Prime among these are the glasses of the Fichtelgebirge (from 1656). They show the Ochsenkopf, the second highest mountain of the Fichtelgebirge, with its rivers, the Main, Naab, Saale and Eger (page 147). The similarity to Kreussen ceramics of the peace-glasses (from 1649) with allegories and words of thanksgiving for the Peace of Westphalia points to the district round Bayreuth. Whereas most of the early armorial glasses come from south Germany, the *Hofkellereigläser* or royal cellar glasses (from 1610) are found in Saxony and Thuringia, while the *Hallorengläser* (from 1679) come from the district of Halle (page 144). The Halloren were salt-workers in and around Halle, who had a guild-like organisation and their own customs and dress. In Thuringia again *Passgläser* showing playing cards (page 148) — a link with the playing-card industry of Altenburg — were extremely popular.

Only rarely does the metal, the enamel-colour, the shape or the ornament provide a pointer to the centre of manufacture. Bohemian glass is usually of a smoky topaz colour; that of Hesse varies: in 1630 it was pale green. The coloured reproductions on page 152 show these differences clearly. The combination of yellow and cobalt-blue — with applied gold as well — is common in Bohemia; in Franconia light enamel-colours — white, yellow and pale blue — predominate. The sides of the Bohemian *Humpen* are straight: the Franconians tended to prefer bulging vessels. Filling-in ornament in the shape of white scrolls and coloured flowers is regarded as a distinguishing feature of the Bohemian enamel-painted glasses, as are the straight borders of dots resembling strings of beads, while a common Franconian border takes the form of a broad band of dotted lines resembling hanging garlands (page 146).

The brightly-coloured, naive enamel-painting just described was admired mainly in Germany. It did, indeed, exist in France too, but there did not achieve the same popularity as in the German countries. There was a revival of enamel-painting in the second half of the eighteenth century, but this time the colour-schemes were more reticent and covered the surfaces more sparingly. Most popular of all was white enamel-decoration as executed in both Germany (page 150) and England. William and Mary Beilby, a brother and sister from Newcastle, were well known in England for this style of painting (page 223).

In Holland, however, painting *en grisaille* with *Schwarzlot* was evolved at the beginning of the seventeenth century; from Holland it spread to northern Germany, whence Johann Schaper took it to Nuremberg in 1655. He became the chief practitioner of a particular kind of *Schwarzlot* painting on glass, which continues to be found in southern Germany until 1700. Painters in this style liked figural scenes, mythological themes, battle-scenes (page 151) and landscapes (page 150). Other artists who belonged to this group were Johann Ludwig Faber, who also invented a few transparent colours, Hermann Bencherlt and Johann Keyll, all of whom signed their work. Some of them were also *Hausmaler* painting faience on their own account. Interlaced strapwork and foliage and chinoiseries began to appear frequently in *Schwarzlot* painting at the beginning of the eighteenth century. The best-known painters on glass in this style are Daniel Pressler and his son Ignaz (page 178), who worked

Painting on glass, the painters and their signatures

Most of the painted decoration on glasses between the fifteenth and the nineteenth centuries was anonymous enamel-work in opaque colours on *Humpen* and *Stangengläser*. It was not until the seventeenth century that transparent colours began to be developed with *Schwarzlot*, iron-red and manganese-purple. *Hausmaler* on porcelain and faience had a hand in this (Faber, Preissler and others). The *Hausmaler* (only the principal ones are noticed here) were free with their signatures. Great numbers of painted milk-white glasses made in imitation of porcelain were produced during the eighteenth century in Venice, Thuringia, France and England. But the great age of miniature-painting on glass was the Biedermeier period (Mohn and Kothgasser).

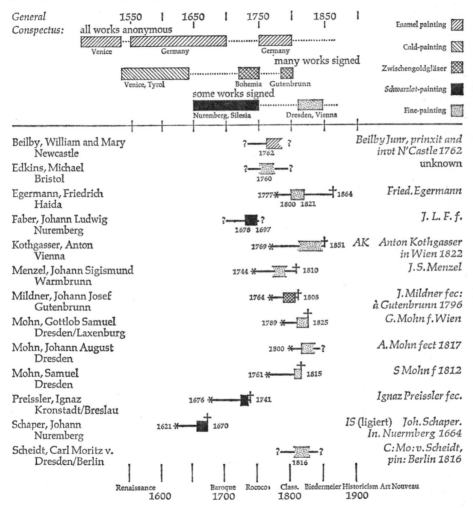

Gold-decoration on Venetian glasses consisted from the 15th century onwards of applied gold-leaf and from 1530 until 1570 of gold-painting behind the glass. The anonymous *Zwischengoldgläser* with their engraved gold-leaf decoration made their appearance during the second quarter of the 18th century. This technique was revived in the Classical period in Mildner's glasses, which have gold-engraved medallion panels. Exposed gold-painting became more frequent in the mid 18th century, most of it consisting of gold borders to engraved glasses.

in Bohemia and Silesia. *Schwarzlot* painting — with the addition of gold heightening and iron-red flesh-colour — stands virtually on its own in a century dominated by cut glass.

Schwarzlot represents the beginning of the development of transparent colours for hollow glasses, such as had, indeed, appeared on Islamic glasses of the twelfth to the fourteenth centuries but had so far remained unknown in Europe. Opaque colours only — they were basically no more than coloured tin or faience glazes of the type employed in Europe since the ninth century — had always since their first appearance in Venice been used for enamel-painted glasses. In contrast to these, the transparent colours are coloured transparent glass-pastes. The numerous porcelain factories which emerged around the middle of the eighteenth century were interested in perfecting them. These factories with their true porcelain came up against the milk-white glasses which had been fashionable before the invention of porcelain in 1708.

The origins of the milk-white glasses ('bone-glasses') go back once more to Egypt, where 'Egyptian porcelain' was made in the fourteenth century. 'Egyptian porcelain' differs from 'Persian porcelain' in that it was not, as in Persia, faience, but glass. By the first half of the fifteenth century this *lattimo* already existed in Venice and by the seventeenth and eighteenth centuries it had spread to all parts of Europe. Special mention should be made of the Venetian milk-white glasses of the eighteenth century (page 178) with their iron-red painting *en camaïeu* (page 178) and the milk-white glasses painted in polychrome transparent colours in Bohemia, Thuringia, France and England. The principal themes, however, were chinoiseries, Watteau-scenes, mythological subjects and genre-paintings, all of which also form the repertoire of Rococo porcelain. One of the best-known painters of chinoiseries on milk-white glass — and on Delft earthenware — was Michael Edkins. Edkins worked in Bristol, where, besides milk-white glass, blue glasses were made and painted with gold (page 178).

Somewhere in Bohemia at the beginning of the eighteenth century the technique of the *Zwischengoldgläser*, as it had been known in antiquity (pages 214–215), was revived. The engraved leaves of gold or silver foil were inserted at first into beakers and later into goblets also, as well as other double-sided vessels. This type of gold decoration is sometimes combined with coloured glass or cold-painting. The numerous portrayals of saints and the relationship of this technique with the early Christian glasses in Rome have led to the supposition that it was first revived in the monasteries. Later pieces carry hunting scenes, mythological subjects, allegories and, towards the end of the century, silhouettes. Mildner of Lower Austria revived the technique of the *Zwischengoldgläser* yet again in 1787.

Diamond-engraved glass and Netherlandish glass

Glass was scratched with flints or other hard implements in antiquity and the practice continued in Mesopotamia and Persia during the Middle Ages. Diamond-point engraving, however, is not found in antiquity, despite the fact that the diamond was known to the Greeks. They named it 'the invincible' or *adamas* — hence our word. Ludwig von Berquem, a Flemish lapidary, was the first to use diamond-dust for polishing stones in Bruges in 1456.

The earliest diamond-point engraved glasses are to be found in Venice and in Hall in Tirol in about 1550. Schwanhardt the Elder first employed this technique in Germany. Giacomo Verzelini introduced it into England.

Certain characteristic qualities were favoured in a few districts — but they do not enable us to draw rigid distinctions. Fine, cobweb-like engraving is the rule in Italy, where it is found either on dark-coloured glasses or on *cristallo* gilt. The Hall decorators preferred straight hatches combined with cold-painting and engraved gold. Schwanhardt and his successors utilised the diamond to perfect intaglio engraving; only Schwanhardt himself also practised pure diamond-engraving. So great was his skill with the diamond-point that the Emperor Ferdinand III summoned him to Regensburg during the Imperial Diet in order to learn diamond-engraving from him. This technique was widespread in Germany, however, only from about 1570 until the outbreak of the Thirty Years' War, when enamel-painting supplanted diamond-point engraving; then in the seventeenth century engraved glass gradually replaced enamel-painting. In the Netherlands diamond-point decoration continued to be exercised with mastery right to the end of the seventeenth century.

In Germany three groups worked in this technique: in Nuremberg, Saxony and Silesia. Diamond-point engraved *Humpen* and *Römer*, many of them with armorial bearings, constitute the majority of these anonymous wares. Only three names are known and they date from a later period: one is that of Peter Wolff of Cologne (page 158), who signed three glasses dated 1660, 1669 and 1677; the second is August Otto Ernst von dem Busch, a canon of Hildesheim, who produced signed diamond-engravings from 1745 onwards; and the third is C. A. F. Werther in Cologne, epigone of his colleague Busch. Busch's particular manner was to resolve his subjects — mostly landscapes with ruins or figural scenes — into fine hatches, which he then stained with soot, thus adapting dry-point etching to glass; he also decorated porcelain in the same style. At the end of the eighteenth century Johann Josef Mildner in Lower Austria also produced glasses with pure diamond-point decoration.

The earliest diamond-point decoration in the Netherlands also dates from the sixteenth century. The earliest known piece is dated 1581. Beakers, *Humpen*

The diamond-point engravers and stipplers and their signatures

The decorative finishing of glasses with the diamond-point had been, as far back as the early, anonymous period of the 16th century, one of the provinces of the Dutch artists. The earliest diamond-point glasses are found in Venice, followed soon afterwards by centres in northern Europe.

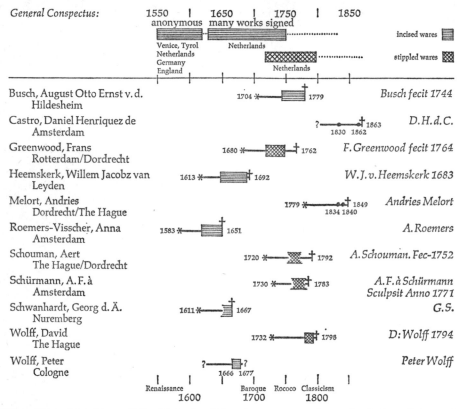

The calligraphic glasses of the Netherlandish artists represent the peak of the technique of diamond-point engraving. The principal practitioners were Heemskserk and Anna Roemers-Visscher. Besides these, there were a number of other artists in the eighteenth century, all of whom signed their work: B. Boers, C. H. v. Boselager, Jan Bot, van Bull, de l'Hommel, Pieter Kibon, C. Koster, H. V. Lockhorst, C. J. Meier, M. Petit, A. C. Schonk, Anna Maria van Schurmann, Izaak Spaan, Maria Tesselschade, H. Zweerts.

The German exponents of this branch of decoration were outsiders: Schwanhardt was mainly a glass-engraver. He and his Nuremberg school executed fine works of glass-engraving with the diamond. During his last years the diamond-point engaged him more closely; he found no followers in Nuremberg. His only pupil in this art was the Emperor Ferdinand III (1653). Canon Busch was an impassioned amateur who produced engravings which he blackened with soot, as did his contemporary and colleague, C. A. F. Werther of Cologne, a follower of Busch's but of lesser importance. Another of the Germans who signed their work was Peter Wolff of Cologne.

The technique of stippling is found only in the Netherlands. It was introduced by Greenwood. D. Wolff and Aert Schouman were painters. There are signed works in stipple of the same period by Jacobus van den Blijk, Willem Fortuijn, G. H. Hoolaart, P. Luyten, Andries Melort and W. Sautijn; and of D. H. de Castro from the first half of the 19th century.

and giant *Römer* were at first the favourite glasses here too (page 172). From the seventeenth century onwards the most widespread were the ever-popular *Römer,* the native flute-glasses (page 120), the wing-glasses (page 121) made by Venetian glasshouses in the Netherlands and bulging bottles with long necks. Predominant in the eighteenth century were imported English lead-glasses in their characteristic form with stems (page 175). Holland had at this time given itself over almost exclusively to decorating glass.

The seventeenth century, after the Wars of Liberation, brought a remarkable economic and cultural boom to the United Netherlands; it also saw Dutch glass at one of the peaks of its development — represented by calligraphic glasses (page 173). First in the field in this instance was a woman, Anna Roemers-Visscher of Amsterdam. Her sister, too, Maria Tesselschade (1594—1649), was an early practitioner of the art. The third woman who made a name for herself with this type of decoration was Anna Maria van Schurmann (1607—78) — not to be confused with A. F. à Schürmann who in the 1780s used both stippling and hatching on the same piece. The most celebrated of the men was Willem Jacobz van Heemskerk of Leiden, cloth-merchant and poet, who liked round green glass bottles with long necks. He must also have been the most industrious, for he left 259 works. Like himself, most of his successors down to the nineteenth century were amateurs who engraved glass simply as a hobby.

The stipple-engraved wares of the eighteenth century represent the greatest triumph of Dutch glass. This technique, which was exclusive to the Dutch, was introduced by Frans Greenwood. It consists in striking the diamond or steel point against the glass with a small hammer. Mezzotint engraving had been invented by Ludwig van Siegen of Utrecht in 1643 and was very popular in both Holland and England at about this time. Mezzotint is a type of copper-plate engraving in which the plate is roughened and produces a soft velvety tone. Stippling on glass produces a similar effect. Greenwood was a master of this technique (page 174). His followers, particularly the two painters, David Wolff and Aert Schouman, who worked from their own designs, are also among the great masters of glass-decoration (page 175).

Wheel-engraved glass is found rather more rarely in Holland. It was intro-duced by Germans in the first half of the eighteenth century. Simon Jacob Sang and Jacob Sang — first recognised as two distinct artistic personalities by H. E. van Gelder in 1958 — went to Amsterdam from Erfurt (page 177). Christian Schroeder (page 176) was a Berliner and Christoffel Grisnich Schröffel came from Austria. Their figures with brightly polished eyes and their style of representation point unmistakeably to the Berlin-Potsdam school centred round Elias Rosbach. Wilhelm Otto Robart (1696—1778), whose works date from the mid-eighteenth century, was a Dutchman.

The great 17th century Nuremberg glass-engravers, their contemporaries and followers

The development of the art of engraving preceded glass by degrees so small that innovations were barely perceptible and only in the final result was progress apparent. Thanks largely to the Venetians, the art of glassmaking had gained prestige and was in a position to enjoy the favour and patronage of the mighty and of those who wished to cut a figure. The art had, however, become restricted — by Venice, the principal maker — to thinly blown utilitarian glasses of all possible varieties and by the provincial glasshouses to the typical *Waldglas*. It was, of course engraved crystal, not glass, which had been used since the fourteenth century to satisfy the demands for greater luxury evinced by the courts of Europe — foremost among them Prague under the Emperor Rudolph II (1576—1612), 'a true father and foster-father of the arts and of artists'. Neither in the robust form of *Waldglas* nor in that of *cristallo* could glass be expected to produce results comparable to those executed, for example, in Prague by the rock-crystal engravers of the Milanese family of Miseroni. Joachim von Sandrart, who himself lived in Prague and Nuremberg and saw with his own eyes, writes of Octavio Miseroni that he 'made for the most honoured Emperor such marvellous rarities and utensils which may be seen in the Imperial treasury, that, besides very great rewards and high favour, Your Majesty has on their account most graciously raised him not only to the office of master of the salt but also to the degree of Freiherr, providing him with all civil authority and lands pertaining thereto'.

Not until the knowledge of how to make glass of sufficient purity and freedom from bubbles had spread to the indigenous glasshouses did the conditions exist in which artists could achieve effects with glass superior to those of rock-crystal. Another contributory factor was that the sources of crystal were limited and could not permanently satisfy the needs of the aristocracy and the rising patricians. Nevertheless, prejudices would not be counteracted nor recognition of engraved glass won until a convincing artistic personality emerged. The reconstruction which followed the Thirty Years' War was cal-

Opposite: Glass from the Chapter of Mainz Cathedral. Probably a gift from the Chapter to Archbishop Johann Schweikard von Kronberg (1604—26). Arms of the Archbishop, St Martin, arms of the 24 members of the Cathedral Chapter, 12 suffragans, 8 hereditary and Imperial offices, 18 domiciliars, a view of Mainz and the inscription: 'Celsitudo atque nobilitas florentissimae metropolitanae ecclesiae et civitatis Moguntinae, ut es anno 1617 constitu', all engraved with the diamond-point. Signed by the artist: 'I R. fecit'. Height 32 cm.

Left: Sturzbecher (the contents had to be quaffed at one draft before the glass could be inverted and laid down) by Georg Schwanhardt the Elder (1601–67), Nuremberg. Height 22.8 cm. *Right: Sturzbecher* with head and shoulders of King Gustav Adolf, flanked by monogram 'GA' and 'R'. Georg Schwanhardt the Elder, Nuremberg. Height of the glass 21.4 cm.

Left: Cylindrical beaker with scene from a bear-hunt. School of Schwanhardt. Nuremberg. Height 10.5 cm. *Right:* Beaker and cover, signed 'Hermann Schwinger inven'. Dated 1672. Inscription round the beaker: 'Wer gemeinen Nutzen schafft, Dessen Ruhm bei allen hafft'. (He who procures general benefit remains in the minds of all.) Nuremberg, Height 26.7 cm.

Left: Cup showing the raising of the siege of Vienna (1683). Nuremberg, Hans Wolfgang Schmidt. Height 52.5 cm. *Right:* Goblet. Double-eagle with the Imperial arms, engraved by Heinrich Schwanhardt (d. 1693). Nuremberg. Height of the goblet 30 cm.

Left: Reverse showing the monogram of the Emperor Leopold I with calligraphic flourishes. *Right:* Goblet with the portrait of a woman, reverse shows woman with crown and shield with monogram E. G. Signed 'Christoph Dorsch. Fecit. Anno. 1712. den. 23. 7bris'. Height 40.5 cm.

Left: Goblet showing crowned lion. Inscription on reverse: 'Je mehr sich in Kriegen meine Feinde mehren, je mehr sich in Siegen mehren meine Ehren'. (The more my enemies multiply in wars, the more my honours multiply in victories.) Georg Friedrich Killinger (active 1694–1726). Nuremberg. Height 36.5 cm. *Right:* Goblet with pseudo-facetted baluster-stem. Signed: 'Joh. Adam WAPPler fecit 1728'. Nuremberg. Height 22.5 cm. *Opposite:* Bottle with chinoiseries, partly after engravings by Paul Decker. Nuremberg, Anton Wilhelm Mauerl, c 1720. Height 18.5 cm.

Left: Goblet with facetting and mat and polished engraving. Arms of Friedrich Heinrich von Seckendorf (1673–1763). Signed 'KILLINGER fec. Norib'. Nuremberg, c 1720. Height 30 cm. *Right:* Tablefountain by G. E. Kunckel. Thuringia before 1721. Height 42 cm.

Goblet by C. E. Kunckel, Gotha, with the arms of Frierich II of Gotha-Altenburg (d. 1732) and 'F' on shield below prince's hat. On the foot 'A' and 'G. E. K. fec.' Height 24.8 cm. (Detail and whole glass.)

Left: Goblet with the arms of the Drach family, probably by Johann Benedikt Hess the Elder, Frankfurt, c 1670. Height 31.4 cm. *Right:* Goblet with large Saxon coat-of-arms. Thuringia or Saxony, c 1720–30. Height 35.5 cm.

Top left: Goblet with view of Schloss Friedenstein in Gotha, Saxon arms on reverse. Attributed to Caspar Creutzburg. Height

33.7 cm. *Bottom left:* Goblet with hollow baluster stem showing the Saxon Electoral arms. Caspar Creutzburg, Gotha. Height 29.7 cm. *Right:* Goblet and cover with Saxon arms 'E' with crown (Duke Friedrich I). Inscription relating to the founding of the family Order of Ernest on the occasion of the inauguration of the princely Residence of Friedrichswerth. Signed 'Am 19. July 1689. Casp. Creutzburg fecit'. Height 35.6 cm.

Left: **Humpen** with diamond-point engraving showing the Pope on horseback and Christ the beggar on a donkey (above: the full scene). Netherlandish, beginning of the 17th century. Height 26.5 cm. *Right:* Goblet with diamond-point engraving of a female figure below the Eye of God, also orange-trees in tubs and an inscription. Dated 1787. English glass c 1700, Netherlandish decoration. Height 21.3 cm.

Stem-glass with diamond-point engraving. Dated 18 November 1756, signed 'P. K.'. English glass, Netherlandish decoration by Pieter Kibon, Haarlem 1756. Height 21.5 cm.

Left: Glass cup with diamond-point stipple engraving of man with a clay pipe. Signed 'F. Greenwood fecit 1764. Holland'. Height 28 cm. *Right:* Glass cup with diamond-point stipple engraving by David Wolff, The Hague, end of the 18th century. Height 14.5 cm.

Left: Diamond-point stipple-engraved English glass carrying the portrait of Prince William V of Orange. David Wolff, The Hague, 1796. Height 17.5 cm. *Right:* Goblet by David Wolff, The Hague, 1794. Height 15.2 cm.

Left: Stem-glass showing allegories of the seasons. Decorated in the manner of C. Schroeder. 18th century. Height 23 cm. *Right:* Stem-glass with combined arms of William V of Orange and his consort Friederike Wilhelmine Sophie von Preussen. Netherlandish decoration, after 1767. Height 31.5 cm. *Opposite:* Goblet. Signed: 'Jacob Sang Fec. Amstr. ao. 1763'. Height 23.5 cm.

Opposite top left: Plate in milk-white glass with iron-red painted decoration. Venice, 1738–1741. Diameter 14 cm. *Opposite top right:* Scent-bottle with cover, with painted decoration in *Schwarzlot* and gold. Bohemia, Ignaz Preissler, 2nd quarter of the 18th century. Height 12 cm. *Opposite bottom left:* Plate in milk white glass with chinoiseries. Lauscha, Thuringia 1720–30. Diameter 20.7 cm. *Opposite bottom right:* Painted decoration in gold on cobalt blue glass in the manner of cobalt-blue porcelain. Bristol, c 1780. Height 8.5 cm. *Top:* Bowl and vase in milk-white glass with polychrome enamel-painting. Venice, 18th century. Height 7.2 and 8.2 cm. *Bottom:* Plates in Venetian milk-white glass with gold decoration. 18th century. Diameter 12 cm.

Vase and two Wig-stands in milk-white glass with the royal arms of France in polychrome enamel-painting. France, c 1715–1730. Height 25.4 cm., 35.7 cm. and 25.1 cm.

culated to favour the use of glass even further, since glass was immediately available from sources which the land everywhere provided — a similar observation will emerge later in connection with the Biedermeier period after the hardships of the Napoleonic Wars. The invention of chalk-glass did not come until later; this was the first glass which was completely suitable for engraving and was as clear as water even at rather greater thicknesses, lent itself even to engraving in cameo relief and was also of more stable composition, in contrast to the Nuremberg glass which tended to suffer from 'glass-disease'. These first intaglio-engraved glasses would also only stand up to surface treatment. They became typical of the engraved glass of Nuremberg which for fifty years represented the pinnacle of the glassmaker's art.

As in so many instances when prevailing circumstances have favoured and assisted a discovery, so in this case of the revival of glass-engraving a controversy has arisen over questions of priority, and the possibility remains that glass-engraving was first resumed in Munich under Duke Wilhelm V during the 1580s. Whatever the truth of this, there can be no argument about the leading part played by Caspar Lehmann and his favourite pupil, Georg Schwanhardt.

Lehmann arrived in 1588 at the court of the Emperor Rudolph II in Prague, having worked for two years in Munich at the court of Duke Wilhelm V. A passage which he wrote later may be taken to mean that he had already learnt the art of glass-engraving from someone while he was still in Munich. His contemporary Joachim von Sandrart, however, describes Lehmann as the inventor of glass-engraving: 'and Your Majesty has handsomely rewarded the author and inventor Caspar Lehmann, Your Majesty's royal lapidary and glass-engraver, for his new invention and has bestowed upon him the great favours and privileges of the most high and greatly landed Emperor in Prague'. In 1609 Lehmann was raised to the nobility as 'Löwenwald' and given a hereditary privilege permitting him to work as a glass-engraver. These distinctions should no doubt also be regarded as compensation for the harassment suffered by Lehmann at the hands of Lang, a groom of the Imperial bedchamber, which went so far as to force him to move to Dresden for two years from 1606 until 1608. In the following years, from 1610 onwards, there were two glass-engravers in Dresden, Caspar and Wolfgang Schindler; and in 1635 there was a Georg Schindler, whose signature GS caused confusion between him and Georg Schwanhardt. Thus in practical terms the privilege so grandly bestowed upon Caspar Lehmann represented no more than recognition, whereas in Dresden engravers upon glass practised without licence.

Caspar Lehmann signed one beaker and dated it 1605. Robert Schmidt attributes to him also a second beaker, with ball-feet, and four glass tablets, two of which are dated, one 1619 and the other 1620. Only two more names of glass-engravers working in Prague at the same time as Caspar Lehmann are known:

Zacharias Beltzer, who followed Lehmann there from the court of Wilhelm V in Munich, and David Engelhart. One Johannes Hess is alleged to have been working in Bohemia at about this time; during the Thirty Years' War he fled to Frankfurt am Main, where he died at the age of eighty-four. The goblet illustrated on page 170 was engraved by his son Johann Benedikt; he died at the age of thirty-eight, leaving two sons, Sebastian and Johann Benedikt, who are mentioned in connection with engraved armorial window-panes, after which they took to gem-cutting. Peter Hess, son of Johann Benedikt the Younger, was also a lapidary.

Whereas glass-engraving in Frankfurt virtually came to an end with Johann Benedikt Hess the Younger in 1699, the same art — also of Bohemian origin — was destined to flourish in Nuremberg for many years.

In 1618 Georg Schwanhardt of Nuremberg, then a boy of seventeen, joined Caspar Lehmann's workshop in Prague as an apprentice. The master died four years later and bequeathed the imperial privilege to Schwanhardt, who in the same year returned with it to his native city. He was not the first glass-engraver in Nuremberg. The art had been introduced before his return by Hans Wessler, the goldsmith, whose signed glass disc showing the beheading of Cyrus, King of Persia, is preserved in the Chambon collection at Marcinelle, Belgium. Nevertheless, Schwanhardt and his school far outstripped Wessler in importance.

The technique of Georg Schwanhardt the Elder differs from that of Lehmann in that he used the diamond-point to complete the details and practised clear engraving, which he is regarded as having invented. The polishing of engraved surfaces became a means of creating a design much favoured by the glass-cutters of Nuremberg and the artists whom they influenced. Schwanhardt the Elder was also responsible for placing the first (1632) polished diminishing lense on the reverse of a glass — a fashion which later became extremely popular; in his case they usually represented the disc of the sun. The cup illustrated on page 162 with the portrait of Gustav Adolf — later altered to form a table-bell — has one of these diminishing lenses in the form of the centre of a sun-flower; seen through the lense, the portrait on the obverse appears smaller. The palm-leaves and laurel branches which George Schwanhardt the Elder engraved on his glasses constantly reappear in the works of his followers and remain the characteristic Nuremberg decoration right on to the early days of the all-pervading interlaced strapwork and foliage style.

Georg Schwanhardt had three sons and three daughters, all of whom were skilled glass-engravers, although no works signed by them are known. The work was presumably divided up in some way. Heinrich, the elder son (pages 164–165), devoted himself, as Sandrart writes, 'at first to studies and became so well qualified especially in philosophy and poetry that he was much loved on account of his skill by persons of both high and low rank. But because natural inclination continually drew him towards his father's art, in which he already had a good grounding, diligent practice made him at last so perfect that he by far excelled his father, mainly because he diligently practised the art of drawing nude and clothed figures at various academies'. In 1730 there appeared in Nuremberg a work by I. G. Doppelmayr entitled *Historische Nachricht von den Nürnbergischen Mathematicis und Künstlern Nürnbergs.* This book says of Heinrich Schwanhardt: 'After 1670 (1671?) he discovered with unexpected good forturne how to etch on glass panes, on which the ground was mat but every character he applied appeared very bright: he also at first progressed far in the art of engraving raised figures on the glasses, all of which has very laudably been proved by his many examples. Died 2 October 1693.' It is true that Heinrich Schwanhardt invented the process of etching on glass, but not that of cameo-engraving, to which the thin walls of the glasses were unsuited. This innovation was left to Friedrich Winter in Silesia ten years later.

Of Schwanhardt's younger son, Georg, Doppelmayr writes that he had achieved a 'good manner' in glass-cutting and 'would have gone even further had not a protracted disease of the limbs interrupted his well-conceived purpose, which in the end death indeed totally destroyed, occurring on 4 February 1676'.

Doppelmayr has this to say of the daughters of Georg Schwanhardt the Elder: 'Three female artists practised in engraving glass were so successful in this art following the good guidance which their father, Georg Schwanhardt the Elder, had given them — for they were mostly occupied in engraving flowers and foliage on glasses — that they were justly praised for it, and many amateurs, having avidly sought these glasses, were contented with them. All three died married, the eldest on the 4 July 1657, the second on the 1 March 1653 and the third on the 2 April 1669.'

And finally Doppelmayr could write of Schwanhardt: 'This old Schwanhardt is supposed to have been not wholly right in religion, for which reason Johann Saubert in his *Sinibalda Postilla,* in the gospel of the false prophets, reproaches him as a man erring in the faith, but culpable though he was held to be, he expressed his confession of faith and hope in a quarto broadsheet in 1639; in 1667 he was buried without a funeral procession and without being registered because he was proclaimed a Weigelian. . . .' More important than the children of Georg Schwanhardt the Elder and another determining influence in the formation of the Nuremberg style was Hermann Schwinger (page 163). He made the flickering landscape of forest and water — already employed by Schwandhardt the Elder — into one of the stock elements of the Nuremberg thematic repertoire, alongside the portraits, coats of arms and mythological scenes executed in so masterly a fashion by Schwanhardt. Schwinger was the pupil, not of Schwanhardt, but of Hans Stefan Schmidt, the engraver of crystal and glass. This fact caused Heinrich Schwanhardt to bear him great malice, which Doppelmayr describes in the following terms: 'Heinrich Schwanhardt was much opposed to our Schwinger because, since he had not learned glass-engraving from a lawful master — Schwanhardt considered no one but his father to be a legitimate master — he regarded him as unacceptable and served a writ with the magistrate, but he achieved nothing thereby and Schwinger continued to work. His enemies then spoke out against him one after the other, claiming that because he had wronged a woman whom he later married he had trifled with the cooper's craft which he had originally followed; but this statement is false, for we find in the written account of his life that he ... cannot ... have offended under Puncto Sexti.' Historians all side with the diligent and skilful Schwinger — who died at the early age of forty-three — against Heinrich Schwanhardt, of whom it is recorded that he 'liked nothing better than to work on Sunday if he had no money'. There are in existence fifteen signed pieces by Schwinger, some of them dated; his preference was for idyllic landscapes with buildings, ruins or little figures.

The engraved glass of Johann Wolfgang Schmidt is closely related to Schwinger, except that Schmidt's landscapes are less atmospheric but rather form settings for animated hunting or battle-scenes (page 164). Three goblets and three beakers carrying his signature are known. Two known pieces show that Schmidt was already using glasses imported from Bohemia, the shapes of which differed from the usual Nuremberg types; in place of the hollow-blown balusters, the goblets had massive stems. Paulus Eder and Georg Friedrich Killinger (page 168) made far greater use of these imported glasses. Eight signed pieces by Eder, who worked in Nuremberg from 1685 until 1709, are known. As a result of using the Bohemian chalk-glass, all the Nuremberg glass-engravers began to execute deeper and more vigorous intaglio engraving — a development which was also in keeping with the trend of the time. Killinger, moreover, made very little further use of the diamond-point. The early form of the interlaced strapwork and foliage pattern found its way into his work and this gives him a place in the growing circle of Baroque glass-cutters. There was now little left that was exclusive to Nuremberg; one of the most important of the typical features to persist was that form of engraving which exploited the contrast between polished and unpolished surfaces. This element is conspicuous in all the works regarded as having been influenced by Nuremberg.

A number of artists, some known by name but less productive, clustered round the group of great Nuremberg glass-engravers of the seventeenth century; among them may be counted Erhard Dorsch and his son Christoph (page 165) and Adam Renneisen. Many pieces must be attributed to engravers who have not yet been identified.

The new generation carrying on the tradition of distinguished handcraft in Nuremberg itself was brilliantly represented by Anton Mauerl, who learned glass-engraving there, moved in 1699 to London and returned to Nuremberg in 1710. With his work, the interlaced strapwork and foliage pattern became a stock form of decoration in the new glass-engraving of Nuremberg; he was also responsible for the first chinoiseries to appear on glass (page 167); this was in about 1720 and thus twenty-five years earlier than in Bohemia and Silesia. Mauerl's contemporaries in Nuremberg included the masters Georg Rost and Christian Ritter.

The fame of the great glass-engravers of Nuremberg brought many young men from afar to serve their apprenticeships in the city. We must assume this to have been the case with Johann Adam Wappler, whose tracks lead to Dresden and of whom nothing is known apart from the signed glass illustrated on page 166. The early unpolished engraving of Bohemia may also have been influenced by Nuremberg. Thuringia, however, came most strongly under the influence of Nuremberg; there the work of Samuel Schwartz (page 221), Georg Ernst Kunckel (pages 168–169) and Caspar Creutzburg (page 171) clearly reveals its models.

Baroque glass

The stylistic phases familiar in the history of art should not be applied un-reservedly to the history of glass, which is concerned not only with artistic but also with technical and economic factors. This applies even to the Renaissance, which was in fact represented solely by the fine Venetian glass impossible to produce in the forest glasshouses.

It is useful, nevertheless, to look for the recurrent features in form, ornament and figural representation which fulfil the expressional requirements of a period. This method not only shows how universal forces act in concert to form styles, but also establishes a connection with wider sociological developments; sometimes also it produces more interesting insights and associations than does the usual method of treating time by studying each country separately. It will be necessary, even so, to lay special emphasis on certain centres in which the style of a given period is most strongly represented. Thus the ornamental Baroque is shown at its most striking in Winter's cameo-engraved glasses of the Hirschberger Tal, whereas the figural style is at its best in the large figures engraved in deep intaglio which stem from the school of Winter and Spiller in Potsdam but are also found in other Baroque princely residences. The Baroque can only be described by pinpointing its achievements whereas the Rococo extends as it were over a larger area since it exerts a wider sociological influence. In the case of the Rococo — so brilliantly exemplified in Silesia — the anonymity of the masters strikes less painfully than with the Baroque. We are more apt to seek the identity of the artist who produces figural work than that of one whose work is purely ornamental and therefore makes a less personal impact. The predominating elements in the Rococo glasses are the ornamental motifs which extend over the whole bowl, whereas the Baroque figures assert their individual existence. It is, indeed, impossible to draw a hard and fast line between Baroque and Rococo, even by ignoring the fact that the Régence too found its reflection in glass.

The principal motifs in the ornamental repertoire of the Baroque are palm-fronds and laurel branches, leafy scrolls and flowers (page 199). Large flowers and bunches of fruit and, especially, acanthus leaves are found among the ornamental motifs of the High Baroque at the end of the seventeenth century. The interlaced strapwork and foliage pattern makes its appearance during the first quarter of the eighteenth century in its early form, with sparsely filled spaces separated by thin bands, garlands of flowers and calligraphic flourishes. The second quarter of the century is dominated by interlaced strapwork and foliage composed of broad, unpolished, engraved bands, with a great variety of accessories, including lambrequins, baldachins, trophies, armorial bearings, monograms and portraits. In figural representation the High Baroque is distinguished by the great nudes of mythology, caught, typically, just at the moment of turning. With the advent of *putti*, galloping horsemen and huntsmen, the figures pass over into the Rococo.

In shape the Baroque glasses are strong and massive. Even the pincered ribs which thicken the undersides of the bowls and first occurred on Venetian and then on Bohemian goblets, and the ball-feet of the cylindrical beakers from Nuremberg, such as were favoured by Johann Schaper, may be regarded as Baroque features. The leaves which extend upwards from underneath the bowl are significant. Cornucopias and shells are also characteristically Baroque forms. Just as in northern Europe the Renaissance made its appearance with enamel-painting, so the period of the Baroque is bound up with deeply engraved glass, although it is not restricted to that alone. There are also Baroque features in the manner and method of shaping glass. The Renaissance forms of goblet-stems, at that time hollow in construction, with interpolated discs, now appear in a more massive style; while folded foot-rings usually give way to smooth-cut ones, surviving only in the goblets of Hesse and Lauenstein with their high-domed feet. The relationship between bowl and stem changes too and the goblets become more squat. Typically-Baroque baluster-stems with air-bubbles (page 168) inside — doubtless originating in Bohemia — made their appearance after 1680. They represent one aspect of the Baroque repertoire of forms — an aspect which early attracted such decoration as facet-cutting, *Kugelschliff* (circular cutting on a vertical wheel) and edge-cutting. As against this, however, the pseudo-facetted stem (page 219) supplanted the hollow baluster because the makers wished to follow the fashion but found that there were not enough facetters available — these were a group whose part in the whole should not be underestimated. The so-called pseudo-facetted stems, for which the glass was pressed to resemble facetting, occur in Hesse and Thuringia during the first half of the eighteenth century.

After Caspar Lehmann's day, the known work from Bohemia consists on the whole only of primitive, flat, unpolished engraving, despite the fact that the splendid Baroque buildings of Prague and other evidence prove that the arts were in a flourishing state. A series of glasses from the Koula Collection in Prague has survived, which, for lack of an exact classification, are known as Koula glasses. One is illustrated on page 198 and must be dated to about 1680. The models for the allegories were engravings by Adriaen Collaert after Martin de Vos. The collection represents an interesting early Bohemian group of Baroque intaglio-engraved glasses with figural decoration on which the first research-work was begun in 1965 by Olga Drahotova. Her investigations seemed to show that these glasses were engraved in the Hirschberger Tal.

The goblet illustrated on page 197 dates from a later period and proves that artistic quality in Bohemia later developed on a broader basis and — together with the first-class character of the material and the good organisation of the glass-trade — laid the basis of the world-wide renown of Bohemian glass. It is a *Meisterstück,* or piece designed to earn the rank of master for the craftsman who made it, and recalls the north-east Bohemian glass-engravers' guild at Kreybitz mentioned by Robert Schmidt. All that has come to light is the draft of their statutes of the year 1750 in which engravers were required to produce an Imperial eagle engraved on glass for their master-work.

Under the patronage of the landed nobility, the Riesengebirge, which belonged partly to Bohemia and partly to Silesia, became a rich source of technical, artistic and economic development in the field of glass-making and its influence began to be felt throughout Europe.

Edmund Schebeck is our source of information about Bohemian glass, E. von Czihak the authority on Silesian wares. The Counts Harrach of the estate of Starkenbach in the Bohemian Riesengebirge played a part parallel to that of the Counts Schaffgotsch in the Silesian Hirschberger Tal. At the risk of simplification it might be said that raw glass, cutting and selling were the provinces of the Bohemians, whereas at this period it was the Silesians who attained to supreme mastery in engraving. The glasshouses on the Bohemian side of the Riesengebirge, for example, supplied raw glass to the Silesian glasshouses, where it was finished. After 1742, when Silesia was ceded to Prussia and Frederick the Great forbade the import of glass, raw glass was smuggled from Bohemia because the product from the glasshouse of Karl Christian Preussler in Schreiberhau — the only Silesian glasshouse which might have supplied it —

Baroque forms

Distinguishing marks of the Baroque are the baluster-stems of the goblets and the ball-feet of the beakers. The stems of the goblets are squat and massive. The foot-rings and rims are engraved. Stems, ballknops and knops on covers, as well as the lower part of the bowl, are all facetted or pseudo-facetted (stems of Thuringian glasses). Domed feet are typical of Hesse and Lauenstein.

1680

1725

Rococo and *Louis Seize*

By about the mid-18th century the forms become more graceful. Engraving is the prevalent form of decoration and Silesian work is outstanding. Sweetmeat-dishes on tall stems are typical. During the last quarter of the century Neo-Classicism gained ground with new formal elements. The principal form of the *Louis Seize* style is the goblet on a square foot.

1775

Opposite page. First row shows early Baroque forms: beaker painted in *Schwarzlot* by Johann Schaper, Nuremberg 1665; marbled goblet from Grimnitz in the Uckermark, dated 1602; glass of a Dresden shooting-gallery, Saxony, dated 1678. Second row, High Baroque: Beaker and cover made of ruby glass with engraved scene by Gottfried Spiller, Potsdam c 1700; Bohemian goblet c 1700; Silesian cameo-engraved goblet, c 1700; Potsdam goblet and cover with acanthus-leaf frieze and lozenge border 1715—25; Bohemian beaker and cover with interlaced strapwork and foliage, c 1720. Third row, Late Baroque: Silesian goblet, c 1740; Lauenstein goblet with domed foot; Thuringian goblet and cover with pseudo-facetted stem and knop on cover, engraved by G. E. Kunckel, 1726; goblet and cover with air-bubbles in the facetted knops, round-headed border with oval eyes, Zechlin 1760; Saxon goblet and cover with baluster-stem, double knop, tear and skill-facets.
Above. First row, Rococo forms: 'ambrosia' dish, Silesia c 1750; Silesian goblet and cover, c 1760; Hessian goblet and cover, c 1750; Berlin goblet with portrait of Frederick II; Silesian bottle with gold-painted decoration. Second row, forms of the *Louis Seize* style; Zechlin beaker; Bohemian goblet; Silesian beaker and cover; with silhouette medallion-portrait, bead border, cellular facetting on the bowl and square plinth.

was not good enough. The prohibition was afterwards let drop and a thirty *per cent* duty levied on imports. Not until 1764 was a general prohibition placed on the importation of all Austrian and Saxon glass. The glass-finishing industry in the Silesian Riesengebirge was established by the Counts Schaffgotsch who owned rich estates in the district. It is recorded that at the beginning of the seventeenth century Hans Ulrich Freiherr von Schaffgotsch brought back from his travels an Italian gem-cutter whom he settled in the Hirschberger Tal. The Italian was commissioned to train native craftsmen in gem-cutting. The Schaffgotsch estates belonged at that time to the Wallenstein duchy of Friedland. When in 1630 Wallenstein forsook the Emperor, Hans Ulrich Schaffgotsch, who wished neither to betray his master nor, indeed, to break faith with the Emperor, was condemned to death and executed in Regensburg in 1635. His son Christoph Leopold and his grandson Hans Anton then founded an order called Von der alten Hacke, which took as its device a small silver hatchet and the motto 'Redlich Seltsam'. The confiscated works of art belonging to the Schaffgotsch family included valuable pieces of rock-crystal.

By 1685 the seed had taken root and the numbers of glass-engravers and glass-cutters in the Hirschberger Tal had so greatly increased that Count Christoph Leopold Schaffgotsch was obliged to promulgate a decree forbidding masters to accept apprentices without special permission.

In 1686 Friedrich Winter, a young steward also known as a good glass-engraver, addressed a letter to the Count, in which he wrote that the 'glass-engravers and glass-cutters were becoming so numerous that one harmed the other and hardly anyone earned his bread properly in the process and everyone trained two or three apprentices, who, when they had spent a year or so and could only scratch a few lines, left their masters, set up their own apparatus and so everyone went on working for himself'. Having given this proof that he understood the situation correctly, Winter in 1687 received a privilege from Count Schaffgotsch who set up a workshop for him and built him a house as well. The numerous commissions which Winter executed for the count and his family included a 'shell' after a prototype in rock-crystal in the Imperial treasure in Vienna.

While the other glass-engravers were pursuing Winter with their jealousy because of the favours granted him — one of them, Hans Christoph Richter of Warmbrunn, even complaining to the Count that he begged to be allowed to pursue his art without having his rights infringed by Winter — Winter was planning an enterprise that would work to the common good. He interested the Count in setting up an engraving workshop which was to derive its power from horse-windlasses. When the plans came to be worked out, Winter hit upon the idea of using water-power. Thus the Petersdorf engraving workshop came into being in 1690—1 and a great advance in technique had been made. Winter's projects in connection with the workshop are revealed in a letter to the Count: 'Had not Your Excellency so graciously determined to build an engraving-workshop, I had thought, though without proper authority, that a room should be built for cutting and next to it I wished to have another large room built, in which from ten to twelve glass-engravers could sit, some of whom would do fine glasses, some ordinary engraving, for which there is a large sale; to help many people, I wished to start sales in the winter; I would have had a booth built in the "warm bath", where a fellow was to sell wares, the rest we wished to take into the country, which would mean that the glass-master would be obliged to make good glass.' Winter's desire to set up a retail establishment in the 'warm bath' — that is, in Warmbrunn — was not at all to the liking of the glass-merchants of Warmbrunn, so they too became his enemies. When the engraving-works were ready, nobody was willing to work with Winter. So at Warmbrunn, with two journeymen, Winter created his distinguished cameo-engraved glasses which, with their vigorous leafy scrolls, represent the best that Baroque glassmaking had to offer in the sphere of ornament (page 200). Friedrich Winter also executed fine intaglio-engraved works, which are obviously related to the Potsdam glasses of the Winter-Spiller school with their large figures. Martin Winter of Potsdam was Friedrich's brother and had presumably served the same apprenticeship. Friedrich Winter died in 1712. After his day only precious stones were engraved at the Petersdorf works.

Engraving works driven by water-power represented the technical advance of the period. They were set up at three places besides Petersdorf. All were associated with outstanding Baroque cameo-engraved glasses which are found nowhere else. One was set up in 1687 near Potsdam by Friedrich Wilhelm, Elector of Brandenburg, the *Grosser Kurfürst;* Carl, Landgrave of Hesse-Cassel, placed his gem-engraving works by the castle moat in Cassel; while Augustus the Strong owned an engraving and polishing-mill on the Weisseritz near Ostra, with the setting up of which Tschirnhaus and Böttger were concerned. This works is particularly notable for the fact that Böttger's 'jasper porcelain' was cut and polished there. The most important of the three was Potsdam, for it exerted influences of which traces may be found in Dresden, Thuringia, Cassel and Amsterdam.

In its early days the glass-industry of Brandenburg was based on Bohemian experience. Even Martin Friedrich, the first glassmaker in Brandenburg, whom the Elector Joachim Friedrich installed in 1601 in Grimnitz, came from Bohemia. He brought his journeymen with him from Bohemia and thus the glasses were also Bohemian in manner and form. The glasshouse at Marienwalde near Küstrin, set up in 1607, also employed Bohemian journeymen, one of whom was tortured to death in 1636 by the Swedes and another beaten until he became crippled. The Imperial troops had in their turn plundered and robbed the glass-master Dressler. In 1653 the Great Elector founded a new glasshouse at Grimnitz, of which the glass-master Georg Preussler of the Riesengebirge

The masters of glass-engraving and their signatures

The general synopsis which heads the following list shows the periods during which each of the various cutting and engraving techniques prevailed. Whereas cutting was always anonymous, works of engraving — a craft to which higher artistic value was attached — were sporadically signed from the beginning. Unsigned engraved glasses far outnumber the rest. The few signed glasses provide important clues for assessing the personal style of a given artist. In many cases only a single signed piece has survived. Artists who left several signed glasses often varied the form and even the spelling of their names. Only a few examples of the forms used at any given time are included in the following list.

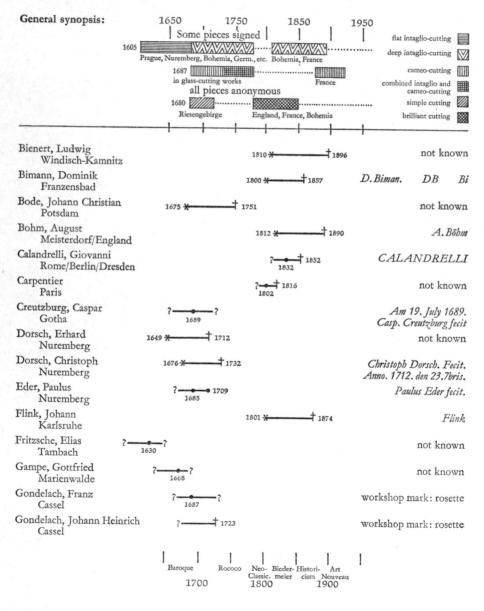

General synopsis:

flat intaglio-cutting	
deep intaglio-cutting	
cameo-cutting	
combined intaglio and cameo-cutting	
simple cutting	
brilliant cutting	

Some pieces signed

1605 — Prague, Nuremberg, Bohemia, Germ., etc. — Bohemia, France

1687 — in glass-cutting works — France

all pieces anonymous

1680 — Riesengebirge — England, France, Bohemia

Bienert, Ludwig Windisch-Kamnitz	1810 ✶———✝ 1896	not known
Bimann, Dominik Franzensbad	1800 ✶———✝ 1857	*D. Biman.* *DB* *Bi*
Bode, Johann Christian Potsdam	1675 ✶———✝ 1751	not known
Bohm, August Meisterdorf/England	1812 ✶———✝ 1890	*A. Böhm*
Calandrelli, Giovanni Rome/Berlin/Dresden	?———✝ 1852 / 1832	*CALANDRELLI*
Carpentier Paris	?———✝ 1816 / 1802	not known
Creutzburg, Caspar Gotha	?———? / 1689	*Am 19. July 1689. Casp. Creutzburg fecit*
Dorsch, Erhard Nuremberg	1649 ✶———✝ 1712	not known
Dorsch, Christoph Nuremberg	1676 ✶———✝ 1732	*Christoph Dorsch. Fecit. Anno. 1712. den 23.7bris.*
Eder, Paulus Nuremberg	?———● 1709 / 1685	*Paulus Eder fecit.*
Flink, Johann Karlsruhe	1801 ✶———✝ 1874	*Flink*
Fritzsche, Elias Tambach	?———? / 1630	not known
Gampe, Gottfried Marienwalde	?———? / 1668	not known
Gondelach, Franz Cassel	?———? / 1687	workshop mark: rosette
Gondelach, Johann Heinrich Cassel	?———✝ 1723	workshop mark: rosette

Baroque | Rococo | Neo-Classic. | Bieder-meier | Histori-cism | Art Nouveau

1700   1800   1900

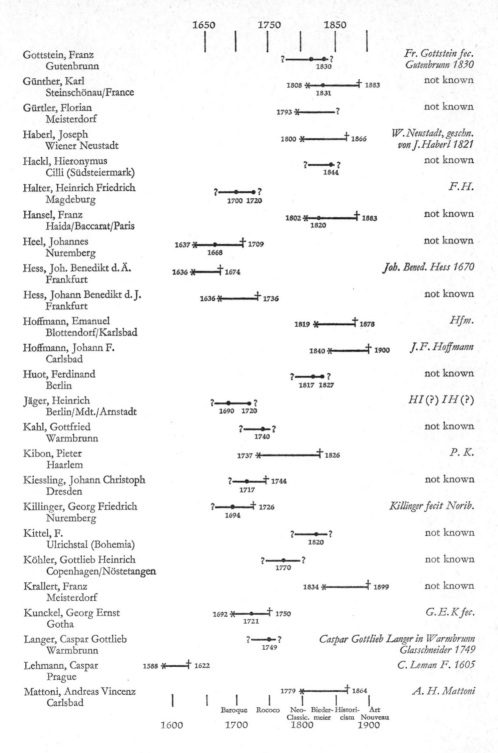

	1650	1750	1850	
Gottstein, Franz Gutenbrunn		?——•—•? 1830		Fr. Gottstein fec. Gutenbrunn 1830
Günther, Karl Steinschönau/France		1808 ✳—•——+ 1883 1831		not known
Gürtler, Florian Meisterdorf		1793 ✳——?		not known
Haberl, Joseph Wiener Neustadt		1800 ✳—•—+ 1866		W. Neustadt, geschn. von J. Haberl 1821
Hackl, Hieronymus Cilli (Südsteiermark)		?—•? 1844		not known
Halter, Heinrich Friedrich Magdeburg	?—•—? 1700 1720			F. H.
Hansel, Franz Haida/Baccarat/Paris		1802 ✳—•——+ 1883 1820		not known
Heel, Johannes Nuremberg	1637 ✳—•—+ 1709 1668			not known
Hess, Joh. Benedikt d. Ä. Frankfurt	1636 ✳—+ 1674			Joh. Bened. Hess 1670
Hess, Johann Benedikt d. J. Frankfurt	1636 ✳——+ 1736			not known
Hoffmann, Emanuel Blottendorf/Karlsbad		1819 ✳——+ 1878		Hfm.
Hoffmann, Johann F. Carlsbad		1840 ✳——+ 1900		J. F. Hoffmann
Huot, Ferdinand Berlin		?—•? 1817 1827		not known
Jäger, Heinrich Berlin/Mdt./Arnstadt	?—•—•? 1690 1720			HI (?) IH (?)
Kahl, Gottfried Warmbrunn		?—•—? 1740		not known
Kibon, Pieter Haarlem	1737 ✳———+ 1826			P. K.
Kiessling, Johann Christoph Dresden	?—•—+ 1744 1717			not known
Killinger, Georg Friedrich Nuremberg	?——•—+ 1726 1694			Killinger fecit Norib.
Kittel, F. Ulrichstal (Bohemia)		?——•—? 1820		not known
Köhler, Gottlieb Heinrich Copenhagen/Nöstetangen		?——•—? 1770		not known
Krallert, Franz Meisterdorf		1834 ✳———+ 1899		not known
Kunckel, Georg Ernst Gotha	1692 ✳—•—+ 1750 1721			G. E. K fec.
Langer, Caspar Gottlieb Warmbrunn	?—•—? 1749			Caspar Gottlieb Langer in Warmbrunn Glasschneider 1749
Lehmann, Caspar Prague	1588 ✳—+ 1622			C. Leman F. 1605
Mattoni, Andreas Vincenz Carlsbad		1779 ✳——+ 1864		A. H. Mattoni

			Baroque	Rococo	Neo- Classic.	Bieder- meier	Histori- cism	Art Nouveau
1600		1700			1800			1900

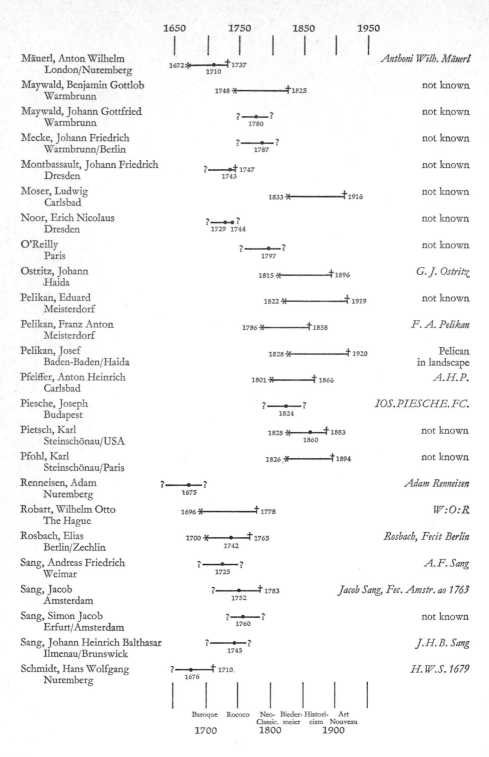

1650 1750 1850 1950

Name / Place	Dates	Signature
Mäuerl, Anton Wilhelm — London/Nuremberg	1672 ✱ — 1710 — † 1737	*Anthoni Wilh. Mäuerl*
Maywald, Benjamin Gottlob — Warmbrunn	1748 ✱ ———— † 1825	not known
Maywald, Johann Gottfried — Warmbrunn	? —— 1780 —— ?	not known
Mecke, Johann Friedrich — Warmbrunn/Berlin	? —— 1787 —— ?	not known
Montbassault, Johann Friedrich — Dresden	? —— 1743 —— † 1747	not known
Moser, Ludwig — Carlsbad	1833 ✱ ———— † 1916	not known
Noor, Erich Nicolaus — Dresden	? — 1729 1744 — ?	not known
O'Reilly — Paris	? —— 1797 —— ?	not known
Ostritz, Johann — Haida	1815 ✱ ———— † 1896	*G. J. Ostritz*
Pelikan, Eduard — Meisterdorf	1822 ✱ ———— † 1919	not known
Pelikan, Franz Anton — Meisterdorf	1786 ✱ ———— † 1858	*F. A. Pelikan*
Pelikan, Josef — Baden-Baden/Haida	1828 ✱ ———— † 1920	Pelican in landscape
Pfeiffer, Anton Heinrich — Carlsbad	1801 ✱ ———— † 1866	*A.H.P.*
Piesche, Joseph — Budapest	? —— 1824 —— ?	*IOS.PIESCHE.FC.*
Pietsch, Karl — Steinschönau/USA	1828 ✱ — 1860 — † 1883	not known
Pfohl, Karl — Steinschönau/Paris	1826 ✱ ———— † 1894	not known
Renneisen, Adam — Nuremberg	? —— 1675 —— ?	*Adam Renneisen*
Robart, Wilhelm Otto — The Hague	1696 ✱ ———— † 1778	*W:O:R*
Rosbach, Elias — Berlin/Zechlin	1700 ✱ — 1742 — † 1765	*Rosbach, Fecit Berlin*
Sang, Andreas Friedrich — Weimar	? —— 1725 —— ?	*A.F. Sang*
Sang, Jacob — Amsterdam	? — 1752 — † 1783	*Jacob Sang, Fec. Amstr. ao 1763*
Sang, Simon Jacob — Erfurt/Amsterdam	? —— 1760 —— ?	not known
Sang, Johann Heinrich Balthasar — Ilmenau/Brunswick	? —— 1745 —— ?	*J.H.B. Sang*
Schmidt, Hans Wolfgang — Nuremberg	? — 1676 — † 1710.	*H.W.S. 1679*

Baroque — Rococo — Neo-Classic. — Bieder-meier — Histori-cism — Art Nouveau

1700 1800 1900

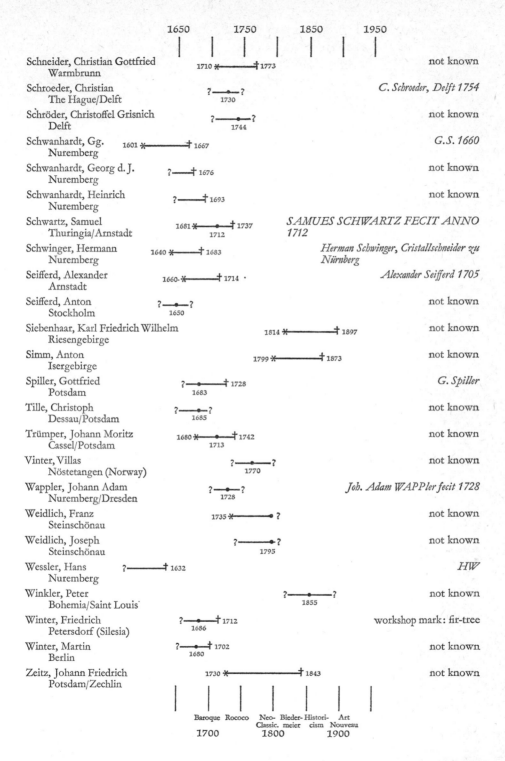

	1650	1750	1850	1950	

Schneider, Christian Gottfried
Warmbrunn — 1710 ✳———✝ 1773 — not known

Schroeder, Christian
The Hague/Delft — ?———? 1730 — *C. Schroeder, Delft 1754*

Schröder, Christoffel Grisnich
Delft — ?———? 1744 — not known

Schwanhardt, Gg.
Nuremberg — 1601 ✳———✝ 1667 — *G.S. 1660*

Schwanhardt, Georg d. J.
Nuremberg — ?——✝ 1676 — not known

Schwanhardt, Heinrich
Nuremberg — ?———✝ 1693 — not known

Schwartz, Samuel
Thuringia/Arnstadt — 1681 ✳———•———✝ 1737 1712 — *SAMUES SCHWARTZ FECIT ANNO 1712*

Schwinger, Hermann
Nuremberg — 1640 ✳———✝ 1683 — *Herman Schwinger, Cristallschneider zu Nürnberg*

Seiffert, Alexander
Arnstadt — 1660-✳———✝ 1714 · — *Alexander Seiffert 1705*

Seiffert, Anton
Stockholm — ?——•——? 1650 — not known

Siebenhaar, Karl Friedrich Wilhelm
Riesengebirge — 1814 ✳———✝ 1897 — not known

Simm, Anton
Isergebirge — 1799 ✳———✝ 1873 — not known

Spiller, Gottfried
Potsdam — ?———•——✝ 1728 1683 — *G. Spiller*

Tille, Christoph
Dessau/Potsdam — ?———•——? 1685 — not known

Trümper, Johann Moritz
Cassel/Potsdam — 1680 ✳———•——✝ 1742 1713 — not known

Vinter, Villas
Nöstetangen (Norway) — ?——•——? 1770 — not known

Wappler, Johann Adam
Nuremberg/Dresden — ?——•——? 1728 — *Joh. Adam WAPPler fecit 1728*

Weidlich, Franz
Steinschönau — 1735 ✳———•——? — not known

Weidlich, Joseph
Steinschönau — ?———•——? 1795 — not known

Wessler, Hans
Nuremberg — ?———✝ 1632 — *HW*

Winkler, Peter
Bohemia/Saint Louis — ?——•——? 1855 — not known

Winter, Friedrich
Petersdorf (Silesia) — ?——•——✝ 1712 1686 — workshop mark: fir-tree

Winter, Martin
Berlin — ?——•—✝ 1702 1680 — not known

Zeitz, Johann Friedrich
Potsdam/Zechlin — 1730 ✳———✝ 1843 — not known

	Baroque	Rococo	Neo-Classic.	Bieder-meier	Histori-cism	Art Nouveau	
	1700			**1800**		**1900**	

became director in 1658. The import of Bohemian glass was prohibited as early as 1656 but, although it was often repeated in subsequent years, the prohibition remained ineffective. Besides enamel-painted glasses, the Marienwalde glass-house from 1654 onwards produced engraved glass. Gottfried Gampe worked here as a painter and engraver of glass, having come from Bohemia with his brothers Daniel and Hans Gregor, who had been granted privileges to engrave glass in 1668. In Grimnitz, by contrast, no engraved work was done, but goblets made of red, white and blue speckled glass were painted in polychrome enamel-colours. The glasses engraved by the Gampe brothers at Marienwalde were of a primitive unpolished style in the manner of the Bohemian provincial wares of the time. Another Gampe, Samuel Gottlieb, was working here as an engraver in about 1750.

In 1674 the Great Elector founded a new glasshouse at Drewitz, near Potsdam. In 1667 Georg Gundelach, a native of Hesse, who had built up the chalk-glass manufacture in Dessau, was installed 'glass-master for making crystalline glass'; and when, in 1678, Johann Kunckel arrived, a new glasshouse was erected on the Hackendamm near Potsdam in addition to the old works at Drewitz, which survived until 1688. The new glasshouse, intended solely for crystal glass and for Kunckel's experiments, was called the 'Cristallinen-Glas-hütte zu Drewitz' but was later known simply as the Potsdam Glasshouse. By the next year Martin Winter from the Riesengebirge had been installed as glass-engraver. And while Kunckel was setting up his private laboratory on the Pfaueninsel, which the Great Elector had in 1685 presented to 'himself and his heirs', Martin Winter was in 1687 endeavouring to persuade the Elector that he needed an engraving-mill for the heavy work of cameo-engraving. This was built in 1688 on the Friedrichswerder near the Berlin Schloss.

There had been engraved glasses at Potsdam even before 1680. Christoph Tille, an engraver, had been summoned from Dessau for this purpose imme-diately after Gundelach. There were also glass-engravers in Berlin who obtain-ed their raw glass from Potsdam. In 1701 and again in 1704 ten of them requested permission to found a guild. The combination of unpolished intaglio-engraving and polished circular concavities was much favoured. At a later date circular cutting *(Kugelschliff)* and round-headed hollow cutting came to extend over the stem and the lower part of the bowl. By the end of the seven-teenth century pointed leaves reserved in the round-headed borders (page 204) had become frequent and from now on were fairly typical of the Potsdam-Berlin glass.

Opposite: Goblet showing Imperial eagle in polished and unpolished intaglio-engraving. Inscribed: 'Vive L'empereur Léopold et Tout L'empire Romain'. Bohemia, late 17th or early 18th cent. Height 25 cm.

Beaker with intaglio-engraved allegories of the four quarters of the globe from copper-plate engravings by Adriaen Collaert after Marten de Vos. Bohemia, 3rd quarter of the 17th century (Koula group). Height 11.5 cm.

Left: Goblet with facetted decoration. Germany, 2nd half of the 17th century. Height 24.2 cm.
Right: Goblet with large Baroque flowers in unpolished intaglio-engraving with fine polished round fruits. Bohemia, beginning of the 18th century. Height 18 cm.

Goblet and cover
with shell-shaped
protruberances
from bowl and
stem. Cameo-cut
birds and leafy
scrolls. Silesia,
Friedrich Winter,
end of the 17th
century. Height
28 cm.

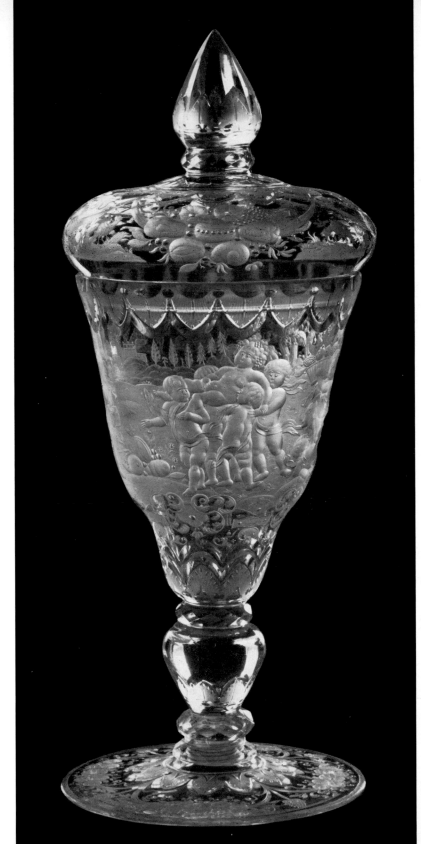

Goblet and cover showing the child Bacchus with train of children in intaglio from copper-plate engravings by Pieter van Avont after Wenceslaus Hollar. Silesia, Friedrich Winter, c 1710. Height 39 cm.

Left: Goblet showing cameo-engraved combined arms of Melchior Ducius von Wallenberg, steward of the Kynast estates of the Counts Schaffgotsch, and Sophie Elisabeth von Knobelsdorff. Silesia, Friedrich Winter, c 1710. *Right:* Goblet with cameo-cut arms of Brandenburg. Berlin-Potsdam, c 1700. Height 27 cm.

Left: Beaker and cover made of ruby glass with cameo-engraved decoration. Berlin, Gottfried Spiller, end of the 17th century. Height 15 cm. *Right:* Beaker and cover with woodland scene, faun, nymphs, amoretti in unpolished intaglio-engraving; cameo-cut laurel frieze. Berlin, Gottfried Spiller, c 1700. Height 27 cm.

Left: Goblet and cover showing Bacchanalia of children in intaglio-engraving. Cameo-engraved scallopped frieze and acanthus leaves. Berlin, Gottfried Spiller, c 1710. Height 44 cm. *Opposite:* Goblet and cover in ruby glass by Johann Kunckel, with 'fruit-children' in intaglio-engraving. Berlin, Gottfried Spiller, c 1710. Height 30.2 cm.

Left: Goblet and cover showing Leda and the swan in intaglio-engraving. Monogrammist HI, beginning of the 18th century. Height 36.5 cm. *Above:* Beaker with intaglio-engraved figures. Monogrammist HI, beginning of the 18th century. Height 14 cm. *Opposite: Left:* Goblet and cover showing Mars and the inscription 'vivat CAROLV. XI. REX. Svec.' Monogrammist HI, Potsdam glass, before 1697. Height 42.5 cm. *Right:* Goblet with intaglio-engraved scene showing a sleeping nymph (Antiope?) and satyr (Zeus?) being struck by Amor. Elias Rosbach, Zechlin-Berlin, 1735–1740. Height 24.5 cm.

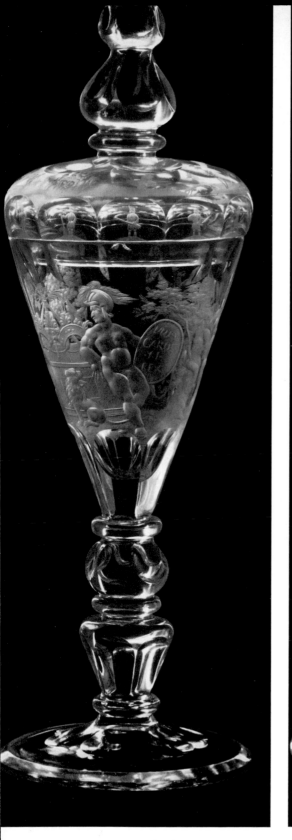

Left: Beaker with foot showing intaglio-engraved scene of children hunting with inscription 'Valiska Zeige dich putz weg den wilden bahren dort wiel dich auch ein schwein ein hirsch ein ochse schehren' (Valiska, show yourself, clear away the wild bears, a boar, a stag, an ox will vex you still). Signed 'JW'. Silesia, c 1730. Height 15 cm. *Right:* Goblet and cover with view of Warmbrunn. Silesia, Gottfried Schneider, c 1740. Height 27.5 cm.

Beaker with foot showing shepherd and shepherdess. Inscribed 'Du Zierd der schönen du, O Amarillis singet, in lieb und Freud ergetzt da du der wolkengott Zum frischen Regen Zwingest der Saat und wiesen netzt' (O jewel of the fair, O Amaryllis sing, you delight the cloud-god with love and joy so that he sends fresh rain to moisten seed and meadow.) Amaryllis is the heroine of C. B. Guarini's pastoral drama of 1590. *Il Pastor Fido*, Silesia, Christian Gottfried Schneider, c 1740–50. Height 10 cm.

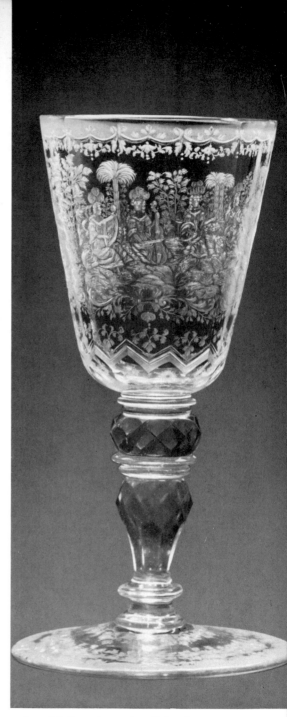

Left: Goblet and cover with interlaced strapwork and foliage decoration. Bohemia, c 1730. Height 25.5 cm. *Right:* Goblet with chinoiseries. Johann Wolfgang Schmidt, Franconia, c 1750. Height 18.5 cm. *Opposite:* 'VIVAT FRIEDERICUS REX BORUSSIAE', Masonic emblems. On the foot: 'Vive Carsine Tanhausen Altwasser à Warmbaad le 20 Aoust 1742'. Height 32.5 cm.

Left: Goblet with hunting-scene. Silesia, c 1750. Height 18 cm. *Right:* Goblet with cover, facetted, engraved in polished and unpolished cameo and intaglio engraving, gilt. Silesia, Christian Gottfried Schneider, Warmbrunn, c 1760. Height 23.5 cm.

'Ambrosia' bowl, facetted and engraved in polished and unpolished intaglio engraving. Silesia, Christian Gottfried Schneider, Warmbrunn, c 1730–60. Height 13.2 cm.

Gold-engraved glasses. *Top left:* Scent-bottle with hunting-scene. Bohemia, 2nd quarter of the 18th century. Height 9.5 cm. *Bottom left:* Beaker showing St Anthony. Bohemia, 1st third of the 18th century. Height 8 cm. *Bottom right:* Gold-engraved glass painted in transparent colours. Bohemia, 2nd quarter of the 18th century. Height 9.5 cm.

Left: Goblet and cover with gold-engraved decoration. Bohemia, 2nd quarter of the 18th century. Height 25 cm. *Right:* Goblet and cover, facetted, engraved and gilt. Portrait of Frederick II of Prussia. Zechlin 1740–45. Height 30 cm.

Left: Goblet with cameo-engraved portrait of Carl, Landgrave of Hesse-Cassel. Cassel, Franz Gondelach, c 1700. (The glass has disappeared since the war.) *Right:* Goblet with emblem of Carl, Landgrave of Hesse-Cassel, monogram on reverse. Cassel, workshop of Franz Gondelach. Rosette under the foot. Beginning of the 18th century. Height 19.5 cm.

Three-sided foot-beaker with biblical scenes and corresponding inscriptions: 'The Child Moses', 'The Promised Land' and 'Idolatry'. Workshop of Franz Gondelach. Beginning of the 18th century. Height 11 cm.

Left: Goblet and cover with a mythological scene of *putti* and fauns drawing a chariot. Probably Russia, 1st half of the 18th century. Height 18 cm. *Right:* Goblet with facetting and unpolished intaglio-engraving, floral decoration with *putti* and banderol: 'Vivat G. F. Z. S.' (= Günther, Prince of Schwarzburg-Sonderhausen). Brunswick, probably A. F. Sang, c 1725. Height 19.5 cm.

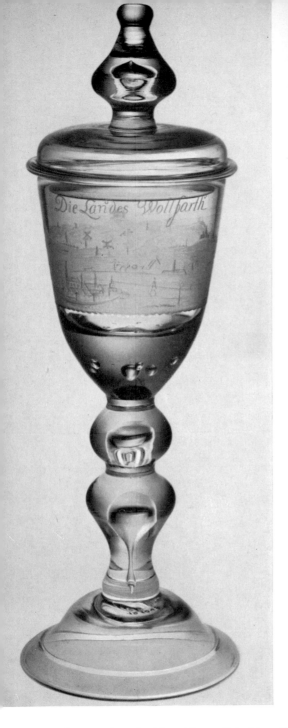 

Left: Dome-footed goblet with unpolished intaglio-engraving. Westphalia, Wittgenstein glass-house, Laasphe 1720–30. Height 23.2 cm. *Right:* Goblet and cover with pseudo-facetted stem and knop. Horse from the Brunswick arms. Monogram AW (= August Wilhelm von Braunschweig-Wolfenbüttel). Brunswick or Hesse, c 1730. Height 39.5 cm.

Left: Goblet and cover, with facetting, polished and unpolished intaglio engraving and the inscription: 'He: He: du saubrer Vogel du, Jetzt kom ich eben recht dazu, geh fort, lass diesen Wind-bruch liegen. Sonst wirst du brave Schlage kriegen.' (Hey, hey, pretty bird, I have come at the right moment, make off, let this windfall be or I will deal you a fine blow or two.) Saxony, c 1750. Height 38 cm. *Right:* Goblet with inlaid ruby glass and gold. Dresden, Johann Christoph Kiessling, c 1740. Height 17 cm.

Goblet to commemorate the 200th anniversary of the Confession of Augsburg-Thuringia, Samuel Schwartz, 1730. Height 30.5 cm.

Jacobite glasses. Newcastle-on-Tyne, England, c 1750. Inscribed 'Fiat', 'Redeat', 'Success to the Society' 'Audientior Ibo'. Portraits of Prince Charles Edward Stuart. Height 9 and 6.5 cm. *Opposite:* Wine-glass with white enamel-painted decoration by William and Mary Beilby. English glass (Newcastle-on-Tyne) 1765–75. Height 19.3 cm.

Martin Winter was appointed in 1680 with an annual salary of five hundred thalers. No glass can be definitely attributed to him. A request he wrote in 1683 asking to have his salary increased shows that he had worked at cameo-engraving even before the engraving-mill was built: 'Your Electoral Highness having so far been pleased to show a gracious liking for my work and desiring more, both of raised work and other rare glasses, with this in mind I set to work with confidence.' He appears, however, not to have been entirely satisfied with his own efforts, for he promises 'to produce something more and better than has resulted so far'. The occasion of the attempt was the ending of the articles of his cousin Gottfried Spiller, who had accompanied him from the Riesen-gebirge and had been apprenticed to him for eight years. He was now employ-ed with a yearly salary of two hundred thalers. Winter died in 1702. Spiller now became 'royal glass-engraver'.

Spiller's most celebrated piece is the so-called 'Orpheus' beaker, on which Orpheus wearing a laurel-wreath at the foot of a tree-trunk plays his harp to a great company of beasts. All the literature from 1786 onwards attributes this beaker and cover to Spiller; it is therefore a fairly reliable guide to further classification. One of his best works in intaglio-engraving of which he was likewise a master, expresses the creative purpose of the Baroque. The figures on this beaker are cut to a depth of 7 mm into glass measuring 1 cm in thickness. Another of Spiller's characteristic subjects are the 'fruit children' or air-borne *putti* with garlands, such as appear on the ruby glass illustrated on page 205.

Heinrich Jäger, reputedly a native of Reichenberg, was a friend of Spiller and stood well with Friedrich III. He became a citizen of Berlin in 1704; only then was he accepted into the glass-engravers' guild, despite the fact that Fried-rich III had intervened in 1701 in favour of his acceptance and had refused to recognise the guild without Jäger. In view of the small quantity of confirmed information about Jäger in existence, this fact is important; indeed, it provides the sole argument which permits us to conclude that Jäger was responsible for the splendid works signed HI or IH (pages 206–207). Having analysed on stylistic grounds the glasses used by Jäger for his intaglio-engraving, R. J. Charleston in 1962 reached the conclusion that Jäger must have worked from 1690 until 1706 in Berlin, from 1706 until 1715 somewhere in central Ger-many and from 1715 until 1720 in Arnstadt in Thuringia. The fact, however, that some of the glasses signed HI or IH are crisselled argues against a Thurin-gian provenance, since the Thuringian sands, at least those from the Ilmenau district, were rich in alumina and thus produced a particularly stable glass.

Heinrich Friedrich Halter, warden of the mint at Magdeburg, signed his goblets clearly — they stood over 50 cm high and carried views of towns and

Opposite: Vase and cover in cobalt-blue glass with gold garlands. Lion mark. Lauenstein, end of the 18th century. Height 26 cm.

castles or portraits of princes — with the letters 'H. F. H.' in an unpolished engraved sun. Since the importation of Bohemian glass into Brandenburg was prohibited in his day (from 1700 until 1720), the obvious assumption — for which there is much supporting evidence — is that he obtained his raw glass from Potsdam.

Elias Rosbach was another who worked as a glass-engraver in Berlin from 1727 onwards. In 1735 and 1736 he was senior master in the Berlin guild of glass-engravers. He has left eight intaglio-engraved glasses signed with the diamond-point 'Rosbach Fecit Berlin'. All date from the period before 1741, when he was still working as an independent artist in Berlin before moving to a position at Zechlin.

In 1718, ten years before the death of Gottfried Spiller, Johann Christian Bode is named as a glass-cutter and engraver at Potsdam. He must have been a highly-regarded personality, for when, around the middle years of the century, sales began to fall off — doubtless due partly to the manufacture of porcelain — Bode, then seventy-six years old, was permitted to organise a lottery. Johann Friedrich Zeitz (after 1730), who moved to Zechlin after 1736 and died there in 1743, and Johann Moritz Trümper, who arrived in 1713 from Cassel and in 1718—19 held the lease of the Potsdam works, were among the best known of the engravers at the Potsdam glasshouse.

'Because the wood of the Churmark can be more usefully converted into money', ran a royal command of 1734, 'all tar-kilns, potash-distilleries and glasshouses must be moved to the Neumark'. In 1736, therefore, the Potsdam glasshouse ceased production and a beginning was made with building the one at Zechlin, which survived until 1890. But in about 1760 glass-engraving came to a standstill and was not revived until the nineteenth century.

Close stylistic links between distinguished artists outside Brandenburg has led scholars to assume that other glass-engravers besides those whom documentary evidence has securely linked to Potsdam, Berlin and Zechlin learnt their craft in Berlin. This, however, does not apply to the most important of German glass-engravers, Franz Gondelach, who was apprenticed in Cassel to the gem-cutter Christoph Labhardt the Elder. At the end of the seventeenth century Carl, Landgrave of Hesse-Cassel, had an 'Edelstein-Schneid-Kunstmühle', or cutting-mill for cutting semi-precious stones, set up in the castle moat. In 1689 Gondelach became court glass-engraver, for which he received the respectable remuneration of 333 thalers. Apart from Spiller, Gondelach is regarded as the best glass-engraver of his day. One example of his outstanding art is the goblet with cameo-engraving and the portrait of Carl, Landgrave of Hesse-Cassel, illustrated on page 216. The three-sided beaker illustrated on page 216 with intaglio-engraved biblical scenes in cartouches formed of cameo-engraved acanthus leaves, comes from Gondelach's workshop, which must have been very considerable. It was carried on by Johann Heinrich Gondelach, who also became court glass-engraver, and later by Johann Franz Trümper. The workshop used as its mark an eight-pointed unpolished engraved rosette on the underside of the foot of its goblets.

It must be assumed that links also existed between Berlin and Dresden. In 1712 there were nineteen glass-cutters and engravers working in and around Dresden. On the instructions of Augustus the Strong, Freiherr von Tschirnhaus set up a number of new glasshouses, for which he brought specialists from Bohemia. To begin with, goblet-forms were borrowed from there as well. As regards decoration, however, the Saxon glasses lean rather towards Potsdam. This applies both to the facetting in horizontal rows and to the engraved portraits which were stuck on. Between 1717 and 1744 Johann Christoph Kiessling was the most important Saxon glass-engraver working in Dresden (page 220). From the time when glass-engraving began in Saxony (page 181) Johann Neumann, a native of Zittau, worked from 1680 until 1697 under Duke Johann Adolf I of Saxe-Weissenfels and Johann Georg Müller of Lauscha until 1783, both as court glass-engravers.

The art of glassmaking in Thuringia early possessed a zealous patron in Duke Bernhard von Weimar (cf page 126). He owned the glasshouse at Tambach, where during the Duke's lifetime Elias Fritzsche worked as a glass-engraver. Andreas Friedrich Sang (page 218) is found at the court of Weimar between 1720 and 1744; while his brother Jacob Sang (page 177) and his son Johann Heinrich Balthasar Sang worked as court glass-engravers in Amsterdam and Brunswick respectively.

Another centre of Thuringian glass-engraving was Arnstadt. Alexander Seifferd, son of Anton Seifferd, court glass-engraver to Charles Gustavus, worked there as a glass-engraver from 1685 until 1714, as perhaps, from 1715 until 1720, did Heinrich Jäger. Samuel Schwartz was there in the service of Prince Günther I of Schwarzburg-Sondershausen from 1731 until 1737.

The third Thuringian centre was Gotha. The goblet illustrated on page 171 and signed by Caspar Creutzburg indicates that he was there in about 1689. This glass bears an inscription (EF with crown) relating to the founding of the family Order of Ernest on the occasion of the inauguration by Duke Friedrich I of the princely Residence of Friedrichswerth on July 19th, 1689. The work is entirely in the manner of the Nuremberg school. Georg Ernst Kunckel worked at the court of Gotha from 1721 until 1750.

That Arnstadt was obviously subject to the influence of Berlin while Gotha was largely influenced by Nuremberg is surely chance, for Schwartz, for example, would have been employed at Gotha too had he not also insisted upon a privilege for trading in glass, which the duke was unwilling to grant him. He also worked at various other courts.

The most celebrated of the glass-engravers of Thuringia were Samuel Schwartz and Georg Ernst Kunckel — who may have been, as Robert Schmidt surmised, a pupil of Schwartz. Pazaurek in 1933 conjectured that Samuel Schwartz in his turn was a pupil of Spiller. The earliest known signed and dated piece by Schwartz was of the year 1712; it has now disappeared. As far as date is concerned, therefore, he could have been trained before 1712 in Berlin. In 1713 he applied for the position of court glass-engraver at Gotha, but failed to obtain it. Kunckel was appointed to this position in 1721. Until 1731, when he was fifty, Schwartz worked independently for various patrons. In that year he was appointed glass-engraver to Prince Günther I of Schwarzburg-Sondershausen in Arnstadt. He held this position for six years, until his death in 1737. When he was forty-nine he engraved the commemorative goblet illustrated on page 221, the inscription on which refers to the bi-centenary jubilee of the Augsburg Confession and to Duke Friedrich II of Saxe-Gotha. This shows that he engraved this goblet at a period when G. E. Kunckel was court glass-engraver to that duke. It may have been for this reason that he felt bound to sign the goblet, for it is the only glass signed by Schwartz to have survived.

There are three pieces signed by Georg Ernst Kunckel in existence. One of these is illustrated on page 169 and shows the arms and monogram of Friedrich II of Gotha-Altenburg. The signature comprises an 'A' and 'G. E. K. fec.' and he may have borrowed it from Killinger. This conjecture is suggested by a comparison between Killinger's goblet illustrated on page 168 and Kunckel's typical intaglio-engraving (page 169).

Rococo glass

The tendency to use optical means to increase the brilliance of glass became more pronounced during the Rococo period. Facetting, enclosed bubbles of air (from 1720 onwards in Potsdam) and gilding were all used simultaneously. New forms included the asymmetrical, tall-stemmed sweetmeat-dishes in the shape of little boats (*Nautilusbecher* and *Ambrosiaschälchen*) with wavy rims and typical Silesian cameo-engraved palmettes (page 213). Similar dishes but with straight rims had existed from as far back as 1680. Chinoiseries, too, now becoming very common, had already been executed by Mäuerl in Nuremberg in about 1720 (page 167). The *rocailles* and *Fledermausflügel*, or bats' wings, so typical of the Rococo, occurred, of course, on glasses too. Silesia, which at this period had the best to offer, also produced meticulous small landscape views. The whole bowl was usually densely covered with the most delicate intaglio-engraved decorative motifs (page 212). There are numerous Rococo goblets carrying portraits of Frederick the Great and Maria Theresa.

By the first half of the eighteenth century Warmbrunn in the Hirschberger Tal had become a flourishing centre of Silesian glass-engraving. In 1733 six independent artists lived there; in 1743 the number had risen to over forty. The senior master was Christian Gottfried Schneider (1710–73). Others in the top rank were Gottfried Kahl, Benjamin Maywald, and Johann Gottfried Maywald who became senior master after the death of Schneider. There was, however, no guild at Warmbrunn.

Christian Schneider's work usually combined cameo and intaglio engraving. Sixty-four impressions of his designs on paper, collected by Schneider himself, are preserved in the Schlesisches Museum in Breslau. Franz-Adrian Dreier has stated that, with the exception of a few earlier ones, they are all derived from Augsburg prints of the ’50s and ’60s. They consist of allegories, portraits (Prince Heinrich Ludwig of Prussia), *rocaille* ornaments and pastoral scenes. Six drawings by C. G. Schneider have also been preserved and these show how awkward a draughtsman this great master of glass-engraving was — an observation which applies equally to a later master, Dominik Bimann. One drawing from nature forms a basis for the engraving on the goblet illustrated on page 208. On the obverse it shows Warmbrunn in the Hirschberger Tal below the hills of the Riesengebirge and on the reverse the fir-tree of the Schaffgottsch arms in a reserve formed by *rocailles* and scroll-work. None of the Silesian glass-engravers of the eighteenth century — Schneider included — signed his work. Caspar Gottlieb Langer provides the sole exception with his goblet of 1749 for a Leipzig corporation. It is impossible to classify the works of the other glass-engravers. Since Warmbrunn was a health resort and therefore had a brisk flow of visitors, it is not impossible that it was the home of the earliest ‘spa glasses’, which bore inscriptions such as: ‘Zum Zeugniss das ich offt mein Freund an Dich gedacht, hab ich Dir dieses Glass von Warmbrunn mitgebracht’ (To show, my friend, you were not absent from my thought, I have for you this glass from Warmbrunn brought) (1740). These early souvenir glasses are eagerly collected today.

Gilt rims and foot-rings and relief palmettes were extremely popular during the period of the Rococo.

In 1735 an Imperial edict from Vienna laid down that ‘men skilled in making and cutting crystal glass shall not be lured out of the archduchy of Silesia into foreign lands or be in any way permitted to repair thither’. When in 1742 Warmbrunn, the centre of the Silesian glass-engraving industry, fell to Prussia, the Silesian glass-industry underwent a crisis. There were a number of contributory causes: Silesia was cut off from the glasshouses which had hitherto supplied her with raw glass; she no longer had access to the well-organised glass-trade which had until now assured her sales; and finally she had no entry to Berlin, the new capital, or to the other provinces of the new fatherland, because the monopoly was held by the Zechlin glasshouse. Until 1792 no Silesian glass was permitted to be imported into the Kurmark or the Neumark, into Halberstadt or Magdeburg, nor was permission given until 1784 to import any into the province of Prussia. In these circumstances, many glassmakers in Silesia were obliged to move to Bohemia. It is true that Frederick the Great repeatedly took a personal interest in the Silesian glass-industry, but his policy oscillated between good-will and the impossibility of putting it to practical effect; the interests of Zechlin and Warmbrunn, whose wares were not 'everyman's purchase but have to be solely and exclusively sold to high personages and capitalists', could not be reconciled in this impoverished country. Frederick II had many new glass-factories set up, most of them in Upper Silesia, commanding his servants to 'discover where glasshouses should be installed and how best to incite their owners thereto', but failed at the same time to improve the possibilities of selling. This was why only a few of the new foundations survived. Recognising the situation, he had earlier even had glass transported from Marienwalde, where it could have been sold on the spot, for sale in Breslau. It found no market, for it was more expensive and of poorer quality than the Silesian glass. But he could not be dissuaded from importing Brandenburg glass into Silesia and instead suppressing Bohemian glass 'without *éclat*'. Notwithstanding the fact that there were already too many artist glass-engravers, in 1764 he issued a pronouncement promising the glasshouses a premium of twenty-five thalers for every foreign glass-cutter, engraver or gilder who joined the establishment; or if an independent artist joined, he was excused all taxes for several years, was given a plot of ground on which to build a house, free building-material, a cash advance and a further fifty thalers 'granted as praecipuum to his establishment so that the glass-manufacture of Silesia could be pushed as much as possible to further attainments'. The Bohemian glass-workers, to whom these inducements were principally directed, received — in a 'ruling for the glass-masters and glass-workers in the Kingdom of Bohemia' dated October 5th, 1767 — a warning from Philipp, Count of Kollowrat, acting for Maria Theresa, which said: 'Since it is of main concern that the glassmakers' fusing and other artifices should not be known and discovered by foreigners or any strangers, such an occurrence is most strongly prohibited, and any infringement will be severely punished by the Imperial Commercial Concession.' And it went on to say that Her Imperial Apostolic Majesty had been pleased to increase the fines 'of those ringleaders who entice others to emigrate and those who recruit glassmakers, whether they be foreigners or natives, to one hundred ducats'. And 'further, should parents be shown to have had any knowledge of the departure of their children or to have been involved in it, they too shall receive suitable punishment'. Here, too, then, the relatives shared liability although they did not, as in Venice, risk assassination.

In 1786, when Frederick the Great was dead, the Prussian government was bound to admit that the Silesian glass-industry had declined. Von Hoym, a Prussian minister, consoled himself with the thought that engraved glasses were old-fashioned anyway. Many glass-engravers had changed over to cameo-cutting since this art was in greater demand in a Neo-Classical age. Thus in 1790 when Goethe was travelling in Silesia he was able to marvel at the achievements of the cutters at Warmbrunn. He even counselled Duke Karl August of Saxe-Weimar to send the engraver Facius to Warmbrunn to learn gem-cutting: 'In Warmbrunn gem-cutting is a craft and mechanisation is quite common there.'

English influence

As far as central Europe was concerned, Bohemia had by the seventeenth century already become the home of a new art of glassmaking, while western Europe in the first quarter of the eighteenth century still remained under Venetian influence. France, having under the *Roi Soleil* become the leading cultural force in Europe, concentrated her technological efforts on the production of mirror-glass, basing herself in the first instance on Venetian experience (see page 102). It was as a consequence of these endeavours — catering for the embellishment of the great Baroque palaces — that the art of glass-cutting also came into existence and was fostered.

In England Charles II of the house of Stuart (1660–85), a francophile and a patron of the arts, set up a glasshouse for making mirror-glass on the French pattern at Vauxhall in London. Although Venetian glasses were imported, the native glass-manufacture did not remain idle.

As early as 1674 George Ravenscroft obtained a patent for crystal glass but he did not try using a proportion of oxide of lead until 1676. Buckley says that the idea was given him by the Italian Da Costa. This was the genesis of English flint-glass. Ravenscroft marked his glasses with a seal of a raven's head in relief, which resembles the Venetian seal of the head of the lion of St Mark.

The close association between England and the Netherlands following the accession in 1689 of William III of Orange to the English throne enabled the English glass-of-lead to gain an early footing on the Continent. There arose in the course of the eighteenth century a relationship between England and the Netherlands similar to that between Bohemia and Silesia, the Dutch obtaining raw glass from England and decorating it with the diamond-point.

Now that a new metal had been evolved, glassmakers were no longer restricted to producing delicate shapes on the Venetian pattern. Solider forms began to emerge. The first goblets to be made of English glass-of-lead possessed the Baroque baluster-stem, such as was usual towards the middle of the seventeenth century, with a straight-walled bowl. Towards the middle of the eighteenth century the baluster dwindled to one or more thickenings one above the other in the straight, tall, thin stem (page 176); the bowl opened out and became bell-shaped. The early pieces also include cordial-glasses with sturdy cylindrical knops such as are found nowhere else. Pseudo-facetted stems made their appearance in about 1715 and are regarded as the fruits of German influence under George I of Hanover (1714–27), since they were popularly called 'Silesian'. Ample feet are in general typical of English glasses, the diameter in the early pieces being greater than that of the bowl. Towards the middle of the century a form became common in which the funnel-shaped bowl merged without a break into the long stem, which in turn ended in a massive foot (page 223).

Four manners may be distinguished in the decoration of these glasses. The first forms part of the business of working the glass and therefore devolved upon the glasshouses. As on the Continent, bubbles had been inserted as early as 1725. This technique was further developed by pulling out and twisting the bubbles, thereby producing the air-twists typical of English glasses between 1745 and 1770. Milk-white glass threads and bands inlaid in spiral form were a later development (page 223), belonging to the period between 1755 and 1780. Combinations of the two forms of twist occur between 1760 and 1770.

The second style of decoration was enamel-painting. This has already been discussed (page 156) in connection with imitations of porcelain in milk-white glass and with cobalt-blue glass. Polychrome painting is found in England around the period 1760–1820. Painting in white enamel, executed most notably by William and Mary Beilby of Newcastle-on-Tyne, was widespread between 1720 and 1780.

The third manner of decorating was engraving; engraving is seldom found on English glasses. It did, however, produce a noteworthy English speciality, which, regarded as a historical document, illuminates the political background of the middle years of the century; these are the Jacobite glasses, so-called after the adherents of James Francis Edward Stuart, the Old Pretender (1688–1766). Most of these glasses were made at Newcastle-on-Tyne and were produced there even before the defeat of Charles Edward Stuart, the Young Pretender, at Culloden in 1746; bearing the Pretender's portrait, they served as a mark of political affiliation. After 1746 the portraits had to be replaced by symbols: one- or two budded roses, an oak leaf growing out of a thorn-covered rosebush, a thistle, a star, a briar-rose with a heraldic lily pointing north-eastwards, the word 'Fiat' (let there be), or 'Redeat' (let him return); these symbols were all widely used and examples still survive (page 222).

Sugar bowl. New Bremen Glass Manufactory, Frederick, Maryland. Height 21.3 cm.

Top: Opalescent pressed 'Robinson' boat salt. c 1830–36. Pittsburgh, Robinson's Stourbridge Flint Glassworks Length 9 cm. *Bottom left:* Beaker, enamelled with friendship motif and inscribed: 'Friendship/Amity'. 2nd half of the 18th century. Possibly Henry William Stiegel's glassworks. Height 8.5 cm. *Bottom right:* Jug with lilypad decoration. c 1842–55. Stoddard, New Hampshire, probably blown by Matt Johnson.

234

Left: Tumbler and cover made for C. Ghequière. *Right:* Engraved goblet made for George Jocob Schley by Frederick Amelung. Height 30.2 cm. Both c 1790, New Bremen Glass Manufactory, Frederick, Maryland.

Left: Columbia flask. c 1806–07. *Right:* Decanter blown in a three-piece mould. Possibly Boston and Sandwich Glassworks, Mass. c 1825–35. Height 24.8 cm.

Pressed dish in lacy pattern, a style developed by Deming Jarves at the Boston and Sandwich Glassworks, Mass. c 1830.

Vase in 'Aurene' style developed by Frederick Carder. Steuben Glassworks. New York c 1920.

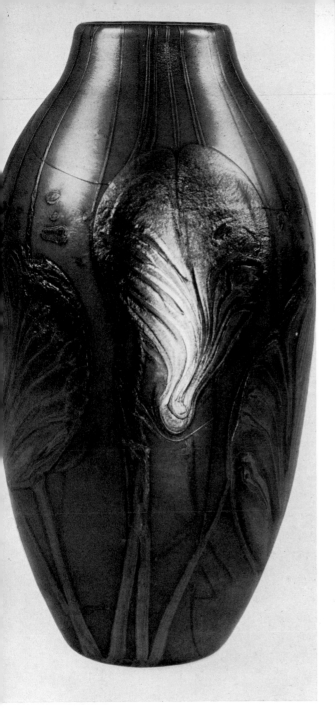 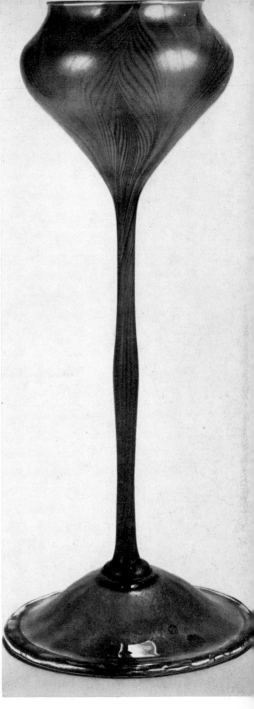

'Favrile' glasses by Louis Comfort Tiffany, New York. *Left:* Vase with palmettes. Honey-coloured glass iridising purple and blue. Signed 'L.C.T.E. 638', c 1900. Height 26 cm. *Right:* Golden-yellowish-brown, transparent glass iridising purple. Green, pale blue and whitish combed threads. Signed 'L.C.T. 12170', c 1904. Height 35.6 cm.

Bowl with scene of a merry-go-round. Glass engraved after the design by Sidney Waugh. Presented to Queen Elizabeth II of England when Princess Elizabeth on the occasion of her marriage in 1947 by the President of the United States of America and Mrs Truman. Steuben, New York. Height 25.4 cm.

English glasses

In the course of the 18th century English glasses broke free of their Venetian models and developed original, firmly based forms. Air-twists and twists of milk-white glass became popular during the second half of the century. Facetting was in general use between 1760 and 1810.

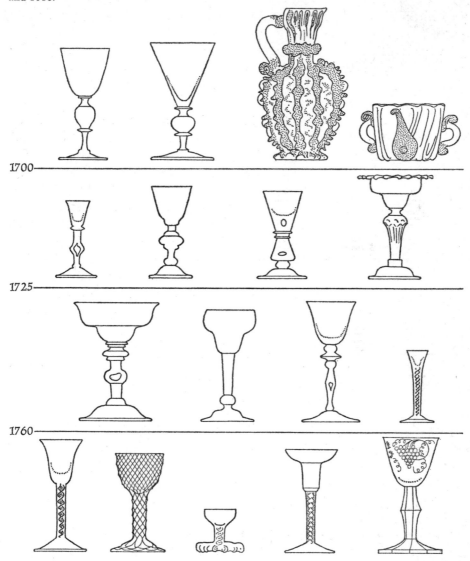

First row: Chalice of Mansell's period, c 1642; Flint glass, c 1680; Jug attributed to George Ravenscroft, c 1680; Punch-bowl. Second row: Cordial glass; Chalice of soda glass, c 1705; Dram glass, c 1710; Sweetmeat glass with dentated rim. Third row: Champagne glass; Chalice; Wine glass, c 1750; Cordial glass. Fourth row: Wine-glasses with air-twists and twists of milk-white glass; glasses with facetted stems, that on the right with vertical flutes; at centre of row a dram glass.

The fourth type of decoration is cut-glass. It began in 1760 when the stems of glasses were cut in facets, and reached its height in 1770 as crystal-cut glass. The technique was to make deep, diagonal criss-cross cuts. Pazaurek claims, on the basis of documents in a Bohemian factory in Cadiz dating from 1751, that this technique was a Bohemian invention, but the question remains unsettled. What is certain is that the art reached its highest standard with the cutting of English lead-crystal glass.

The technique developed similarly in Ireland, where English flint-glass was introduced in 1690, and the industry received a fresh impetus in 1784 when John Hill, financed by George and William Penrose, set up the Stourbridge glassworks near Waterford.

The brilliance of English cut crystal in the eighteenth century was such that it influenced continental glass also. France went over to the 'façon d'Angleterre', although the Venetian concession had been renewed in 1727 and production after the 'façon de Bohème' had only been introduced in the second half of the eighteenth century. The most important 'Bohemian' centres were those of 1752 at Lettembach (Moselle) (*Manufacture royale de cristaux et de verres en table*), of 1764 at Baccarat (*Verreries royales de Sainte Anne*) and of 1767 (*Verrerie de Saint-Louis*). Certain Venetian glasshouses in France — as, for example, that of B. Bayel in 1780 — had also changed over to the *façon de Bohème*. The first glasshouse making glass in the *façon d'Angleterre* was established at Saint-Cloud in 1783 by Lambert and Boyer. Marie-Antoinette became the patron of this establishment which called itself *Manufacture des Cristaux et Emaux de la Reine*. In 1784 Mayer Oppenheimer of Pressburg, who had worked for several years in Birmingham, also obtained a privilege for manufacturing English glass in Normandy. And in the end the English style of cutting became the principal one in Bohemia too. By about 1800 this form of decoration had become widespread throughout Germany and remained so throughout the Biedermeier period.

Cut decoration was not, however, the sole result of the English discovery of glass-of-lead; glass-of-lead, with its strong refraction of light, was also used as 'composition' glass and became a stock-in-trade of many glasshouses. On the basis of this metal a flourishing industry in glass-jewellery grew up, especially in north Bohemia, where the centre in the nineteenth century was at Jablonec.

This, however, was not the end of English influence. After the Napoleonic Wars England emerged as the leading nation in the field of technics, contrasting with the backwardness of the Continent. While locomotives and steamships were beginning to revolutionise transport and trade with distant countries, the production side saw the advent of industrialised mass-production. England and America began to market machine-made pressed glass designed to imitate the English deep-cut glass. French *entrepreneurs* followed in their footsteps.

In France it was the crystal-glass factory at Baccarat which showed most interest in developing and producing pressed glass. Like France, the United States of America had by the eighteenth century made a showing in the field of hollow glass and only now did both become leading nations in the art of glassmaking.

Early American glass

Within a year of the founding of the earliest permanent English settlement in America, at Jamestown, Virginia, the first eight glass-workers had landed in the New World and had built a glasshouse outside Jamestown, in which they made blown bottles. This glasshouse did not last long: no glass was fused there after 1617. There were half a dozen such attempts, spread over the seventeenth century, to settle a glass-industry in America with the support of the London Company, one of its purposes being to make the glass beads which served as inexpensive objects of barter in trade with the Indians. In the early days, however, the colony sent back to England not only the skins which had been acquired in exchange for glass beads but also a large proportion of the glass bottles produced.

History records that one Captain William Norton was concerned with this bead-making; and in 1621 the same man summoned six Italian glassmakers to Virginia. In 1622 he was running a glasshouse in Jamestown, which continued to manufacture beads after his death under the management of George Sandys. Excavation of Indian graves suggests that there were a number of other glass-houses in America making beads, although many of the beads from these graves are of European, mainly Venetian, manufacture.

In the year 1641 Ananias Cocklin, Obadiah Holmes and Lawrence Southwick of Salem, Massachusetts, obtained a loan of fifty pounds to set up a pot-furnace for making glass for bottles. During the period 1650–74 the Dutch settlement at New Amsterdam also possessed two glasshouses established by Johannes Smedes and Evest Duycking. They made bulbous, long-necked bottles of a type that were being blown in the Netherlands at that time. Yet another glasshouse is said to have been built in 1683, in what is now Philadelphia, by Joshua Tittery of Newcastle-on-Tyne, a manufacturer of window-glass.

All the glasshouses set up in the seventeenth century were short-lived. The first to survive for a longer period — forty years to be exact — was the one founded by the German, Caspar Wistar, in 1739 in South Jersey on an arm of the Allo-way Creek, between Salem and Philadelphia. Wistar went to Philadelphia when he was twenty-one. He became a Quaker and a businessman but knew nothing about glassmaking. On December 7th, 1738, he signed an agreement with John William Wentzell, Caspar Halter, John Martin Halton and Simon Kreismeier which guaranteed these glassmakers a free passage to America and a third of the net takings of the proposed glass-works, which were to manufacture bottles and table-ware. The factory was built in the summer of 1739 and production began at the end of the year. As a sideline and rather for their own needs and for friends, they also made domestic ware. The factory ran at a profit. Wistar died in 1752; after this his son Richard continued to run the factory until 1780, the year before his own death, when he put it up for sale.

The style of the hollow glasses manufactured at Wistar's factory matched the puritanical outlook of the colonists, an outlook which in all fields contrasted markedly with what they considered to be the reprehensible way of life of the home-country. The sturdy, free-blown glass of the southern part of New Jersey, with its metal varying between natural green and amber-yellow and its applied decoration in the form of threads or medallions, was pre-eminent in the region in which the leftist puritans, that is, the Quakers, formed the majority of immigrants. Despite its predominant individuality, the general features of this type of glass may be followed through into the nineteenth century. The 'lily-pad' decoration (page 234) was an original creation, being a form of thread decoration first in upright garlands and after 1830 in the cursive form of the 'running dog'. The range of colours for glasses also increased during the nineteenth century, because the natural colours were now supplemented by artificial ones, especially — after 1840 — blue.

The earliest imitation of Wistar's glass was made at Glasboro, in Gloucester County, where a glasshouse was set up in 1780—1 by the four brothers Stanger. They themselves and many of their workmen came from Wistar's factory. In 1813, after various changes in ownership, during the course of which the factory took the name of 'Olive Glass Works', a number of workmen moved further south to a newly-founded glasshouse, in which, again, the Stangers held an interest. From these beginnings, the type of sturdy, free-blown glass spread north and south, to New York and New England. Even the Owens Bottle Company, which dates from much later and gained world renown through its pioneering achievements in the automatic production of bottles, can be traced back to the early glasshouses of South New Jersey.

Henry William Stiegel — popularly known as 'Baron' — represents quite a different line of development. The fine American decorated glass of the eighteenth century, with its engraved and painted embellishment, which stood in the way of imports from the old world, is bound up with his name.

Stiegel was a Rhinelander and a native of Cologne. On August 31st, 1750, when he was twenty-one, he landed with his widowed mother and his brother in Philadelphia. His marriage gained him entry to the ironworks belonging to his father-in-law Huber in Lancaster. He was efficient, succeeded in becoming a partner and in acquiring sufficient resources to build a glasshouse. He began work in 1763 at 'Elizabeth Furnace' with a whole team of German glass-blowers. In November 1765 he moved to a new glasshouse which had in the meantime been prepared at Manheim. But he was not satisfied with making bottles and window-glass and occasional simple table-ware. He envisaged a great top-ranking flint-glass works on the European pattern which would sweep the American market. A visit to London strengthened him in these aspirations. Finally in 1768 the foundation-stone of his second Manheim glasshouse was laid and work began at the end of 1769. Here he employed more than 130 workmen, bringing to America engravers, painters and glass-blowers who were masters of the Venetian techniques, and glass-workers from Bristol. But the success of the undertaking lasted for only four years and was followed by economic ruin. Stiegel was unable to recover from this set-back. He was compelled to take a situation as a clerk and later became a teacher in Schaefferstown. He died in poverty on January 10th, 1785.

Stiegel's glasses were often made of glass-of-lead and were either blown in metal moulds or engraved or enamelled. It is true that probably even before 1769 the Glass House Company of New York, and later the Philadelphia Glass Works too, were making blown and decorated table-ware, but the qual-ity of the glasses made at Stiegel's second Manheim glasshouse was superior. Of the glasses blown in metal moulds — which probably accounted for the greater part of the output — some followed the English example and were executed by the Bristol glass-blowers while the surfaces of others were decor-ated with Venetian patterns. But both the enamelled and engraved glasses, with their symmetrical stylised tulip, heart and bird patterns on both sides of the glasses, remind one rather of Dutch or Spanish decoration. From June 1773 until the factory ceased production Stiegel employed the English glass-engraver Lazarus Isaac. Thereafter Isaac pursued his art independently, using Philadelphian and imported glasses.

When in 1774 production halted at Stiegel's glasshouse, many of his workers moved to the Philadelphia Glass Works. This factory was set up in 1771 by Robert Towars and Joseph Leacock and operated, with one intermission, until the beginning of the nineteenth century, latterly under the name of 'Dyottville Glass Works'. The Saxon glass-engraver, William Peter Eichbaum, was man-aging-director here in Philadelphia from 1793 until 1796. A year later he went to manage the 'Pittsburgh Glass Works', the first glasshouse in the Pitts-burgh district, which had just been founded by General James O'Hara and Major Isaac Craig.

Records of the history of American glass include as well the old German glass-makers' name of Greiner. An agreement signed on September 18th, 1763, between Stiegel and a team of glassmakers mentions one Martin Greiner, while a surviving document dating from 1752 of the Glass House Company of New York names a Johann Martin Greiner of Saxe-Weimar. This is probably one and the same man, which would mean that Greiner from New York moved over to Stiegel in Manheim. Stiegel's list of employees also includes the names of Balzer and Martin Thramer of Hesse. The unusual name of Balzer — for Balthasar — makes it certain that these are the brothers Kramer, who landed in Philadelphia on September 18th, 1773, with two more brothers and cousins as well. They worked for Stiegel and when production came to a standstill at the Manheim factory moved to Frederick, Maryland, to Amelung, and finally — when work at his factory also came to a halt — pressed further west, founding the first glasshouse west of the Alleghenies.

John Frederick Amelung and his New Bremen Glass Manufactory occupy a commanding position in the history of American glass of the eighteenth century. Amelung was a native of the Hanseatic city of Bremen. In 1784, in partnership with Benjamin Crocket, a Baltimore businessman, he founded a glasshouse in Frederick County, Maryland. This was followed between 1787 and 1790 by a second works. In 1788 economic difficulties forced Amelung to take up a loan of one thousand pounds. In 1795 he was obliged to offer the works for sale.

Amelung's factory produced the only American glasses of the eighteenth century to carry dates or other particulars. Mention should be made of two celebrated goblets and covers. One, with the key in the arms of the city of Bremen and the inscription 'Old Bremen Success and New Progress' and dated 1788, is in the possession of the Metropolitan Museum of Art. The second, similar but more perfect in form, is illustrated on page 235. It was a present from Amelung to Georg Jacob Schley, who lived in Frederick, Maryland, but came originally from the Palatinate, having emigrated to America in 1746. Although this goblet and cover are undated, they may be associated with the Bremen goblet. The inscription and the whole character of the beaker and cover illustrated on page 235 show that it too was made in Amelung's glasshouse. All the pieces with this provenance are soda-lime glasses; many of them are somewhat smoky in colour. The engraving of these glasses is deeper than that of Stiegel's glasses and reveals a greater mastery. The engraved glasses are certainly the best-known though not the only kind of glasses produced at this factory. There were also rather inferior utilitarian glasses blown in metal moulds, which remind one of Irish models, and enamelled glasses too.

Towards the end of the eighteenth century glassmaking spread to the Middle West. The glasses which were blown throughout the Pittsburgh-Monongahela district, in Western Virginia and Ohio much resembled Stiegel's wares, although they were a little more delicate and had thinner walls; the metal also came in a greater variety of colours. It may be assumed that glassmakers from

Empire and Biedermeier forms

Nineteenth-century glasses are always cut. The final shape is in many cases only achieved by deep cutting. Following upon the Neo-Classical forms of the goblet and urn so common during the Empire period, small beakers predominate during the Biedermeier period. The imitations of earlier styles which characterise Historicism — current from 1830 until 1890 — continue throughout much of the century.

Empire forms: Berlin goblet with scalloped foot and brilliant-cutting, dated 1825; Bohemian beaker with brilliant-cutting and cylinder-cutting, c 1830; urn made at Baccarat 1810–20; Bohemian *Kuglergravur* 1820; beaker by Samuel Mohn, 1812; double-medallion beaker by Mildner, 1806. Biedermeier forms: *Knopfbecher* made of lithyalin, 1830–40; Hyalith beaker, c 1830; flashed beaker with cut decoration, c 1840; *Ranftbecher* by Kothgasser, c 1828; cut-glass beaker, c 1840; bowl with foot, brilliant-cut decoration, c 1840. The forms of Historicism: 'Etruscan' vase; 'Medici' vase; both c 1840.

247

Stiegel's factories played a part in spreading the glass-industry westwards. The fact that the old German technique known as the half-post method is found in the blown bottles of the Middle West is an indication that German glass-blowers were involved.

Albert Gallatin, a Swiss Republican and native of Geneva — after which New Geneva was called — is credited with having founded the first glasshouse west of the Allegheny Mountains. In 1797, when a sizeable group of glassmakers who had been employed by Amelung moved out of Frederick County under the leadership of Balthasar ('Balzer') Kramer of Frankfurt am Main, in the direction of Kentucky, Gallatin managed to persuade them to go no further west but to set up a new factory in New Geneva. Gallatin and his brother-in-law, James Nicholson, placed their capital at the glassworkers' disposal for the purpose. In 1803 ownership of the works passed to the glassmakers Reitz, Reppert, Eberhart and the Kramer brothers. In 1807, when coalfields were discovered on the Monongahela River, they built a new glasshouse on the western bank near Greensboro, where the furnaces were heated with coal. In 1847 the glasshouse was destroyed by fire.

Albert Gallatin, who showed so much initiative while the glass-industry was being settled in the Middle West, was a representative of the new America. When the Constitution was proclaimed in 1787 he was only twenty-eight years old. In the year in which the glasshouse was set up at New Geneva John Adams succeeded Washington as president. Towards the end of the eighteenth century Jefferson, framer of the Declaration of Independence, was elected president of the United States. Gallatin worked as a high official under him and Madison until 1814. He represented the United States of America at the Peace of Ghent, was ambassador in France and England and co-founder of New York University. Many intellectual and libertarian ideas — and others, later, in the field of industrial techniques — emerged this period in the new world and influenced thought in old Europe.

Neo-Classicism

The new mood of intellectualism and criticism which began to make itself felt in Europe towards the end of the eighteenth century was hostile towards the traditional forms and exuberant decoration which still dominated the middle years of the century. The first result of the negation of what had until then been acceptable was a decline in quality.

Surprisingly enough, the art of glassmaking responded less readily to those

Ranftbecher beaker with Tarot-cards. Inscription on reverse: 'Leur union est notre force'.
Anton Kothgasser, Vienna 1815–20. Height 10 cm.

Left: Beaker with Masonic symbols and motto. Germany, c 1800. Height 11.8 cm. *Right:* Bottle with inserted medallions and out decoration, Joseph Mildner, Gutenbrunn, c 1800. Height 25 cm. *Opposite:* Beaker with portrait of J. von Fürnberg, one-time owner of Gutenbrunn. Portrait painted in colours on parchment within border of reddish-gold leaves, sur-

rounded by olive-cut border; reverse of medallion carries signature in silver and date. Lower Austria, Joseph Mildner, Gutenbrunn, 1792. Height 11.5 cm. *Above right:* Beaker with reddish-gold inserted medallion, diamond-engraving, cut rosette on base, rim and foot-ring olive-cut Mildner, 1802. Height 16 cm.

Opposite: Chalice in glass of purple tinge with gilt decoration. Inserted gold medallion carrying monogram CGH. Silesia, J. S. Menzel, Warmbrunn, late 18th century. Height 13.5 cm. *Left:* Empire goblet with portrait. Dresden, c 1810. Height 15 cm. *Right:* Empire goblet with silhouettes. Silesia, J. S. Menzel, Warmbrunn, 1805. Height 14.1 cm.

Top left: Beaker with fish motif, signed 'A. K.', Anton Kothgasser, Vienna, c 1812. *Top right:* Beaker with butterfly motif, Samuel Mohn, c 1810. Height 10 cm. *Bottom left:* Goblet with view of Schloss Steyersberg. Signed 'Mohn fecit 1816'. Gottlob Samuel Mohn. Height 19.5 cm. *Bottom right:* Beaker with view of garden pavillion. Workshop of Viertel and Siegmund, c 1813. Height 10 cm.

Glasses by Kothgasser, Vienna. *Top left:* Memorial *Ranftbecher* with star, c 1815. *Top right:*
Ranftbecher with view of St Stephan's Cathedral, Vienna, 1815–30. Height 11.7 cm. *Bottom-
left: Ranftbecher* with inscription 'Ehret die Frauen . . .' c 1825. Overall height 10 cm. *Bottom
left: Ranftbecher* showing Schloss Schönbrunn, c 1820. Height 10 cm.

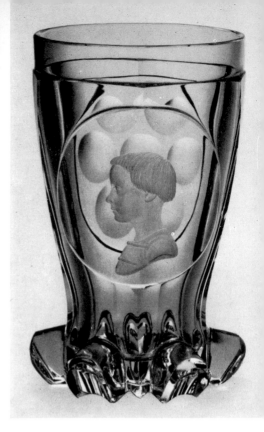

Opposite: Top left: Beaker with engraving of hunting-party. Probably Dominik Bimann, Bohemia, c 1830. Height 13 cm. *Top right:* Beaker with portrait of a child. Signed 'B'. Bimann, c 1830. Height 13 cm. *Bottom left:* Beaker with foot and cut and unpolished intaglio-engraved decoration. Lower Austria, Franz Gottstein, c 1820. Height 11.8 cm. *Bottom right:* Beaker in blue flashed glass with intaglio-engraved views of Carlsbad in the cut away ovals. Signed 'WI'. Bohemia, c 1850. Height 12.5 cm. *Above:* Brilliant-cut beaker with portrait of Ernst, Duke of Coburg-Gotha. Signed BIMAN. Bohemia, 1830–31. Height 13.4 cm.

Top left: Beaker showing the chariot of Venus. Paris, Charpentier, before 1813. Height 9.5 cm.
Top right: Beaker with cut decoration, polished and unpolished engraving, brilliant-cut base.
Bohemia, c 1800. Height 9.5 cm. *Bottom left:* Beaker portraying Amor in unpolished intaglio
engraving, diamond-cutting. Signed 'IOS. PIESCHE. FC.', after an engraving by F. Stöber,
Vienna. Budapest, c 1820. Height 12.7 cm.

Opposite: bottom right: Crystal-glass goblet (English glass) with diamond-engraving. Amsterdam, D. H. de Castro, dated 1856. Height 13.7 cm. *Above:* Beaker showing Venus and Amor. Paris, Charpentier, before 1813. Height 10.1 cm.

Glass illustrating the different Ages of Man. Northern Bohemia, c 1810. Height 14.5 cm.

Left: Humpen and cover with brilliant-cutting, coloured etching, clear and mat engraving. Bohemia, c 1850. Height 21 cm. *Right:* Goblet and cover, with cut decoration silvery-yellow etching, mat intaglio engraving. Bohemia, c 1830–40. Height 30 cm.

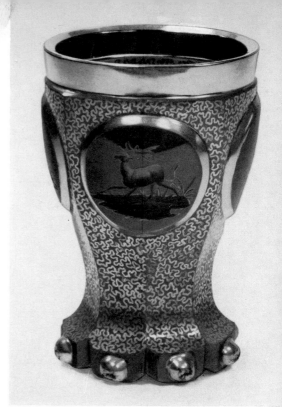

Lithyalin and hyalith glasses. *Top left:* Enamel-painted container and cover. Atelier of Egermann, Bohemia, c 1830. Height 6.5 cm. *Top right: Knopfbecher* with intaglio-engraved motif
and gold vermicular lines. Atelier of Egermann, Bohemia, c 1830–40. Height 11 cm. *Bottom
left:* Box with cover, effect of wood-graining. Atelier of Egermann, Bohemia, c 1840.

Opposite: bottom right: Plate in black hyalith glass. Southern Bohemia, Bucuoy factory, c 1830. Diameter 22.5 cm *Above:* Beaker with foot in lithyalin glass with gilt decoration and miniature-painting. Friedrich Egermann, Blottendorf near Haida, North Bohemia, c 1830. Height 14 cm.

Top: Two beakers encased in beads; between them a beaker flashed white, cut and enamel-painted. Bohemia, c 1850. Heights 8, 9.5 and 10 cm. *Bottom:* Two beakers, cylinder-cut and enamel-painted; between them a beaker with a portrait, decorated by the transfer process. Russia, mid—19th century. Heights 6, 6.5 and 7.5 cm.

Top left: Beaker painted in gold, silver and enamel, transfer process. St Petersburg, 1830. Bohemian beakers. *Top right:* Beaker with green flashing, cut spaces, inserted paste portrait of Justus von Liebig, dated 1859. *Bottom left:* Cobalt blue glass with polychrome enamel-painting and gilding. *Bottom right:* Blue glass with cut white flash and miniature-painting. Heights 9.6–12.5 cm. c 1850.

Bohemian beakers, c 1840. *Top left:* Opalescent green *(Annagrün)* glass beaker, painted in gold. *Top right:* Blue flashing, silvery-yellow etching and gold painting. *Bottom left:* Opalescent green glass painted in enamel colours and gold. *Bottom right:* Ruby glass, with intaglio-engraving silvered. Heights 10—14.5 cm.

Left: Goblet and cover, with pink, black, pale blue and purple painting in transparent colours, yellow etching, cutting and engraving. Bohemia, dated 1836. Height 32 cm. *Right:* Blue glass goblet with cold-painted decoration. Height 18.5 cm.

Beaker with foot, relief flashing and gold relief painting. Bohemia, c 1850. Height 14.3 cm.

two fundamental virtues of Neo-Classicism, severity and clarity, than to Romanticism. The English glass, with its bright, water-like purity and its linear cutting, most nearly matched the Neo-Classical urge for purity. On the Continent, however, the bourgeois-Romantic counter-movement gained a far more powerful hold on glassmaking. It persisted even after 1830, when Neo-Classicism had in general faded out. The Biedermeier preserved and fostered the Romantic element up to the middle of the century. And just as the *Gesamt-kunstwerk*, or synthesis of all the arts, corresponded to the Romantic ideal, so a new universality entered the field of glassmaking, bringing every artistic technique into play.

Simple, clear shapes — rectangular socle or plinth used as a foot for goblets and vases — are distinguishing features of the Neo-Classical repertoire of forms. *Putti*, flower-garlands and trophies are still found in the transitional *Louis Seize* style, while medallions became fashionable as decorative features for glass towards the end of the century, as did silhouettes in the first half of the nineteenth century. Glasses made in imitation of various stones, however, did not occur until the nineteenth century and even the marble-like mat-cut opaque glass made to look like agate first appeared in 1809, that is, during the Empire period — made by Egermann, despite the fact that it was as much in keeping with Neo-Classical taste as was biscuit-porcelain and could have been manufactured much earlier, since the technical requirements for making this type of glass already existed in the eighteenth century. It was left to the nineteenth century to discover and put these potentialities to use.

An important discovery was made at Sèvres, where experiments were carried on between 1796 and 1798 in fusing biscuit-porcelain medallions into glass. These so-called 'encrusted cameos' remained in favour until the middle of the nineteenth century. A thin layer of air between the porcelain and the glass lends these cameos and medallions a silver sheen well suited to the cold Empire style. The principal exponents of this technique were Desprez *père et fils* (active from c 1806 until 1830) and P.-H. Boudon de Saint-Amans (active between 1818 and 1858) in Paris. They signed their works 'D. P.', 'Desprez' and 'S. A. Paris'. Another celebrated piece is a vase and cover 52 cm high with seven relief portraits by L. Posch, which the Zechlin glasshouse presented in 1813 to Frederick III. Here the portraits are on a ring which can be removed from the body of the vase.

A certain technical super-subtlety had already set in with the gold-engraved glasses *(Zwischengoldgläser)* of the 1730s, which Mildner followed up in 1787 with his technically even more complicated double-walled glasses with inset medallions (pages 250—51). Mildner, a native of Lower Austria, let glass medallions into concavities in the double glasses which had been cut out to receive them. The inner sides of the medallions usually carry an inscription of etched silver on red lacquer and the outer sides a monogram in etched gold-leaf or black laquer silhouettes or portraits painted in colours on parchment between the protective layers of glass. Mildner evolved a style of his own in this technique which remained without imitators.

Those Rococo beakers in the double bases of which dice were enclosed must be included in the category of double glasses.

J. S. Menzel (pages 252—53) of Warmbrunn is also celebrated for his gold-engraved goblets with silhouette medallions. Both his works and the silhouette glasses made between 1806 and 1810 by Samuel Mohn are examples of the Empire style which brought Neo-Classicism to an end. Mohn became the leading artist of the great days of Biedermeier miniature-painting which came in at the beginning of the nineteenth century with the revival of painted table-glass.

Biedermeier glass

Glass for the middle-classes enjoyed a period of triumph during the decades which separated the Wars of Liberation (1813—15) from the Revolution of March 1848. The period before the Revolution was great in small things. Attention to detail, appreciation of thorough workmanship, emotional friendships and memories, romantic contemplation — all these mark the atmosphere in which the numerous *Ranftbecher* (beakers with cut steps) and *Knopfbecher* (beakers with button-like medallions), the memorial beakers with their painted decoration, the bead-surrounded, flower-adorned love-tokens came into being and were displayed in the glass-cabinet to decorate the home. A type of inflexible, class-conscious art-criticism has always despised these wares as mere lower-middle-class handicrafts. By 1839 the art-historian M. A. Gessert was already writing of Samuel Gottlob Mohn that he 'dragged stained glass down into one of its unworthy eras' and misused it for 'all sorts of *Quincaillerien*'. Today we are able to appreciate the faithfulness with which these *Quincaillerien* bring to life a not so distant past.

In fact, the story of Biedermeier glass ends neither with hand-painting nor with bead-embroidery nor yet with dilettante work done at home; on the contrary, it is technically extremely varied and some of it reaches artistic heights unattained by the achievements of previous centuries. This is particularly true of the Bohemian masters of glass-engraving.

First to be discussed must be Dominik Bimann. This outstanding portraitist was born in 1800 in Harrachsdorf-Neuwelt and began his studies at the Academy of Arts in Prague in 1826. His first signed ('D.B.') and dated work, Raphael's *Madonna della Sedia* engraved on glass — a recurrent motif on Biedermeier glasses — dates from that year. In 1829 he settled in Prague as a glass-engraver and later moved to Franzensbad, where he engraved on glass the portraits of visitors to the spa. An advertisement which appeared in the *Franzensbader Kurlistern* during the years 1851—54 runs: 'Portraits on crystal-glass engraved in his glass-shop at the Berliner Hof in the Kirchengasser, Dominik Bimann, academic glass-engraver.' However, by the 1850s the demand was already diminishing. Bimann fell ill, attempted suicide in 1855 and died in 1857. He left autobiographical notes and a manuscript of 170 pages entitled *Anmerkungen über Gesichtsphysiognomie 1841*, in which he discussed 121 portraits. A copy of this work is preserved in the Narodní Technické Museum in Prague.

Bimann signed his works 'D. B.', 'B.', 'D. Bimann', 'D. Biman', 'Biman', 'Bimann', 'D. Bieman' or 'Bi'. After 1830 he spelled his name Biemann. One of his best-known pieces is the beaker illustrated on page 257; it dates from the year 1831 and carries the portrait of Ernst I, Duke of Saxe Coburg-Gotha. So pleased was the duke with this work that he commissioned a second beaker from Bimann. The first beaker is signed 'Bimann', the second 'D. Bieman'. One of the most charming portraits must surely be that of Countess Wrangel which Bimann engraved in about 1835. It is a flat medallion such as he often used for his portraits. Besides these he engraved portraits, horses or hunting scenes on many drinking glasses and goblets.

The centres of glass-engraving lay in northern Bohemia. Gustav Pazaurek in his fundamental study, *Gläser der Empire- und Biedermeierzeit*, 1923, has described in detail conditions in Bohemia during the first half of the nineteenth century and has brought together the names of all the glass-engravers. The Bohemian tradition, which dates from the beginnings of glass-engraving in Europe, saw some of its greatest days during the nineteenth century.

We may take first the district of Steinschönau, which can claim two of the outstanding glass-engravers of the Biedermeier period: Franz Anton Pelikan (1786–1858) and August Böhm (1812–1890), both natives of Meistersdorf, south of Steinschönau. Franz Anton Pelikan had four sons and four daughters, all of whom practised as glass-engravers. Special mention should be made of his sons Anton and Josef. There was a second family Pelikan in Meistersdorf, consisting of Franz, the father, and two sons, Eduard and Josef. Josef sometimes placed a pelican in his landscapes. All members of both families made excellent engravings of horses and hunting scenes. Franz Anton Pelikan was the most important. His only known signed piece is a memorial goblet commemorating the twenty-five-year jubilee of the battle of Culm (1813).

August Böhm, the other great glass-engraver of Meistersdorf, signed his pieces more often. After 1833 he went to Stourbridge, London and America, where he earned good money but spent it open-handedly. He returned home as an old and impoverished man and died in Meistersdorf in 1890.

Other glass-engravers of the Steinschönau district who deserve mention are: Franz and Joseph Weidlich, Karl Günther, Karl Pfohl, Franz Knochel, David and Karl Pietsch and Franz Zahn.

Haida lies not far from Steinschönau to the east. The Ostritz family of Haida fostered the tradition of glass-engraving until the end of the nineteenth century. They have left only one signed work — by Johann Ostritz (1815–96), signed 'G. J. Ostritz'. Johann's sons Julius and Hermann belong to the second half of the century. Franz Hansel (1802–83) emigrated to France and worked at Baccarat.

One of the most skilful glass-engravers in the Isergebirge was Anton Simm (1799–1873). The famous glass-manufacturing family of Riedel is represented among artists of the Biedermeier by Franz Anton Riedel; he was also a manufacturer like his nephew and son-in-law Josef Riedel (1816–94), known as the 'Glass-king of the Isergebirge'.

On the Bohemian side of the Riesengebirge, the families Pfohl and Pohl of Harrachsdorf-Neuwelt, birthplace of Dominik Bimann, produced many glass-engravers. Among the artists who engraved both glass and precious stones at Warmbrunn, the old centre on the Silesian side of the Riesengebirge, we find Karl Friedrich Siebenhaar (1814—95), to whom Frederick William III sat in 1855 for his portrait engraved in onyx. After this he became court gem-cutter. Following his great model, Christian Gottfried Schneider, he left rubbings on paper of his engraved work on glass.

A school formed round Andreas Vincenz Peter Mattoni (1779—1864) at Carlsbad, the renowned spa in north-west Bohemia. Outstanding among Mattoni's pupils was Anton Heinrich Pfeiffer (1801—66). Anton Urban (1845—1909) was in his turn a pupil of Pfeiffer. The Urban family continued to produce glass-engravers into the twentieth century. Among Mattoni's other journeymen were Rudolf Hiller (1827—1915) and Anton Rudolf Dewitte (1824—1900). Emanuel Hoffmann (1819—78) moved to Carlsbad from Blottendorf near Haida. There is a goblet of about 1870 carrying a hunting scene and signed 'J. F. Hoffmann' by his son, Johann F. Hoffmann (1840—1900). One of the most famous of the Carlsbad men was Ludwig Moser (1833—1916). Moser originally learned glass-engraving as a pupil of Mattoni but afterwards became a glass-merchant and supplier to the Imperial court and in 1857 founded the factory of 'Ludwig Moser & Söhne AG' at Meierhofen, near Carlsbad.

And finally Austria was represented by yet other glass-engravers of the first rank among nineteenth-century artists. Foremost among these was Franz Gottstein, a distinguished artist from Gutenbrunn, whose works (page 256) should presumably be dated to the period between 1810 and 1830. Two signed glasses of his are known. According to the inscription on one of them he worked at the Strany glass-factory in Moravia; he was active at Gutenbrunn from 1823 until 1830. The refined style of his works reminds one of Charpentier in Paris. Joseph Haberl of Wiener Neustadt (1800—66) is known by signed works dating from 1821—2. Joseph Piesche was working in Budapest during the 1820s; a signed beaker of his is illustrated on page 258.

In about 1830 Johann Flink (1801—74) of Karlsruhe in south-west Germany signed a beaker with foot carrying a portrait of the Grand Duchess Sophie Wilhelmine and a chalice with a portrait of Wilhelm, Margrave of Baden.

In France, the engraver Charpentier of Paris was responsible for a series of finely engraved glasses showing goddesses and *amoretti* in the Empire style (pages 258—59). Franz-Adrian Dreier has established this attribution on the strength of an inscription on the inside of the cover of the *étui* of one such beaker. It is certain that Charpentier was active in Paris between 1813 and 1819. After that date the firm was successfully carried on by Madame Desarnaud-Charpentier. The raw glass was obtained from the glasshouse belonging to Aimé-Gabriel d'Artigues in which lead-crystal glass was made; the

Nineteenth century decorative techniques

The following table should enable the student to date the glasses of the 19th century according to the manner in which they are decorated.

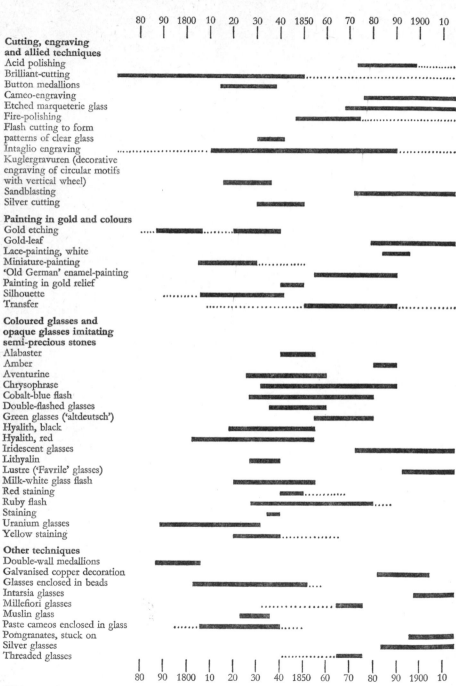

works was at Vonêche near Brussels and had been set up in 1802 on the English model.

We also find a number of Bohemian glass-engravers in France during the nineteenth century; they were always welcome at Baccarat, Vallerysthal and Saint-Louis. They are found in both England and America too. One of the earliest emigrants from Bohemia was Joseph Weidlich of Steinschönau, who went to Rome and, in 1795, to Naples. In France we find Franz Hansel of Radowitz, in about 1820, Karl Günther, after 1831, and Franz Knochel, in about 1860 — all three from the Steinschönau region. August Böhm went to England and America. The brothers Johann and Ludwig Görner, from the district round Haida, also emigrated to America. Karl Pietsch of Steinschönau returned home after six months. These are only a handful of names cited to demonstrate that it was not only the Syrians in antiquity and the Venetians in the sixteenth and seventeenth centuries whose art spread throughout Europe, but that the Bohemian *Glasraffineure*, too, followed their urge to travel and so carried the Bohemian style of glassmaking all over the world. The Biedermeier differs from earlier periods in that its glass is impossible to imagine without the embellishment of cutting; and as a rule it carried other forms of decoration as well.

The great importance now attached to glass-cutting resulted in a notable advance revealed in the new styles of cutting and a refinement of cutting techniques. The *Kugler* (cutters of circular and oval motifs) often took upon themselves to produce not only the favourite diamond-cut borders, diminishing lenses, button-medallions, star-cutting, sheaf-cutting, brilliants and cylinders, all of which were revived during the Biedermeier period, but also ventured into the field of engraving. *Kugelgravuren* occur during the period between 1814 and 1835. Since the same man was responsible for both cutting and engraving, the two represent a total composition in which engraving gives an even more finely elaborated effect to the cutting, itself usually very finely done.

Favourite motifs of the Biedermeier period included portrayals of the Three Fates, Sybils or prophetesses, Madonnas, Paternoster beakers with the Seven Supplications, Faith, Hope and Charity, the dignity of women, forget-me-not beakers, glasses showing the ages of man, flowers, beakers with the figure of Amor, hunting, horses and portraits.

The Biedermeier glasses decorated by miniature-painting were entirely in tune with the times, not only in their external appearance but also in the commercial method by which they were produced in 'small factories', such as Mohn senior set up in Leipzig and Dresden. The glasses painted to his requirements in these factories were signed by him and, from 1812 onwards, by the artist who painted them as well. By 1809 Mohn was already using transfers.

Transparent painting was derived from *Hausmalerei*, or studio painting, on porcelain and was influenced by its elder sister, stained glass, which enjoyed a revival at the beginning of the nineteenth century as part of the gothicising trend of the Romantic movement. Samuel Mohn of Merseburg, who himself wrote that he had rediscovered the 'lost' art of transparent painting, had begun life as a *Hausmaler* of porcelain. His son Gottlob Samuel, who had also started out as a *Hausmaler*, later became a stained-glass artist. In 1810 he took drawing lessons at the Leipzig Academy and, thanks to this training, he excelled his father as an artist. Samuel Mohn, the father, however, was able to muster far-reaching connections, which — as the age demanded, he carefully and respectfully cultivated. The first glass made at the workshop which Mohn ran with his son, on which Gottlob Samuel had painted armorial bearings, was in 1805 dedicated to Frederick William III. And a year later on March 10th, the birthday of Queen Louise of Prussia, he presented her with a glass with a dedicatory inscription, for which she ordered him to be paid three *Friedrichsdor*. Having laid this foundation of good public relations, he did profitable business with other glasses associated with Queen Louise, especially after her death in 1810. He took advantage of the Treaty of Tilsit in 1807 to dedicate a glass with a painted verse to Duke Friedrich Franz I of Mecklenburg (1756–1837) on the occasion of his birthday. The verse began: 'Zu deiner diesmahl frohern Jahrtags Feier Schickt Dir Erhabner Fürst Dein Mohn die Leyer...' (On this your most joyful birthday, noble Prince, Your servant Mohn addresses you this song). In 1807 he moved his workshop from Neubrandenburg to Leipzig. This workshop was followed in 1812 by a second 'small factory' in Dresden; while in 1811 his son Gottlob Samuel went to Vienna to carry out commissions for stained glass and to extend his knowledge of colour technique at the Polytechnic Institute in Vienna. This brought him into contact with the porcelain factory, where he met Kothgasser, a porcelain painter, who joined him. In Vienna Mohn also made glasses after his father's style.

The motifs which occurred with greatest frequency on the glasses of the Mohns (page 254) in Leipzig, Dresden and Vienna were views of these cities, palaces and noteworthy sights suitable as travel souvenirs. Mohn the elder favoured flowers and butterflies — 'in which the connoisseur will find all the known colours together' since these exemplified the high standard of colour technique he achieved. He followed fashion in using the language of flowers as well, sometimes in the well-known rebus *Wandel auf Rosen und Vergissmeinnicht*, sometimes in an acrostic made up of names of flowers, as, for example, in the one — not easy to solve — which produces the name Luise *(Lilie, Ursinie, Immergrün, Silene* and *Efeu)* on one of the 'Louise' glasses of about 1810.

When Mohn the elder died in 1815, his son Gottlob Samuel — who had meanwhile risen to the position of palace painter at Schloss Laxenburg — continued to run the Dresden factory from Vienna. From 1809 onwards the brothers August and Wilhelm Viertel, Christian Siegmund, a copper-plate engraver, and C. von Scheidt, a painter, had all been working in Dresden. In 1812 Wilhelm Viertel and Siegmund opened a workshop of their own (page 254) and Samuel Mohn took proceedings against this competition, but was unsuccessful. From this year onwards the counter-signature 'C. v. S.' (von Scheidt) occurs on Mohn's glasses. There were other counter-signatures but so far they have not been identified. In 1826 C. von Scheidt went to Berlin.

Besides those in Dresden and Vienna, there were other workshops of this kind in Germany. They were usually run by *Hausmaler* of porcelain who practised transparent painting on glass as well: Franz Anton Siebel (1777–1842) and his daughter Klara at Lichtenfels am Main, Fritz Wedemayer (1783–1861) in Göttingen and the brothers Eduard and Feodor Kehrer at Erbach in the Odenwald, sons of the founder of the ivory-carving establishment.

The most popular miniature-painter of the Biedermeier period was undoubtedly Anton Kothgasser (1769–1851) of Vienna. Kothgasser was employed from 1784 until 1840 at the Vienna porcelain factory and painted glasses from 1812 at least until 1830. Following Mohn's example he also employed other painters. In 1823 he demonstrated his own art with a portrait in stained glass measuring 60 cm by 52 cm of the Emperor Franz I in coronation regalia. For his other works he preferred the *Ranftbecher*. His flower-paintings are among his best works. At forty-five florins the *grosse Rosen Parthy* was one of his most expensive pieces. Kothgasser was catholic in his choice of motif (page 249). Inscriptions in French often occur on his glasses, a fact attributable to the cosmopolitan nature of Viennese society at the time. Kothgasser was also most anxious that his customers should be able to find him and he sometimes marked his beakers accordingly: 'The maker lives on the Spanischer Spitalberg No. 227 in Vienna.' Kothgasser's glasses were much imitated and fakes are not easy to detect. By the 1830s Friedrich Egermann's *Atelier* in Haida had already adopted Kothgasser's style. Egermann (1777–1864) soon gave up painting on glass and took to developing new types of glass and new techniques. With him began an era of coloured glass; this had begun by 1820 and lasted until 1870, the coloured wares taking the place of painted glasses. The dawn of the technical age, the first really characteristic mark of the nineteenth century, found in Egermann exactly the right type of technically able, universal artist.

The nineteenth century

The various phenomena of the nineteenth century are all so closely interconnected that, although there are recognisable climaxes, it is impossible to draw hard and fast dividing-lines.

The forms of Art Nouveau and New Functionalism

The reaction to the stylistic recapitulations of Historicism took the form of Art Nouveau. The pioneers of the movement were concerned that it should be a genuine expression of the age and they advocated consistency of form and decoration. By about 1905 Art Nouveau had hardened into an ornamental, linear, purely decorative art and was challenged by the champions of Functionalism. They saw the idea of a New Objectivity in pure harmonious form.

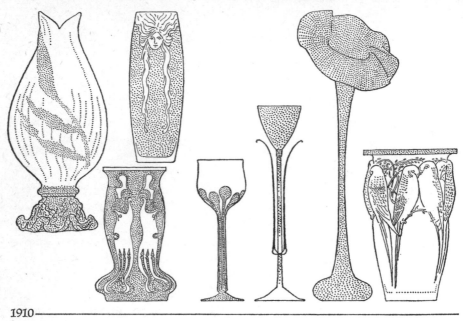

1910

Art Nouveau forms: vase with bronze foot by Emile Gallé; vases from Val Saint-Lambert and by Carl Goldberg of Haida; wine-glass made by the Rheinische Glashütten AG, Köln-Ehrenfeld; ornamental glass by Karl Köpping; ornamental glass by Louis Comfort Tiffany; vase by René Lalique. Examples of New Functionalism: vases by Timo Sarpaneva and Richard Süssmuth; beaker by Wilhelm Wagenfeld; stacked mixing-jugs by H. H. Engler; wine-glass by A. F. Gangkofner; vases by Heinrich Löffelhardt and Kaj Franck.

278

The master-images of the Biedermeier glasses were created by powerful artistic personalities, the nature of whose practical experience had been determined around 1815 by the metropolis of Vienna; the next generation, however, was compelled to recognise that the key-problems of development were shifting to other parts of the world and other planes of interest. Handcrafts which had previously been carried on in an amiable, uncommitted manner became increasingly subject to rational economic theories. Many who tried to escape these changes by leaving their native land found in foreign countries the recognition they hoped for since to take on specialist workers — not least because of the continuing decline in quality — helped to strengthen the internal economy at a period of nationalist protectionism and blocked imports. Just as states modelled themselves to meet the problems of the future so were the standards of industry improved. Technical and social advances had to be forcibly brought into conformity. Many outmoded ideas disappeared in the process; the new machines necessitated new laws; life was changing. Those processes which were easiest to mechanise were the first to succumb to the revolutionary changes. The linen-workers of Reichenberg destroyed the machines in 1844 but the glass-bead makers of Jablonec did not wreck theirs until 1890.

America led the field in the technical revolution. Robert Fulton crossed the Hudson in his steamship *Clermont* in 1807; in 1819 the *Savannah* made the Atlantic crossing. The American glass-industry made up for lost time too. Around 1800 nine glasshouses were in production; in 1820 there were forty, including such celebrated factories for fine hollow glass as Bakewell & Company of Pittsburgh, the South Boston Crown Glass Company and the New England Glass Company in East Cambridge, Massachusetts. By 1837 a further sixty glass-works had been added to this number. The period between 1820 and 1837 saw a boom in all fields. Revolution and war were over and the time for universal peaceful development had at last arrived. This 'era of good feeling' provided an atmosphere which allowed the American talent for invention, or 'Yankee ingenuity', to develop. The new contribution of the American engineers to the development of the glass-industry was their mechanisation of the process of preparing the mass. The pressing machine made its appearance during the 1820s. It was soon followed by the lace-like glass (page 237) which was produced between 1825 and 1850 and is regarded as the finest type of American pressed glass. It was shown for the first time at the industrial fair in New York in 1829.

The first known patent for pressed glass dates from September 9th, 1825. It was granted to John P. Bakewell of the glasshouse of Bakewell & Co, Pittsburgh, for pressing knobs for furniture. A year later, on the 4 November 1826, Enoch Robinson and Henry Withney of the New England Glass Company in Cambridge, Mass. obtained a patent for the same purpose. In 1827 Enoch

Art Nouveau artist-glassmakers and their centres of activity

The new decorative style which emerged during the second half of the nineteenth century and supplanted the trend known as Historicism was espoused both by universal artist-glassmakers and by factories and workshops. Artists like Gallé and Tiffany represent the type of artist-craftsman who understood the use of every variety of glass and every technique. The high cost of fusing forced factory-owners to turn their installations to better account by going over to mass-production and employing foreign labour. In these cases the signature does not guarantee that the glass in question was in fact made by the artist. The Grossherzögliche Edelglasmanufaktur in Darmstadt is an exception: there different signatures were used by the factory and the artist.

D. Christian & Sohn Meisenthal, Lothringen		
Daum, Auguste Nancy	1853—1909	
Daum, Antonin Nancy	1864—1930	
Gallé, Emile Nancy	1864—1904	
Archducal Fine-glass factory Darmstadt		
Koepping, Karl Dresden/Berlin	1848—1914	*Koepping*
Lalique, René Jules Paris	1860—1945	R. LALIQUE
Joh. Loetz Witwe (Max Ritter von Spaun) Klostermühle, Bohemia		
Poschinger, Ferdinand von Buchenau/Theresienthal		*Ferd. von Poschinger Buchenau*
Prouvé, Victor Nancy	1858—1943	(»Gallé« with star)
Schneckendorf, Josef Emil Darmstadt	1865—1949	
Tiffany, Louis Comfort New York	1848—1933	
Val St. Lambert Belgium		
Vittali, Otto Munich/Frankfurt	1872—	

A further group of artists included Van de Velde, Ludwig Sütterlin and Gustav Schneider, Kolo Moser and Josef Hoffmann, all of Vienna; these men were only distantly involved in glassmaking in so far as they produced designs for glasses. They are not included in the table.

Only those few industrial enterprises are listed in the table which can be said to have done a certain amount of pioneering work for the new style. Besides these the following firms were well known: E. Bakalowits Söhne in Vienna, the court suppliers, the Cristallerie de Kosta in Stockholm, the Graf Harrach'sche Glasfabrik at Neuwelt, Fritz Heckert at Petersdorf, the Glasindustriegesellschaft Ludwig Moser & Söhne in Carlsbad; A. Landier fils at Sèvres, Legras & Co. at Saint-Denis, J. & L. Lobmeyr in Vienna, Meyr's Neffe at Adolf in Bohemia, Josef Fallme König at Steinschönau and Kosten, The Rheinische Glashütten-AG under Friedrich Oskar Rauter at Köln-Ehrenfeld, Joseph Riedel at Harrachsdorf.

Robinson in Cambridge and Deming Jarves in Boston succeeded in pressing hollow glass. In 1830 John M'Gann of Kensington, Philadelphia, obtained a patent for pressing bottles. Further patents were given to other glasshouses on the Eastern sea-board. Most of the pressed glasses were made at the above-named glasshouses, particularly those in New England. The Boston and Sandwich Glass Company at Sandwich, Massachusetts, was for a time the sole producer of pressed glass, with the result that most people called any pressed glass 'Sandwich'.

Another product of mechanisation and typical of American glass of the nineteenth century was the 'historical' flask. These were small flasks blown in metal moulds with relief portraits of the presidents, state emblems or goddesses of victory and were made everywhere between 1816 and 1875.

Europe did not fail to emulate the American advance towards mechanised mass-production. The factory of Benedikt Vivat in Styria probably went furthest in imitating the historical flasks blown in metal moulds. Vivat produced various drinking glasses carrying the portrait of Archduke Johann in relief, the Austrian double eagle and agricultural symbols. The factory of Paris in Bercy also produced busts blown in metal moulds, known as *flacons de cheminée*. One such piece, a Napoleon made of opal glass, adorned Goethe's desk in Weimar.

Press-moulded glass too soon came to be widely manufactured in Europe. Developments in this field in England particularly even cast doubt upon America's claim to priority. In 1836 James Stevens in Birmingham succeeded in press-moulding a tall wine-glass. Besides Stevens, mention must be made of John Ogdin Bacchus, George Joseph Green & William Gammon and Rico Harris, all of Birmingham, as well as of Aspley Pellat of Blackfriars Bridge, Surrey, all of whom were pioneers of this process in England. Press-moulding came to be much used in France too. The two Neo-Gothic vases by Launay, Hautin & Cie. of Paris illustrated on page 247 (bottom right) are examples of French press-moulded glasses of the 1840s. Like the Americans, this factory also made glass door-knobs. Other European factories making press-moulded glass were C. W. Scheffler at Haidemühl in Germany, Johann Mayr at Adolph in Bohemia and Josef Lobmeyer at Marienthal in Czechoslovakia.

Economic development brought with it new opportunities, new antagonisms and dangers. The opportunities lay in mass-production, which went hand in hand with increasing population, a boom in trade and the use of machines. New means of gaining riches and good fortune had suddenly appeared: these means were in effect the masses.

In London as early as 1802 the forces of social justice were demanding a law for the protection of children and in 1847 the ten-hour day for women and juveniles became statutory. In the course of the century the continental countries were compelled to follow these examples.

Economic and social problems exerted an overwhelming power of attraction. The scrupulousness of the good old days was over. The new factor which nurtured every artistic activity was the desire of the prosperous middle-class to make a show. Strengthened by its success in bending the forces of nature to useful purposes, the spirit of rationalism then abroad yearned to dominate the past — which could, of course, only be transcended, not changed. The whole range of the artistic expression of past ages was there at hand for use. And so the fashion changed from the homesick Gothic to the nostalgic Exotic; around the middle of the century this yielded to the Revived Rococo, itself to be supplanted by the Neo-Renaissance, until in 1889 at the World Exhibition in Paris Emile Gallé showed his 'tentacular style' in glass.

A second element in this complex development stemmed from a different source: the principle of competition in industrial output resulted in exhibitions of national industries — the first of which was held in Paris in 1798 — becoming a permanent institution. The first half of the nineteenth century saw many such opportunities for comparing achievements in the national field; the second half was the era of the world exhibition. These were a spur to achievement but also caused manufacturers to put all their effort into good selling lines.

Not only that: they also brought the civilisations of foreign countries to Europe. The World Exhibition of 1862 in London included a display of Chinese art, while the newly discovered art of Egypt caused a great sensation at the second Paris World Exhibition of 1867. Together with technics, the applied arts were at the hub of the cultural, industrial and social problems of the period. Time made a solution urgent and tensions cast their shadows on the world exhibitions. Simultaneous with the London Exhibition of 1862 was the founding of the first International Working Men's Association, of which Karl Marx was secret head; and a Pole used the World Exhibition in Paris of 1867 to make an attempt on the life of the Czars. The dominant endeavour in the field of art and culture in Europe at the period of the Restoration was that of renewing the art forms and consciousness of the Middle Ages and antiquity. Chemistry and technics were available as the means of realising this endeavour.

Glasses which had been individually painted and engraved at great cost in time now gave way to coloured glasses, glasses which simulated various semi-precious stones and flashed glasses, all of which were better suited to mass-production. New materials, such as uranium pitchblende (uranium glasses), were used. Able technicians, directors of factories and their inspectors, as well as artists, all worked together to put a constant stream of new varieties on sale. Wedgwood's ceramics constituted one of the challenges and starting-points, for these wares contributed much to the formation of taste during the first third of the nineteenth century, not only in England (page 306) but also on the Continent.

Georg Franz August Longueval, Count von Buquoy's south Bohemian factory under its director Bartholomäus Rosler brought out its sealingwax-red Hyalith glass after Wedgwood's *rosso antico* as early as 1803. The black, true Hyalith (page 262) on the model of Wedgwood's 'Egyptian black' followed in 1817.

In northern Bohemia Friedrich Egermann (1777—1864) was the central figure concerned in these developments. In 1828 he invented a glass which imitated the appearance of semi-precious stones which he called Lithyalin and which he continued to manufacture until 1840. This metal appeared in a wide variety of styles, of which a few examples are illustrated on pages 262—63; they vary from monochrome glasses in pastel colours, with or without painting, gilding, silver-etching, cutting or engraving, to glass with marbling or agate-like patterning. It was not for nothing that Egermann named a type of Lithyalin which he brought out in 1835 *Chamäleon-Glas*. Lithyalin was imitated in both Bohemia and Silesia. With later developments in Cologne, Bunzlau and France, the succession of these opaque glasses — Haematin, Purpurin, aventurine, glasses imitating malachite, lapis lazuli, jasper and porphyry — continued until about 1855.

Egermann's greatest economic success was his discovery of yellow and red 'staining' in 1820 and 1840 respectively, which made it possible to cover raw glasses with a coloured bloom. By 1842 he was already employing two hundred people who handled one hundred and fifty tons of glass annually with an annual turn-over of 100,000 florins.

Egermann was a celebrity in Haida. There was still a postcard in existence at the turn of the century which showed an event which had taken place in 1855: the Emperor Ferdinand of Austria after his abdication walking arm in arm with his 'grateful subject Friedrich Egermann, painter and glass-merchant' — the latter heads taller than his monarch — across the market-place at Haida. Behind them at walking-pace came the royal coach and four.

Despite the rationalisation of colour production achieved by Egermann's technique of coloured staining, flashed glasses remained popular; original effects were obtained by cutting patterns through the white tin-oxide (page 264), copper-red or cobalt-blue upper layers — or, during the 1830s, through several layers, a process known as *Doppelplattierung*.

In 1839 the Verein zur Beförderung des Gewerbefleisses in Preussen announced a prize to be awarded to the glass-worker who could rediscover the Venetian technique of making thread-glasses. The competition was won by Franz Pohl, director of the Gräfliche Schaffgotsche Josephinenhütte in Schreiberhau. Interest in glasses *á la façon de Venise* was thus awakened and Venetian forms, though crudely executed, came on to the market once more in France and Germany. This Neo-Venetian fashion was fostered by the second World Exhibition in Paris in 1867, at which Salviati of the Compania Venetia-Murano successfully showed Venetian glasses. Opposition to this trend was offered at the Vienna World Exhibition of 1873 by Ludwig Lobmeyer. He had employed for the purpose the best Bohemian engravers, to wit, Carl Pietsch, Franz Ullmann and Franz Knochel, all of Steinschönau. He succeeded in restoring cut and engraved glass to its position of pre-eminence, but the Neo-Renaissance, represented by the firm of Fritz Heckert in Petersdorf, was already in sight. Heckert specialised in enamel-painting and from 1889 onwards produced 'Cyprus glasses' in its own glasshouse; manufactured in all shades of green, these glasses recalled the *Waldglas* of former times and carried descriptive names such as *'Princessgrüncypern'*. One of the artists who designed for Fritz Heckert was Ludwig Sütterlin (1865—1917), the Berlin graphic artist responsible for the Sütterlin script which was introduced into the Prussian schools in 1915 and later into those of other German *Länder*.

That America too was involved in this whole development shows that the artistic and technical vogues of the nineteenth century applied throughout the world. During the 1880s especially, numerous new inventions came on to the market; as in Europe they were subject to rapid changes. Among the coloured glasses, amber glass (cf. page 274) was popular in America too. Two-coloured glasses were, however, a speciality of the American makers; the effect was achieved by partial warming-in. Joseph Locke, for the New England Glass Works — where these glasses were called 'Amberina' — obtained the first patent on July 24th, 1883. The lower part of these glasses was the colour of amber, gradually merging higher up the vessel into a ruby-red. Many other glass-houses adopted this technique and produced similarly shaded glasses. In 1886 Joseph Locke himself created another type; this was a mat glass shaded from white to pink which he called 'Agata'; while a year earlier Joseph Webb of the Phoenix Glass Company at Beaver Falls, Pennsylvania, had attracted attention with his mother-of-pearl satin glass. Another metal which belongs in the category of coloured glasses was the dark reddish-yellow one marketed by Hobbs, Brocunier & Company in Wheeling, West Virginia, as 'Peachbloom'; this was transformed by the New England Glass Works into their red and white 'Wild Rose-Peachbloom' and by the Mount Washington Glass Works into red and blue. The true speciality of the last-named factory was, however, its alabaster glass roughened with hydrofluoric acid. Frederick S. Shirley, director of the factory from 1874 until 1887, owned a patent for mother-of-pearl glass as well and another for 'Burmese' glass which was fused with a proportion of uranium oxide and was shaded salmon-pink and lemon-yellow. These wares were painted as well. A set of glasses presented to Queen Victoria and Princess Beatrice were decorated with a floral pattern designed by the artist Albert Steffin; the pattern was afterwards known as the 'Queen's design'. Thomas Webb & Sons bought the licence and called their wares 'Queen's Burmese'. Venetian techniques were revived in America as in Europe, although a little

Bowl with design of ephemeras. Emile Gallé. Nancy, c 1889. Diameter 21 cm.

Opposite: Flask with bat motif. The upper part the colour of ice shading towards the base into a dull yellowish-red. Rough shape of a bat in glass paste applied hot. Cyclamen flower in milky mauve and vivid purple on the throat of the bottle. Emile Gallé, Nancy c 1900. Height 24 cm. *Above:* Vase inscribed 'Le soleil et les vents . . . Des feuilles sur son front faisaient flotter les ombres'. Signed on base: 'Emile Gallé E fect Nancy F 1888 pour la Gallerie d'Honneur Exposition 1889'. Height 12.9 cm.

Cameo-glass plate with red background (detail; left, whole plate). Venus and Cupid. George Woodall, c 1890. Made by Thomas Webb & Sons, Stourbridge. Diameter 45 cm. *Opposite:* Vase with ornamental bands. Colourless glass flashed with iridescent green. Whitish green applied threads round an ornamental relief band of interlaced glass threads and blue spots below the mouth. Probably made at the J. Loetz Witwe glasshouse (Max Ritter von Spaun), at Klostermühle in Bohemia, c 1900. Height 34 cm.

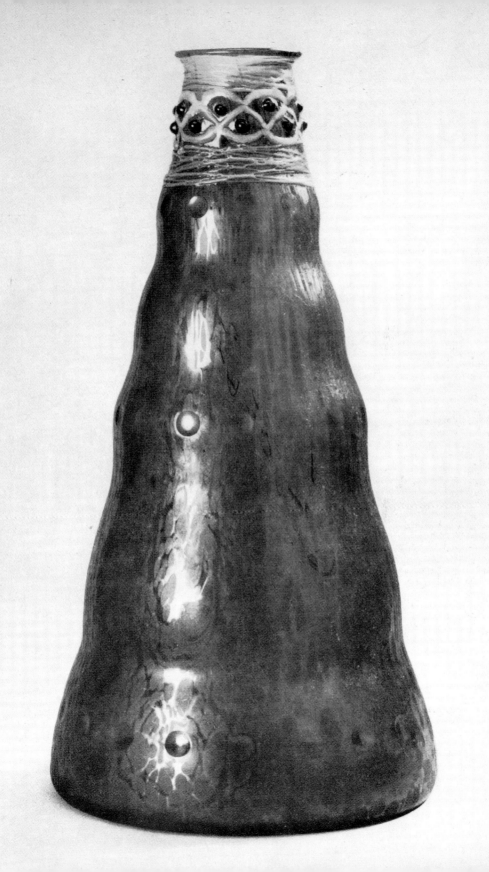

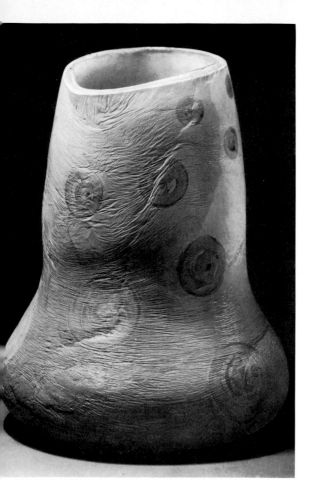

Opposite: Bronze-mounted glass jug. Signed 'R. Lalique'. René-Jules Lalique. Paris 1903. Height 49.3 cm. *Above, left:* Vase with wrinkled surface. Glass treated with metallic salts, tinted beige with bluish and pale purple rings. Impressed mark on the underside of the base EL below a crown (Großherzogliche Edelglasmanufaktur, Darmstadt) and 'J. E. SCH'. Josef Emil Schneckendorf, Darmstadt, c 1908. Height 17 cm. *Above, right:* Small jug with silver gilt mount. Daum frères (Auguste and Antonin), Nancy, c 1900. Height 24.5 cm.

Vase with four trunk-shaped handles (cf. pp. 58—9). Colourless, transparent glass with golden-yellow opalescent surface. 'Loetz Austria' in letters cut on the base. Made by the J. Loetz Witwe glasshouse at Klostermühle in Bohemia, c 1900. Height 25.1 cm.

Round vase made of coloured glass decorated with threads — converging upon purple and olive-green areas on a yellowish-brown iridescent ground. Base gilt. Inscribed in gold letters 'N 224 Ferd. von Poschinger Buchenau'. Ferdinand von Poschinger, Buchenau, c 1900. Height 10 cm.

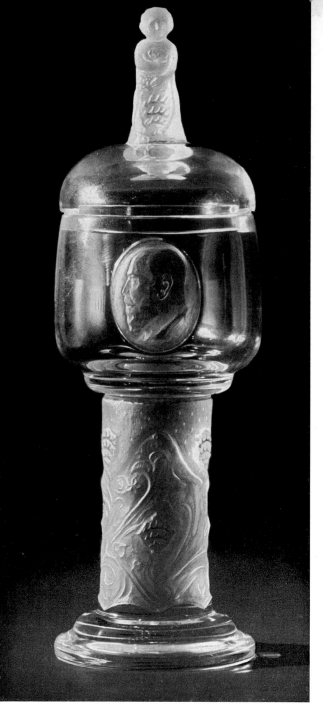

Left: Goblet and cover with portrait (*'geschnitzt'* or 'chipped') of King Wilhelm II of Würt-temberg. Colourless glass. Wilhelm von Eiff, Stuttgart, 1916. Height 28.6 cm. *Right:* Vase with enclosed green and yellow threads. Colourless glass, milky below the mouth. Count Harrach's glasshouse, Neuwelt, Bohemia. From the Jubilee Exhibition, Vienna, 1898. Height 39.5 cm.

Wine-glass. Mat-etched crystal-glass with black bronzite decoration. Designed by Joseph Hoffmann and L. H. Jungnickel. Made by J. & L. Lobmeyr, Vienna, 1910. Height 18.8 cm.
Right: Ornamental glass in the form of a tulip. Polychrome glass, partly opaque. Friedrich Zitzmann, Wiesbaden, before 1900. Height 29 cm.

Left: Glass for white wine with a broad gold band. Designed by Peter Behrens, Düsseldorf. Made by Benedikt von Poschinger, Oberzwieselau, 1903. Height 19 cm. *Right:* Glass for white wine. Designed by Joseph Maria Olbrich, Darmstadt. Made by Backalowitz Söhne, Vienna, 1901.

Double sweetmeat dish. Designed by Wilhelm Wagenfeld, Stuttgart. Made by the Wurttem-
bergische Metallwarenfabrik, Geislingen-Steige, 1962. Height 13 cm.

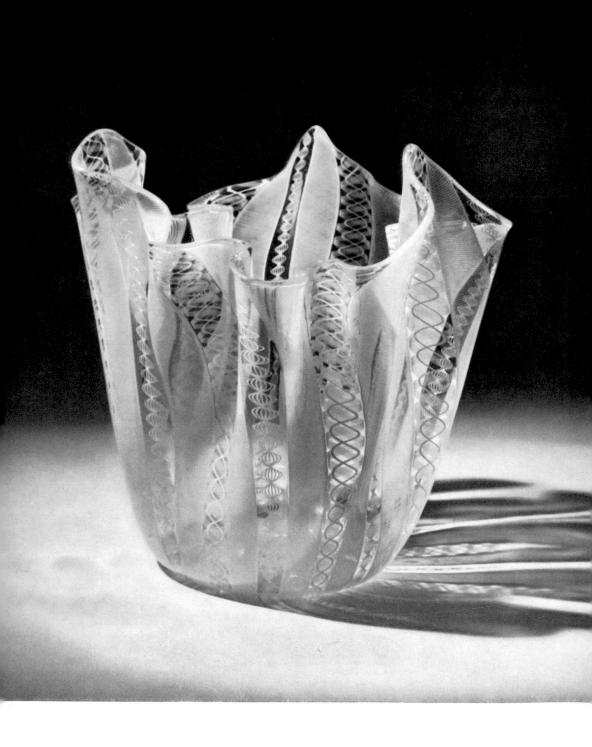

Bowl ('Zanfirico'). Freely-formed glass with enclosed threads of milk-white glass in the early Venetian technique of *vetro di trina*. Paolo Venini, Venice, before 1959. Height 13 cm.

Top: Freely formed bowl. Height 18 cm. *Bottom:* Long-shaped cut glass bowl. Both glasses from the Compagnie des Cristalleries de Baccarat, Paris, before 1965. Height 20 cm.

Vase made partly of colourless partly of violet-purple metal. Designed by Antonio da Ros.
Made by the Vetreria Cenedese, Murano. Venice, c 1960.

Left: Carafe, colourless etched glass. Teuton with five maidens. Orrefors before 1958. Height 27.2 cm. *Right:* Flask and goblet from the 'Brussels' service which won the *Grand Prix* at the World Exhibition in Brussels in 1958. Designed by C. J. Riedel. Made at the Tiroler Glashutte C. J. Riedel KG, Kufstein, Austria. Height 24.5 and 13.8 cm.

Spherical vase by Ingeborg Lundin. Orrefors c 1950. Diameter 45 cm. *Opposite:* Cylindrical vases made of clear glass, one flashed purple the other bluish-green. Designed by Tapio Wirkkala. Made by Karhula Littala Glasbruk, Finnland 1957. Heights 19 and 34 cm.

later. The leading craftsman in the technique of *latticino* and *vetro di trina* was Nicholas Lutz of the Cristallerie de St-Louis in France, who had emigrated to America. From 1868 he worked at the Boston & Sandwich Glass Company, then at the Mount Washington Glass Works in South Boston and finally at the Union Glass Works at Sommerville, Massachusetts. He also made threaded glass. Yet other Venetian techniques were imitated, including ice glass, aventurine and agate glass. Spangled glass in shades of red, brown and gold and a speckled glass known as 'spatter' were developed during the 1880s by Hobbs, Brocunier & Company, the Aurora Glass Company of London having brought out their similarly produced 'Metallised Glass' ten years earlier.

Although the artistic and technical developments were much alike in Europe and the United States of America, the social and economic situation was different. The economic liberalism of America — in no small measure a reflection of the Victorian era — offered the more ingenious entrepreneurs immense scope for development; while in Europe, especially on the Continent, social and economic tensions provided the stimulus to further advances.

Art Nouveau and Jugendstil

The clashes between artistic handcraft and mechanised industry and the social revolution in the nineteenth century affected the whole of Europe. In his *L'organisation du travail* Louis Blanc (1813—82), the intellectual leader of the fourth estate in Paris, was the first to demand a national economic programme. Blanc saw free competition, economic liberalism and Cobdenism as the causes of social abuses. His project for state-supported workmen's co-operative production societies was adopted by the provisional government in Paris after the Revolution of 1848. *Ateliers nationaux* were set up but soon came to a sorry end. John Ruskin (1819—1900) in England based his plea for the renewal of artistic handcrafts on religious and social considerations. William Morris (1832—96) in his revival of arts and crafts set about giving practical effect to the ideals preached by Ruskin. In 1861 he started an interior-decorating business (Morris, Marshall, Faulkner & Co.). He had already in 1859 induced his collaborator, Philip Webb, the architect, to design glasses; these were, in fact, executed by James Powell & Sons, but their puritanical simplicity gained them

Opposite: Ornamental vase by Karl Koepping, Berlin , c 1900. Height 27 cm.

scant approval. The 'official' Neo-Classical trend in art was more successful. Shortly after the Great Exhibition in London in 1851, Benjamin Richardson, proprietor of a glasshouse at Stourbridge, offered a prize of £ 1000 for a copy of the Portland Vase. It was won by John Northwood (1837—1902) in 1876. Northwood had been working at cameo-engraving since 1860. In 1873 he made his celebrated Elgin Vase, a glass in the Greek style measuring 40 cm in height and carrying a copy of the group of riders from the Parthenon frieze. John Northwood's example was followed by his son John, by George Woodall (1850—1925) and his brother Thomas, who worked in collaboration with Thomas Webb & Sons — the 'crystal kings of England' — as well as by Joshua Hodgetts (1858—1933). Besides the cameo-glass (page 288) made by these artists at Stourbridge, mention should be made of the 'Cameo Incrustations', or paste cameos enclosed in glass, made by Apsley Pellat (1791—1863), which attracted attention at the World Exhibition of 1862.

The English cameo-glasses were paralleled in both time and technique by the cameo-cut wares of Gallé.

Emile Gallé (1846—1904) was a native of Nancy. His father owned a factory making ceramics and glass at Saint-Clément. Emile studied mineralogy at Weimar and in 1866 learnt glass-engraving at Meisenthal in Lorraine. By the following year he was showing his own designs at the World Exhibition in Paris and was beginning to attract attention. A visit to London in 1871 during which he had an opportunity of studying Chinese glass at the Victoria and Albert Museum influenced his subsequent development. This experience gave rise to his own style of decorating coloured flashed glasses with engraved plant designs. In 1874 he set up a glass-factory with his father in Nancy. In 1887 he exhibited his new glasses for the first time and had by now become internationally famous. The World Exhibition of 1889 was a triumph for him. A school grew up round the *genre Gallé*. The brothers Auguste and Antonin Daum turned their father's utility glass-factory over to artistic glasses. During the 1890s the artists and artist-craftsmen of Lorraine joined to form a 'School of Nancy'. The leading spirits in this association were Gallé, the brothers Daum, Louis Majorelle, the cabinet-maker, and Victor Prouvé, the painter and sculptor, who in 1892 painted a well-known portrait of Gallé showing him working at his designs.

At the World Exhibition of 1900 Gallé won the *grand prix* twice over and was awarded the Cross of the Legion of Honour. Some of his collaborators — Albert Daigueperce, Emile Munier, Julien Roiseux and Paul Oldenbach — won silver medals. Gallé's factory frequently employed several hundred workmen. All the glasses were signed, including those not actually designed by Gallé but simply released by him for sale. Thus when faced with a glass signed by Gallé, one cannot be at all certain whether it was in fact designed by the master, let alone executed by him. The most one can assume is that he was responsible for those glasses which carry quotations from Victor Hugo. Gallé died in 1904 but the factory remained in operation until the 1930s.

Gallé's pupil Alphonse G. Reyen and E. Leveille in Paris were independent artists in the style of the master. The following firms made glasses in the *genre Gallé*: Daum Frères, Nancy, Verrerie de la Paix, Paris, Cristallerie de Sèvres, Christian & Sohn, Meisenthal, Lorraine, Cristallerie de Kosta, Stockholm, and Val Saint-Lambert, near Liège. The last-named factory was one of the largest enterprises in Europe with an annual turn-over of eight million francs in 1900. Its factory catalogue was illustrated by original drawings by Constantin Meunier. Van de Velde was associated with the factory.

Another glass-designer, Louis Comfort Tiffany (1848–1933), had a sensational success at the World Exhibition of 1893 in Chicago. Son of C. L. Tiffany, a silverware manufacturer of New York, he became a jeweller, artist in stained glass and designer of lighting fixtures. In 1866 he began to study painting in New York, continuing in Paris in 1869. Here he met Siegfried Bing, the art-dealer and patron of Art Nouveau. Tiffany first devoted himself to stained glass. His first church window was placed in the Episcopalian Church at Islip, Long Island, in 1878. In 1879 he established the Tiffany Studios. Tiffany's great invention was his 'Favrile' glass of 1893, distinguished by its lustred effects (page 239). Behind this effect was his desire to make conscious decorative use of the iridescent or weathered appearance of ancient glasses. His love of early works of art took him to Egypt in 1870 and 1908.

Tiffany was not the only maker of iridescent glass. Frederick Carder followed on in 1904 with his 'Aurene' glasses (page 238), most of which were decorated in gold; while in 1916 the Quezal Art Glass & Decorating Company of Brooklyn, New York, made iridescent glasses which they called 'Quezal' (after the ancient Mexican god, Quezalcoatl).

In Europe the chief response to Tiffany's inspiration in manufacturing lustre glasses came from Max Ritter von Spaun at the glasshouse of Joh. Lötz Witwe at Klostermühle in Bohemia (page 292).

Siegfried Bing was Paris agent for Tiffany's glasses. An associate of Bing and scion of Art Nouveau in glass was René-Jules Lalique (1860–1945), jeweller, goldsmith and artist-craftsman. In 1885, after having studied art in Paris and London, he opened his own glass workshop in which he made fully plastic cameo-engraved glasses of curious charm. He preferred figural motifs and colourless glass (page 290).

In Vienna Josef Hoffmann and Gustav Schneider, members of the Secession, were making glass in the new style. The Viennese Secession lasted only from 1897 until 1905. Josef Hoffmann (1870–1955) was also associated with the founding of the Wiener Werkstätte in 1903 and of the Austrian Werkbund in 1912. From 1910 onwards he was designing his *Bronzitgläser* (page 295) for the Viennese firm of Lobmeyr which owned glasshouses in Haida and Stein-

schönau and whose artistic director was Stefan Rath. In Darmstadt the Grosz-
herzögliche Edelglasmanufaktur under Josef Emil Schneckendorf was concerned from 1907 until 1911 in developing coloured iridescent glasses in the Art
Nouveau style.

The most elegant glasses were those designed by Karl Köpping (1848–1914).
He came from Dresden and began by studying chemistry; from 1869 he was
learning painting and the technique of etching from J. L. Raab in Munich and
from 1876 from C. A. Waltner in Paris. In 1890 he was appointed director of
the master studio for etching and copper-plate engraving at the Berlin Academy. One of his finest glasses is illustrated on page 304. Köpping found a
follower in Friedrich Zitsmann (1840–1906) of Thuringia. Zitzmann lived at
Wiesbaden and was an instructor in glass-blowing. Glasses made after the
manner of Köpping were blown at the lamp.

Functionalism and modern glass

In contrast to Historicism, Art Nouveau, a product of reforming movements
in the applied arts, created forms of its own. It did not, however, solve the
problem raised throughout the world by the Industrial Revolution. Revolution
requires radical re-thinking in every field.

The introduction of machines brought a new profession — that of the designer —
into existence. For the first time it became possible for outside talent to become
involved on a large scale in the creation of glasses. The art of glassmaking
abandoned its position of isolation; the horizon broadened. With this, however, came the danger of the decorative misuse of glass. 'Good form', said Hans
Eckstein, 'makes demands not only upon talent but upon character too'.

It was recognised that the new situation represented the initial phase of
modern industrial society and this awareness was bound up with social ideas.
When Van de Velde said that anything that benefited one person only was
practically useless, he was overstating his case. His words of 1907 proclaimed
in advance the functionalism of the 1920s: 'The totally useful object made on
the principle of rational and consistent construction, fulfils the first condition
of beauty, fulfils a necessary beauty.'

Twelve artists and twelve firms appealed for the founding of a militant unit to
protect artistic interests, with the result that on October 5th and 6th, 1907, the
Deutscher Werkbund was inaugurated in Munich. 'The aim of the Bund', runs
the charter, 'is to improve industrial work through the concerted action of art,
industry, commerce and manual work, by education, propaganda and a posi-

tion of solidarity towards questions affecting these things'. The fifteen artists who signed the appeal included Peter Behrens, co-founder of the Munich Secession (1893), Joseph Maria Olbrich, co-founder of the Vienna Secession (1897) and Josef Hoffmann, a member of the Vienna Secession. Behrens and Olbrich were architects and only occasionally acted as glass designers (page 296). One of those who preached most insistently against the decoration of useful objects was the Viennese architect Adolf Loos (1870—1933), a native of Brunn.

The Viennese arts and crafts movement, which — under the inspiration of Rudolf von Larisch — set itself the goal of creating functional forms, was particularly progressive in the sphere of glassmaking. In Germany Bruno Mauder worked to the same end. In selecting shapes for hand-made pieces he went back to basic types. Wilhelm von Eiff (1890—1943) was another who pursued this quiet reform of artistic handcraft. Von Eiff had studied in 1910 in Paris, where as a gem-cutter he had come into contact with René Lalique. From 1921 until 1937 he was head of the teaching and experimental workshops for glass and gem-cutting which were largely financed by the Württembergische Metallwarenfabrik at the Kunstgewerbeschule in Stuttgart. He made these workshops a centre for education in the art of glassmaking, the importance of which was felt throughout Germany. Besides this, he was responsible notably for some distinguished portraits engraved in precious stones and glass. He evolved a new technique of cutting glass, known as *Schnitzen* or chipping. The tradition of artistic handcraft in Grmany has been preserved to the present day by A. F. Gangkofner of Munich with free-blown coloured glasses, Stefan Erdös of Zwiesel, with his love of technical experimentation, and by the elegant forms of Hans Mauder of Zwiesel.

The Deutscher Werkbund had been founded, however, with more far-reaching themes in mind. The sense of social and aesthetic responsibility on the broadest basis was at issue. Since the first thing required of a useful object was that it should be functionally efficient, Functionalism won the upper hand. In architecture Louis H. Sullivan had already in about 1900 espoused this cause with the slogan 'Form follows function', while in painting it first appeared in Kandinsky's geometrical abstractions.

The designers converted the ideas of New Functionalism into fact. This was the tenor of the instruction given to the pupils of the Bauhaus in Weimar, an institution which was of central importance in this connection. The Bauhaus sought contacts with industry. Thus Gerhard Marcks, head of the Bauhaus pottery department, and László Moholy-Nagy, director of the Bauhaus metal workshops, both worked for a time for Schott & Gen. The glass workshop under Josef Albers, however, was concerned only with stained glass. Albers was one of the most important artists in the field of modern stained glass. He went to America in 1933 and in 1950 became professor at Yale University.

Wilhelm Wagenfeld (page 297) was a product of Moholy-Nagy's metal workshop. He promoted the Thuringian glass-industry and established the type of the Jena fire-resistant glass. In 1935 he became artistic director of the Vereinigte Lausitzer Glaswerke in Weisswasser. At the World Exhibition of 1937 in Paris he was awarded two *Grands Prix* and a gold medal. At the Triennale in Milan in 1940 he obtained the *Grand Prix* for his *Rautenglas* wares made at Weisswasser. The Triennale of 1957 brought him the *Grand Prix* for his work in general. His association with the glasshouse belonging to the Württembergische Metallwarenfabrik in Geislingen began in 1949; in 1954 he set up his Werkstatt Wagenfeld as an experimental workshop for developing industrial models.

Wagenfeld's pupil Heinrich Löffelhardt became well known for his Jena glass, for which he won the Grand Prix at the XII Triennale in Milan. He was also the artistic head of the Vereinigte Farbglaswerke AG at Zwiesel.

In Germany, the country of origin of the *Werkbund* movement, New Functionalism provided the starting-point for modern glassmaking. Among its exponents were Richard Süssmuth, Wilhelm Braun-Feldweg, E. and H. von Poschinger, Josef Stadler, H. T. Baumann, Cuno Fischer, Konrad Habermeier, H. Sattler, H. H. Engler, K. H. Eisele and Franz Killinger, in central Germany Ilse Decho, Ilse Scharge-Nebel and Horst Michel. The work of the younger people already transcends the dogmatic austerity of the founders of Functionalism.

This applies not only to Germany. In 1953 Paul Reilly wrote of the English Council of Industrial Design: 'We have worked through the purifying period of Functionalism and are ready for the next step, which might be called a humanising of contemporary architecture and form.'

The international picture of modern glass is, in a certain sense, similar to that of the fine arts. It has, to borrow Reilly's expression, a Doric and an Ionic pole. This can be seen in the Milan Triennale, the series of special exhibitions of the 'decorative and industrial arts and of modern architecture' which have taken place at three-yearly intervals since 1923 and reflect the state of achievement.

In Sweden the Orrefors Glasbruk A-B gathered important artists round itself. Until 1916—17 a series of failures had afflicted the factory; but on the advice of the Swedish *Werkbund* Simon Gate and Edvard Hald were then appointed artistic collaborators. They laid the foundation of the reputation of Swedish glass and among other things developed a type of flashed glass to which the name *Graalglas* was given. Glass was both cut and engraved and a school for glass-engraving set up. Edvin Öhrström, Sven Palmquist, Nils Landberg and Ingeborg Lundin (page 302) were appointed to the artistic side in preparation for the World Exhibition in Paris in 1937.

In Finland the artists Tapio Wilkkala (page 303) and Timo Sarpaneva were concerned in designing wares for the glass-factory of Karhula Iittala. Kaj Frank designed the glass of the Notjö Glasbruk in the Wärtsilä combine.

The Danish designer Björn Wiinblad worked for the Holmegaard glass-factory and — like Wilkkala of Helsinki and Georg Butler Jensen of Chicago — for the Rosenthal-Kristall Studio Linie of the Rosenthal glass-works.

In France Baccarat with its freely formed glasses (page 299) represents an individual style of modern glassmaking. These glasses — pure products of the craftsman's skill — do not lend themselves to industrialisation. Jean Luce was an outstanding designer of industrial products. The artists André Thuret of Paris and Michel Daum of Nancy designed heavy luxury glass.

In Holland as early as the period of Art Nouveau the architects K. P. D. de Bazel and K. P. Berlage were producing designs for the N. V. Koninklijke Nederlandsche Glasfabriek. The artists Floris Meydam and Willem Heesen worked under the artistic director A. D. Copier, who also produced designs of his own. Outside artists who supplied the factory with designs were Frank Lloyd Wright, C. de Lorm, the industrial organiser, and C. J. Lanooy, the potter. The Royal Dutch Glassworks in Leerdam, which date from the year 1765, today belong to the Dutch United Glass-works, which make all types of glass.

In the United States of America the Steuben glass-works which had been founded in 1903 by Carder and Thomas G. Hawkes in partnership with Mr and Mrs Willard Reed were taken over in 1918 by the Corning glass-works. This concern was founded by Amory and Francis Houghton in 1851. In 1933 A. A. Houghton, a grandson of the founder, appointed John Monteith Gates, who brought in the sculptor Sidney Waugh (page 240). In 1940 the firm employed twenty-one painters, sculptors and other artists. On the advice of Matisse, other foreign painters and sculptors were induced to execute designs for glasses. Out of this grew an association with Dali, Cocteau and Isamu Noguchi. (Kokoschka, Picasso, Braque and Chagall all produced occasional designs for glass — for Muranese and other glasshouses.) In the year 1954 the Steuben glass-works temporarily appointed twenty English artists; these included the sculptors Frank Dobson and Jacob Epstein, Lawrence Whistler, the writer and engraver on glass, the painters Graham Sutherland, Duncan Grant, John Minton and Rodrigo Moynihan, Muirhead Bone, the etcher, Leslie Durbin, the silversmith, Eric Gill, and R. Y. Gooden, professor in the department of glass at the Royal College of Art. Contemporary English glass-engravers include John Hutton of London, Mrs Phyllis Boissier of London, a diamond-point engraver, and Sheila Elmhirst of Ipswich.

In Austria Adolf Loos and Oswald Haerdtl produced designs for glass tableware for J. & L. Lobmeyr which was exhibited at the first Milan Triennale in 1923 and which may be regarded as timeless.

The glasshouse in the Isergebirge belonging to C. J. Riedel, the former 'Bohemian glass-king', later moved to Kufstein in the Tirol and secured the services of R. Trawöger and H. Thurner as well as those of the architects Schlesinger and Aubock.

In Bohemia the art of glassmaking has been fostered since the middle of the century in the Advanced School of Industrial Arts in Haida (Novy Bor) and at the State Technical School at Steinschönau (Kamenicky Senov). The most important educational establishment is, however, the High School for Industrial Arts in Prague. Besides the traditional cutting and engraving, the new Bohemian glass-workers make freely formed glass and delicate undecorated glass, such as Pazaurek described earlier as being in the 'Venetian style'.

Venice long remained untouched by the reforms of the arts and crafts movement. It was not until 1921–2 that Venetian glassmakers began to make efforts to overcome their eclecticism by associating themselves with developments in the rest of Europe. The initiators of this movement were Giacomo Cappellin and Paolo Venini, who secured the services of Vittorio Zecchin as designer. Their example was followed by Ercole Barovier and the brothers Toso. During the last years of his life Paolo Venini worked on his own; he used in particular the early Venetian techniques of *latticino* and *vetro di trina*. Much of his work can be counted among the best achievements of modern glassmaking; much, however, like the bowl illustrated on page 298, betrays a carelessly ill-judged use of material which flouts the strict principles of craftsmanship. Barovier too worked on his own. Glasses with vigorous, geometrical, polychrome patterns are characteristic of his work. Alfred Barbini, another artist-craftsman, made freely formed glass. The many industrial concerns included Seguso Vetri d'Arte on Murano, which worked with the artist Flavio Poli to produce clear, undecorated form in heavy coloured glass. Salviati & Co of Venice produced thin-walled coloured glasses in pure forms from designs by Luciano Gaspari and Romano Chirivi. The Vetraria Cenedese on Murano made glasses to designs by Antonio da Ros which remind one of modern paintings (page 300). The course adopted at Orrefors by Simon Gate and Edvard Hald set an example which Venice followed. Those concerned learned that success depends on good co-operation between designers and glassmakers, with the latter acting as interpreters. Following the example of Orrefors, a training centre was set up on Murano where glass-engraving was also done, and which, like the Svenska Slöjdforeningen, 'ENAPI', the National Union of Trade and Light Industry and the Istituto Veneto per il Lavoro has helped to bring artistic standards into industrial production. — The reader may recall that at the beginning of the sixteenth century Peter Månson (page 69), a Swedish pastor, travelled to Italy in order to acquire experience to take back to Sweden.

Urgent need to bring glassmaking into line with changed sociological and economic conditions has everywhere produced a profusion of creative ideas, experiments and original forms which are the expression of the new age.

Technique and history
of glassmaking

The achievements of the ancient glassmakers

The history of glass extends over several thousand years but the glass made for vessels today comprises virtually the same compounds as those given in the recipes — deciphered by R. Campbell Thompson in 1925 — on Asshurbanipal's cuneiform tablets of the seventh century BC. Of the many possible proportions in which sand, natural soda and the ashes of the seaplant *Salicornia* may be mixed, some were then found to be so satisfactory that it would be impossible even at this late stage to propose any that would give an all-round improvement. It is true that our present-day understanding is great. We know at what point in the simple system of three substances — silicic acid, natron and chalk — optimum stability and workability lie. And, having learnt in the nineteenth century how to analyse raw materials, we know all the secondary materials which enter into the glass when a given raw material is used. Analysis of ancient glasses enables us to state how it was that the old glassmakers of more than three thousand years ago were able to fuse a metal which was superior to the diseased glasses produced in some parts of Europe during the seventeenth century.

In his *Beiträge zur Kenntnis alter Gläser* Wilhelm Geilmann has compiled full analyses which include all secondary components and traces and satisfy the most exacting demands. What emerges is that despite the fact that they were fused from only two or three raw materials the ancient Egyptian glasses of the middle of the second millenium have an extremely complicated chemical composition. Besides the main components — silicic acid, natron and chalk — they contain eighteen other constituents and thus amount to a complex system which even today we can only put together empirically without having grasped its theory. Although the ancients did not know that the sand they used supplied both alumina and chalk as well as other oxides, some of which had a stabilising effect while others produced colours, they still devised excellent recipes simply by following their instinct.

Only by judging from visible results could they control the fused glass. This was adequate because in the early days colour was in any case their main concern. As long as they continued to use the same sources of raw materials, they could to some extent reproduce the colours too. Colour was at once worth striving for and attainable; transparency could be achieved only with difficulty at the low temperatures which were all that could be expected of clay crucibles and was probably never attempted.

The possibility of using high temperatures was limited by the material of the crucible, but the glassmakers found a brilliant way out by fritting the mixture beforehand. This method of fusing in two phases remained in use until the nineteenth century.

The fact that transparent glass was made in Assyria and Syria a few hundred years earlier than in Egypt gives cause for thought. It was very probably due to the influence of more advanced metallurgical knowledge. Iron metallurgy was spread by seafaring people and reached the Syrian coastal region — where the Philistines possessed this knowledge — as early as the thirteenth century BC. By the time the (iron) glassmaker's tube came into use in Syria, the Syrians already knew how to make vessels sufficiently large and sufficiently fire-resistant to fuse considerable quantities of transparent glass. In the Egyptian empire, where iron had ceased to have any meaning, no advance was made beyond the lower technical stage of fusing non-transparent coloured glass; with the advent of the Hellenistic era development continued where it had left off in the Iron Age.

Geilmann's analyses show that the Islamic glasses were still of the same composition as the ancient Egyptian, the Alexandrian and the Roman as far as the Rhine-Main country; and that even a glass of the Carolingian period found at Geisenheim was of the same type as regards material. All are natron glasses. Throughout the centuries there have been three important sources of the soda required for making this glass: the natural soda which Pliny called *nitrum*, such as occurs in the Wadi Natrun in Egypt; the ashes of the plant *Salicornia (Chenopodiaca salicornia)*, which contains up to 30 *per cent* sodium carbonate; the Venetians called it *allume*, *rocchetta* or *soda* and it continued until the eighteenth century to be exported to Europe from Syria or the Levant; and the somewhat less valuable ashes of the plant *Barilla*, which reached Venice and England from Alicante in Spain.

Antonio Neri, a Florentine priest, wrote his *L'arte vetraria* in the year 1612. This is a collection of recipes and shows how carefully the glassmakers of the Renaissance in Italy and Flanders purified the soda-ashes and how intent they were upon using white powdered quartzite to obtain a colourless glass. Chalk, tartar and substances containing lead are among the other raw materials mentioned in Neri's book.

The monastic glasshouses went their own way from the tenth century onwards, procuring no soda either from the Near East or from Spain. Geilmann has analysed flat glass of this period and found it similar to the hollow glasses for which we have to wait until a later period to find survivors in any number. This is potash-glass and was made from the ashes of indigenous plants. Straw, rushes, bracken, beech, oak and other woods were burnt to ashes. The composition of the glasses varied according to the ashes; some of them were very rich in lime. Thus, taking the mean value of leaves, trunk and branches, beech ash contains about 50 *per cent* chalk (calcium oxide) and about 10 *per cent* magnesia (magnesium oxide). Because of the large quantity of sulphates and impurities, great skill is required to fuse *Waldglas* and it is particularly important to break up the sulphates, which have no part in forming the glass, before they become 'glass-gall' and spoil the fusion. The great variations in the composition of the ash due to the location, type and the parts of the plants used increased the difficulty of fusing glass in the forest glasshouses. Moreover, the body of traditional knowledge was laced with mystical beliefs, such as the one which recommended harvesting the bracken needed for ashes at full moon. And it was to be done on the day of the beheading of John the Baptist when the sap was at its height. Ash from bracken was commonly used in France and the French expression was, therefore, not *Waldglas* but *verre de fougère*. As late as 1774 when Frederick the Great was enquiring whether it would be possible to make glass of this French type in Prussia too, he was told that 'this would demand quite unusual knowledge and that there was no glass-master even in the whole of Bohemia who had the necessary experience'.

Unwanted colouration was counteracted by adding brown-stone — or 'glass-maker's soap' — by a process familiar everywhere since antiquity. Fritting also helped to purify the substance. When glass-gall appeared at the first fusing it was skimmed off with iron scoops. The fusion was then made to flow into water and became granulated and purified in the process. Thus a granulated 'frit' was obtained which was fused to make it shiny at a second fusing process; this time the fusion had to be sufficiently liquid for bubbles of gas and air to rise and be released from the glass.

When, under the influence of the Venetian style, green *Waldglas* was abandoned and glassmakers were striving to make colourless 'white glass', the forest ashes too were subjected to a purifying process. They were simmered in copper cauldrons *(Potte)* until all the salts were lixiviated from the ashes, after which the lye without the sediment was poured into earthen pots to allow the solid particles to settle. The saline water was then re-heated in cauldrons, until the salts crystallised out. There were special potash distilleries. In Silesia in the eighteenth century a hundredweight of the best potash cost ten thalers.

Useful oxides, however, were also removed from the potash with the unwanted impurities. It may have been this which gave rise to glass-disease, especially in the seventeenth century, before it was understood that substances now known to have a stabilising effect should be added to the richly alkaline glass sediment. Those regions — such as Grossalmerode in Hesse — where there was extremely pure sand containing little alumina or alkaline earth were at special risk. Glass-disease appeared in Germany at about this time in Cassel, Lauenstein, Potsdam and Nuremberg.

It is recounted that Caspar Lehmann in Prague drew the attention of his pupil Schwanhardt to the importance of including chalk. Lehmann died in 1622; he may therefore have known Neri's book, in which the addition of chalk is recommended.

Neri's *L'arte vetraria* provided a blueprint for the invention of Bohemian chalk-glass and — since it was translated in 1662 by Christopher Merret, a physician and fellow of the Royal Society — it may be similarly connected with the invention of English lead-glass. Ravenscroft applied for a patent for his crystal-glass in 1674.

Neri had collected all the recipes and prescriptions he could find. His book appeared not only in three Italian and one English editions but also in two Latin editions in Amsterdam (1668 and 1686). It was translated into German by Kunckel in 1679 (second edition 1689) who himself tested out the recipes. The practical experience which he gained from so doing made him one of the best glass technicians of his age.

As a chemist, Kunckel was caught up in the alchemical endeavours of the time. In Dresden he was engaged in 'making gold' for the Elector, Johann Georg II; later he was called to Berlin, where he had the good fortune to unmask a false adept and thus gained the favour of the Great Elector. In 1678, for a rent of one hundred and fifty thalers Friedrich Wilhelm leased him the 'Cristallinen-Glasehütte zu Drewitz', where he tried out the recipes collected by Neri. They included recipes for making a ruby-glass fusion. Kunckel was no more an inventor than were Neri or Ravenscroft; nor did he ever claim to have invented ruby glass. 'But may I be granted the honour', he wrote, 'of proclaiming as my invention something that others were unable to do whereas I fully succeeded'. By this he meant the reddening of the ruby glass—which starts life colourless—when it is re-heated. Kunckel had one indisputable virtue: that of having subjected the information which had been handed down to him to critical examination, thereby bringing to light much generally useful knowledge. Other glassmakers besides Kunckel made ruby-glass. 'I believe', he wrote, 'that I shall have drawn the earliest and best profit from it; I will leave the rest to others.' Although these words may perhaps have been referring to spiritual gain, many people criticised them as uncalled-for generosity. One such may have been the Elector Friedrich III who wished to know what concrete result had accrued from Kunckel's expensive experiments. The investigation rehabilitated him but there still remained eight thousand thalers to repay. In 1693 Kunckel went to Sweden as an authority on mining. King Charles XI raised him to the nobility, granting him the title of 'von Löwenstern'. Kunckel had nothing further to do with glassmaking; he died in 1703 at the age of seventy-three.

E. von Czihak recounts an amusing story which is marginal to the story of Kunckel's life. When on a visit to Breslau, Kunckel gave Johann Christian Kundmann, a physician who was interested in the re-discovery of porcelain, a small flask made of white bone-glass, and with it the recipe for making such glass; it was fused from sand and the ashes of human bones. When an old burial-place of the 'Quadi or Lycians' was discovered in Breslau, Kundmann commissioned bone-glass to be fused from some of the bones. The Christian conscience was pacified by the fact that the bones were heathen. But in order to do something to further the salvation of the souls of these heathens, 'who, despite the fact that they have already been tortured at the stake and in the glass-furnace, are still being tormented in hell', an alms-bowl was made out of the bone-glass with an inscription calling for a donation of wine for the wretched, unquiet dead.

Kunckel's *Ars vitraria* was translated into French by Haudiquer de Blancourt in 1697 *(De l'art de la verrerie)*; it was re-issued in Nuremberg in 1756 under the title of *Vollständige Glasmacherkunst* and remained the standard work for glass-fusers throughout the eighteenth century. Glasses — with the exception of Ravenscroft's glass-of-lead — still continued to be composed of the basic substances: sand, potash (potassium carbonate) and chalk. There was a distinction, however, between the several qualities, which corresponded to the degree of purity — green glass, white glass and crystal-glass. There was also bone-glass, ruby-glass and glasses of other colours. Thanks to the knowledge disseminated by Kunckel's writings, varieties of glasses multiplied. This afforded a basis for selecting and developing individual types for specific uses. The trend towards achieving specific qualities (colour, refraction of light, hardness, chemical stability) necessarily entailed the need to use purer raw materials. The emerging chemical industry gradually became able to meet this need too. While natural sand and chalk continued to be used, glassmakers began to obtain their alkalis from the industry: sea-salt in 1764, then sulphate of sodium, from 1823 (Liverpool) the crystalline soda made by Leblanc's process and which contained water, and finally soda made by Solvay's process which contained no water; the first factories for making this were set up in England in 1871, in France in 1874 and in Germany in 1880. Chemistry took a great leap forward economically and industrially in the nineteenth century with the result that the art — as it had once been — of fusing glass was transformed into glass technology. The results of this are found mainly in the specialised glasses which made it possible greatly to extend the number of uses to which 'glass' could be put.

Understanding glass as a material

There have been various stages in the understanding of the character of glass and these have been linked to the wider understanding of nature. The Egyptians included blue glass, lapis lazuli and the blue colouring obtained from copper *(chesbet)*, also green glass, emerald and malachite *(mefkat)* among the metals — possibly because fire was used in preparing them all (cf page 13). Al-Razi (865—925), a Persian, however, regarded glass as one of the stones; in his opinion it was a kind of rock-crystal. Here again the significance of the difference between the coloured glass of the Egyptians and the transparent glass of the east and of later periods is clearly apparent.

The Arabian alchemists distinguished between true astronomy and *astronomis inferior*, by reference to which they differentiated stones which were stable in the fire — these corresponded to the fixed stars — from metals and glasses which melted in the fire — these corresponded to the planets. Albertus Magnus (c 1206 to 1280), however, restored glass to its position among the stones — perhaps partly because of the love of imitating precious stones which existed in his day. During the Renaissance men began to reflect upon the virtues of individual materials. Johann Mathesius, an Evangelical pastor, preached about glass-making at Joachimstal in Bohemia. His sermons were published in Nuremberg in 1562 under the title of *Sarepta oder Bergpostill*. He was probably echoing expert opinions of Bohemian glassmakers when he said: 'From sand, flint, ashes, fire generates glass material so that it flows; but there exists ash, saltpetre and saltwort so that men may stretch, bend, shape and work the material.'

The first theoretical explanation of the structure of glass was advanced by René Descartes (1596—1650). He considered the world to be composed of particles (corpuscles) of the three elements of fire, air and earth. In glass the corpuscles of the element of earth lie on top of one another, while in the spaces between them which have been caused by fire there is air. He endeavoured thus to explain the hardness and fragility of glass on the one hand and its transparency on the other. Opacity is caused by a deposit of earth corpuscles, which withstand fire better than air. Robert Boyle (1627—1691) also in the main subscribed to the corpuscular theory. Kunckel, however, rejected it and directed discussion rather towards chemical procedures. At this period natural science was still incapable of understanding the structure of glass theoretically. It was not until Lavoisier, Berzelius, Klaproth and others had done their fundamental work at the beginning of the nineteenth century that an understanding of the chemical processes gradually began to emerge and formed a basis upon which ideas about the character of glass could be constructed.

Research into the nature of glass entered a new phase when Joseph Fraunhofer (1797–1826) began to measure its optical value and set up experiments concerning the connection between the composition of glass and its optical properties. Otto Schott (1851–1935) systematically pursued this course. Thus began purposeful modern glass research based on scientific principles. It produced many statistics which proved useful to later investigators of the structure of glass.

Thanks to the work of Arrhenius, Van't Hoff and Ostwald, a new scientific discipline emerged during the 1870s in the form of physical chemistry and this supplied the real bases and methods for dealing with questions about the structure of glass. One of the first research-workers to address himself to this problem was Gustav Tamann. He enunciated the notion of glass as an undercooled and hardened fluid (1903). V. M. Goldschmidt found that capacity to form glass depended upon the radius ratio of the ions of the relevant oxides. W. J. Zachariasen (1932) and B. E. Warren (1933) for the first time advanced a theory which made it possible to calculate the properties of a given glass in advance from data concerning the elements of the atoms involved. A. Dietzel (1942), A. Smekal (1949) and W. A. Weyl (1958) further developed and refined this network theory.

The essence of the theory consists in the assumption that the glass-former creates an irregular network. The most important material in the group of glass-formers is silicic acid (silicic acid anhydride). It is the irregularity of the network which differentiates glass from crystal, in which the atoms are arranged regularly. The disorder in glass is caused by quick cooling (undercooling). The components have no time to form an ordered three-dimensional lattice in which they could exist with low energy. They freeze and retain part of their energy. Glass has more energy than solid materials but less than fluids. Its internal energy may lead to subsequent changes, such as devitrification in which the energy is released in the form of crystallising heat.

Network-forming agents and network transformers are embedded in the network of glass-formers. The most important of these are the alkalis (soda) and alkaline earths. The physical properties of the individual components determine the properties of the glass in question. But the manner in which the temperature acts, its duration and degree, also plays an important part. All these influences can produce glasses of extremely varied character. In fact there are only three properties which are common to all glasses: they are not crystallised, not optically similar in all directions nor plastic at all temperatures.

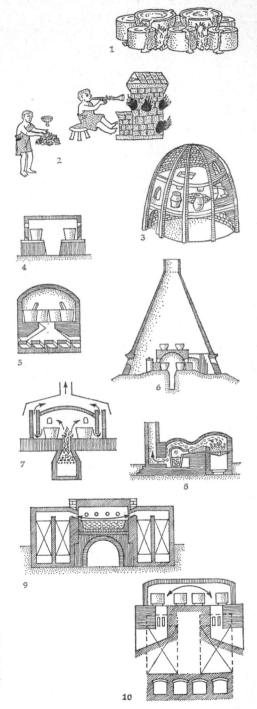

1375–1358 BC. Amarna period, glass fused at two levels in crucibles over open fire ①

669–633 BC. Asshurbanipal's clay tablets name arsenic as a purifying agent and tin-oxide for rendering glass opaque

1023 Hrabanus Maurus's encyclopaedia with a drawing of a furnace ②

1540 and 1556 Biringuccio and Agricola describe bell-shaped furnaces ③

1615 Glass fused with coal as the fuel for the first time in England

1674 Jobst Ludewig builds the usual type of German furnace in Potsdam ④

1675 Glass-of-lead or flint-glass in England, 1683 chalk-glass in Bohemia. *Schürrost* in Bohemia ⑤ and France. English crystal-glass cone furnaces ⑥

1816 Robert Stirling takes out patent for glass-furnace heated by the regenerative process

1840 Description of a Belgian furnace ⑦ with grate firing

1840 J. Crosfield discovers the flame furnace ⑧, forerunner of the tank-furnace

1857 Friedrich Siemens uses regenerative firing for glass-fusing furnaces

1857 F. Siemens builds a furnace in Berlin fired with gas as used for lighting

1858 F. Siemens builds a water-glass furnace at Liesing near Vienna heated with generator gas

1860 H. and F. Siemens design first periodic tank-furnaces in Saxony and England ⑨

1867 The first continuous tank-furnace for fusing glass designed by F. Siemens in Dresden

1871 Soda first made by Solvay's process

1885 Siemen's tank with freely developing flame

20th century Pot-furnaces are used to fuse smallish quantities of different glasses. They are mostly *Bütten* furnaces ⑩ heated by the regenerative process; increasing tendency to use round furnaces heated by the recuperative process. High-powered tank-furnaces are used for fusing large quantities of a single type of glass; working of the glass is automatic

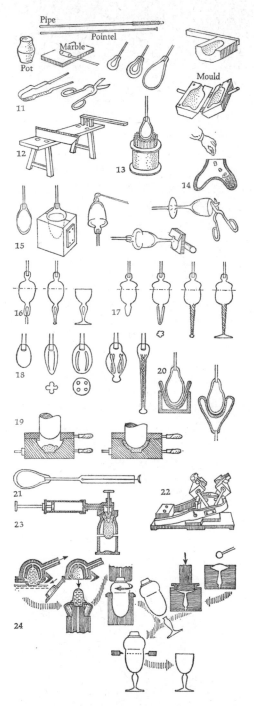

Pipe
Pointel
Marble
Pot
Mould
11
12
13
14
15
16
17
18
19
20
21
22
23
24

3rd millenium BC. Beads and amulets made by pinching, rolling and other plastic means of shaping the glass

1500 BC. Sand-core glasses

1st century BC. The glassmaker's tube introduced, composite moulds used and tools which have remained unchanged to the present day ⑪

1630 The glassmaker's bench or chair ⑫ comes into use, ancient techniques resumed: thread-glass ⑬ and the *millefiori* technique ⑭ in Venice

1720 Bohemian baluster goblets with enclosed tears ⑯ in Potsdam, twist stems ⑰, also with enclosed thread twists, in Bohemia and Silesia. Goblets ⑮ made in quantity to be cut and engraved

1745—70 Goblets with air twist stems in England ⑱, later in the USA

1800 Glass pressed in England and USA ⑲

1802 Charles Chubsee of Stourbridge devises an iron mould which folds together to be opened mechanically ㉒

1820 The technique of flashing ⑳ is perfected in Bohemia

1821 Method of blowing with an air-pressure pump ㉑ invented at Baccarat

1830 Three-part moulds

1859 The British patent a machine for blowing bottles which can make 400 bottles per day

1881 Fahdt's spring cage in Dresden

1886 Ashley and Arnall patent a machine for blowing bottles with preliminary mould and finished mould

1897 Boucher at Cognac builds a machine for making 120 bottles per hour

1898 Owens experiments, sucking in hot glass to feed the blowing machine ㉓

1898 W. J. Miller's fully automatic press at Swissvale, USA

1905 Bock's US patent for a machine for blowing bottles with a turning tank

1920 First fully automatic bottler with double moulds, by M. Owens. Output: 102,000 bottles every 24 hours

20th century. Automatic manufacture of hollow glasses is used to make seamless moulded thin-walled goblets ㉔

Glass furnaces

Until the nineteenth century glass was always fused in ceramic vessels. In the earliest days these took the form of dishes on an open fire. Brick-built furnaces in which the glass was fused in ceramic pots were introduced during the first century BC, probably simultaneously with the development of glass-blowing. The earliest information about the appearance of such pots is to be found in the sixteenth century in the works of Biringuccio and Agricola. They were bulging vessels about 60 cm in height by 45 cm in diameter. For reasons of strength they had narrow necks. How to make a pot which was stable in the fire was a perennially serious problem of glassmaking. Suitable fire-resistant clays had often to be brought from great distances. Biringuccio says that there were deposits at Valencia and Treguanda. According to his account the pots were dried in the shade for between six and eight months, after which they were fired in the glasshouse's fritting furnace until they were red-hot. They were then transferred with iron tongs across to the pot furnace where the temperature had already been adjusted. The wall of the furnace had to be broken open before they could be placed inside. Once all the pots were in position the wall was closed up again and only the working openings — which were also the flue openings — were left.

The earliest illustration of a glass-furnace occurs in the encyclopaedia *De originibus rerum* composed by Abbot Rhabanus Maurus (d. 856). A manuscript dating from 1023 preserved in the monastery at Monte Cassino contains an illustration of a small, tower-shaped furnace, in front of which a glass-blower sits. Next to him stands a man preparing the mixture or seeing to the fritting. The flames burst from the working and firing openings. The finished glasses are placed in the upper part slowly to cool (temper).

The subsequent development of glass-furnaces can be traced from early literary sources. The tenth century *Theophili Presbyterii diversarum artium schedula* contains a description of a chamber furnace fifteen feet long and ten feet wide (about 4.5 m $\times$ 3 m) in which there was room for several pots. Wolfgang Kahlert calculated that in a furnace of this kind, which possessed no hearth, more than four tons of dried beechwood blocks would be required every twenty-four hours to obtain and hold the temperature of between 1300° and 1350° C which was needed to fuse a mixture consisting of sand and beech-ash. A chamber-furnace is also mentioned in Book III of *De coloribus et artibus Romanorum*. The pots stood in the middle chamber; the frit was prepared in one of the outer chambers while the third served as a tempering furnace. All three furnaces were situated above a common firing area.

Biringuccio and Agricola in the mid-sixteenth century described a fusing furnace shaped like a bee-hive which had a diameter of ten feet and a height of eight feet (about 3 × 2.3 m). Besides the fusing furnace, the glasshouses also had a fritting furnace shaped like a baking oven and measuring six feet in length, four feet in breadth and two feet in height (1.75 × 1.20 × 0.60 m) and a rectangular tempering furnace measuring eight feet in length and six feet in breadth (2.3 × 1.75 m). The pots stood in the fusing furnace on the hearth floor situated above the firing space; they were handled through eight working openings. In the middle of the floor of the hearth was a large round aperture through which the flames rose. Some of the smoke escaped through the working openings and some through a duct which opened into the tempering furnace. This furnace could also be heated separately. The glasses, already shaped, were placed in long-shaped fired clay muffles measuring three feet long, one and a half feet high and one foot wide, and left to cool slowly. The smaller glasshouses did not have separate tempering furnaces and their glasses were cooled, also in muffles, on the upper floor of the bee-hive furnace.

During the sixteenth century there were still large numbers of the rectangular type of chamber furnace. A furnace of this type measuring 3.6 × 1.6 m, dating from the Tudor period (1485–1603), has been excavated at Vann Farm near Chiddingfold in Surrey. Since English glassmaking was at that time under the influence of French glassmakers, it may be assumed that similar furnaces were used in France too.

When in about 1600 the forest glasshouses became stationary, larger and more stable furnaces were built. By the end of the seventeenth century in England and later in Germany too, tall furnace-buildings came in; they also served as a chimney because the waste gases still streamed through the working openings into the working area. The tall windowless buildings — they measured between fifteen and thirty metres in height — served other purposes as well. When the chamber was closed and the wind high, their height and tapering shape caused a draught powerful enough to draw the air — led by an underground channel to the stoke-hole — as strongly as was necessary. The effect was the same as using bellows and the high temperature required for fusing was thus obtained. The processes of manipulation were performed with the door open since so high a temperature was no longer needed. Instead, fresh air streamed in and saved the workers from the troublesomeness of the smoke. The conical furnace-building, through the upper opening of which the rain could pour unimpeded, contained a small rectangular chamber furnace containing two pots on either side of the stoke-hole. A similar arrangement is illustrated in Volume 10 of the *Encyclopédie* of Diderot and d'Alembert which appeared between 1751 and 1776. A few of these flue-gas cones still survive. Rudolf Günther has sought out these installations of a past era and has found six in England and four in Germany. They were built between 1740 and 1846 and some of them today rate as architectural monuments. Of the German gas-flue cones two are in Obernkirchen, one in Steinkrug, Kreis Springe, and one in Gernheim near Minden. Of the six in Great Britain, three are at Stourbridge and one each at Catcliffe near Sheffield, Lemington-on-Tyne and Alloa in Scotland. The chamber furnaces in these flue-gas cones are rectangular but in his *Ars vitraria* of 1689 Kunckel still illustrates a round furnace.

We must, no doubt, assume that both round and rectangular furnaces were in use during the sixteenth and seventeenth centuries. Of these two types, the rectangular proved more susceptible of further development. A stone grate half the height of the stoke-hole could be built into a rectangular furnace. The iron grate followed later; conversion to coal-firing, which occurred in England as early as 1615, made it particularly necessary.

The principle of direct firing persisted until the mid-nineteenth century. In 1840 Achilles Christian Wilhelm Friedrich von Faber du Faur, mining director to the King of Württemberg, discovered how to make gas and the gas generator. This invention had an equally revolutionary effect upon glassmaking as upon steel-founding. Direct firing culminated in attempts to use the hot smoke-gases to pre-heat the air for combustion, using a recuperator ('Boeotian furnace' with covered pots) and a gas-generator built into the lower furnace. This arrangement, however, proved too clumsy. Gas was therefore generated away from the furnaces in separate generators and piped to the furnaces with the requisite combustion air.

As in the steel-industry, so in the glass-industry the brothers Siemens played a pioneering part in the stormy development of furnace-building. In 1856 Friedrich Siemens in England took out a patent for regenerative firing, putting it to use for the first time at the Atkinson Steelworks in Sheffield. Regenerators are chambers filled with latticed fire-resistant bricks laid one on top of the other. The hot exhaust gas is piped through these chambers and the bricks store the heat. To use this heat to warm the combustion air, hot smoke-gas and cold fresh air is passed alternately and at fixed intervals — about every half hour — through the chambers. The chambers were also reversed every half hour by means of a reversal drum. The regenerator chambers stood on both sides below the hearth chamber, that is, in the lower furnace. There were usually two pairs of chambers, one for gas and one for air. The flames pass in one direction through the hearth chamber. When the mechanism is reversed they pass in the opposite direction. The openings of the channels which lead from the regenerator chambers are arranged on both sides of the hearth chamber and act both as burners and — upon reversal — as smoke flues.

In 1857 Friedrich Siemens applied the principle of regenerative firing to glass-fusing too. He had been preceded as early as 1806 by an English parson named Robert Stirling who had patented his idea of a regenerative furnace for glass. Between 1857 and 1859, after his return from England, Friedrich Siemens built among other things regenerative furnaces for glass-fusing in Styria and Moravia. The commonest form of glass furnace is to this day known after him as the 'Siemens furnace' and the one which has a separate smoke flue for the period of working is called the 'Siemens-Siebert furnace'. This is a 'Bütten' furnace with between six and fourteen pots. In this type of furnace the two burners (*Bütten*) are on the floor between the two rows of pots.

By pre-heating the gas and air (to 800° or, better, 1000° C) it became possible to obtain with generator gas the high temperatures required for fusing glass — which would have been impossible by other means. It meant also that the firing was easier to regulate. Taken in conjunction with the change-over to industrial soda it fulfilled many of the conditions necessary to improve quality. Exact maintenance of the temperature in itself played a considerable part in glass-fusing. Not merely the working properties but also the quality of the glass depends upon temperature. If the temperature drops, while the pots are being worked, so far that the furnace has to be re-heated, the glass will spoil because new bubbles will form as the temperature rises. In principle the same thing may be observed when an insufficiently cooled champagne bottle is opened: the fluid releases more gases at high temperatures than at lower ones; the cork shoots out.

As the building of pot furnaces developed further, the builders returned to the original idea of pre-heating by means of recuperators. These are heat alternators through which the hot smoke-gas streams, warming the combustion air flowing in the opposite direction, without the mechanism having to be reversed. Round furnaces heated by the recuperative system are regarded as the most up-to-date pot furnaces. The pots of today have a capacity of between 60 and 1000 kg of fused glass. The capacity of the largest pots of the eighteenth century was 120 kg. The pots usually measure between 65 and 140 cm in diameter and about 65 cm in height.

The process of fusing in pots is as follows: using a scoop, the glassmaker fills the heated pots with cullet and glass-mixture. The first stage of fusing or rough fusing is completed when a thread of glass drawn out with an iron rod no longer feels rough. During the successive fusing or refining fusing the mass must be thoroughly mixed: it is 'teased' until it is 'seed-free' or fully refined. A wet block of wood is dipped into the pot on an iron (blowing iron) and moved backwards and forwards on the bottom; or else a piece of arsenic is thrown into the fusion and sinks because of its higher specific gravity. Bubbles are released and complete the thorough mixing process as they rise. If there are no bubbles in the glass-mass it can be stood off, which means that it is cooled from the fusing temperature of between 1300° and 1550° C to a working temperature of some 250° C. This temperature must be maintained during the process of working. Once the pot is empty it is re-filled and fusing begins over again. This periodic procedure has various disadvantages: it is slow and necessitates the whole installation constantly being cooled and re-heated. Consequently there has been no lack of attempts to convert pot fusion into a continous process. Once again it was Friedrich Siemens who designed a continuous pot consisting of three connected chambers. The first was for fusing, the second for refining and the third for working. This arrangement was intended to permit the processes described above to be carried out simultaneously instead of one after the other. Siemen's pot was an early form of the tank-furnace, which is based on the same principle except that in place of the pot there is a brick basin. Friedrich Siemens built the first tank-furnace in 1858 for a water-glass factory at Liesing, near Vienna. The first tank-furnaces for technical glass were built independently of one another by the brothers Hans and Friedrich Siemens in the year 1860. They were periodic tanks and only the rough fusing was done in them. They were then drained and the process of refining was continued in pots. Not until 1867 did Friedrich Siemens convert a tapped tank built in Dresden by his brother Hans — who had died shortly before — to continuous operation. As time went on the tank-furnace was improved in various particulars but the principle has remained unaltered to this day. Besides furnaces heated by the regenerative process there are tank-furnace constructions equipped with recuperators as well. Heating is by gas or oil firing. Electricity is seldom used for fusing.

Even the first continuous tank-furnace in Dresden had a production capacity double that of an ordinary pot-furnace, as well as numerous other advantages. The high performance and quality together with ease of control which made the process of glass-fusing susceptible of being automated also made it possible to employ machines and automata for working glass. The first to derive the greatest benefit from this development were the sheet-glass and bottle industries; these were first in the field with continuous methods of working glass which could be geared to the process of uninterrupted fusing. In bottle production expenditure of labour dropped within a bare century from 15 to 0.1 working hours for one hundred bottles, that is a decrease of 0.7 per cent. The number of pieces produced per hour for each mould rose from 17.5 bottles to 350 — a twenty-fold increase. It was longer before a method of mechanising the making of goblets was developed. Their complicated form necessitated several machines working together, one group blowing the bowl, the stem and the foot and others pressing, putting the parts together and fusing them.

Processing and decorating glass

Glass technicians make a distinction between processing and decorating glass. Processing is a matter for the glasshouses. Ancient, Venetian and forest glasses all belonged to this category. Of the glasses of the ancient world, those of the *diatretarii* form an exception, being decorated rather than processed.

The old, complicated techniques of processing glass, the making of the Mycenean plaque beads with their narrow boring, the Frankish *Rüsselbecher*, the *Kuttrolfe*, the Alexandrine *millefiori* technique and the Venetian *latticino* glass—all these, just as much as the ancient decorative technique of the *diatretarii*, are hedged round with mystery. Reconstructional experiments can show only how such things may be made but never how, in fact, they were made. Many techniques have been reinvented as time has passed. Nineteenth-century historicism was full of such endeavours. Blowing with the tube is the one tradition which has remained alive since antiquity. There is only one other known case of a primitive technique having been preserved and that is the Nigerian method of making jointless glass bracelets. Leo Frobenius, the ethnologist, who died in 1938, was the first to observe that the jointless glass bracelets made at Bida, capital of the region of Nupe in northern Nigeria, were reminiscent of Celtic finds. They continue to this day to be made in a manner which must be the same as that of the La Tène period. The craftsmen at Bida make the soft glass ring rotate round an iron rod until the join disappears.

Historical sources provide information about many ancient techniques, but medieval accounts are confined to sheet glass.

Besides the technique of blowing with the tube, blowing 'at the lamp' (blow-lamp, at that time an oil lamp, and bellows) early came into use in Venice for finer work and for figures. This processing technique was not adopted in Germany until the seventeenth century (page 138). Abraham Fino (d. 1657), an Italian born in Amsterdam, is credited with having taken it to Nuremberg. Kunckel in 1679 described the blowing bench with double bellows which remained in use until the gas blow-lamp was introduced.

In Venice, where artists were 'called to the furnaces', enamel-painting was probably another type of decorating undertaken in the glasshouse. The enamelling could be fired in clay muffles in the tempering furnace. Enamel-painting was a family occupation in the forest glasshouses. The single operation by which the craftsmen delivered the finished wares was first split up with the advent of glass-engraving. The glass-engraver, the *Kugler* and *Hausmaler* of the seventeenth and eighteenth centuries were the earliest representatives and pioneers of a body of independent — and later industrial — glass-processors.

Sometimes they were organised like a guild; the nineteenth-century sequels were the 'glass refineries' where work was further subdivided.

When Frederick II visited Silesia in the year 1774 he was compelled even at that early date to ask of Rohrbach, the glass-manufacturer, to explain the sub-divisions in the work of decorating glass. The story goes that the king asked Rohrbach whether he had good glass-cutters for making figures. Rohrbach replied that he had not, for they were glass-engravers, that 'there was a great difference between cutting and engraving and that it was very seldom that one man understood both'.

The fact that glass-engraving can be done with simple apparatus — the cutting lathe — may have contributed to making it independent. This lathe consists of a horizontal spindle revolved by a belt-pulley worked by a treadle. Different wheels can be attached to the spindle for the engraving, while the engraver holds the glass under the wheel. For unpolished engraving a small copper wheel and a mixture of emery, petroleum and a little rape-oil are used. Wheels made of wood, cork or leather with a thick watery mixture of very fine powdered pumice are used for polishing. Cameo-engraving required more strongly built apparatus, which is the reason why during the seventeenth and eighteenth centuries it was only done at cutting works. In contrast to the earlier form, the cameo-engraving of the nineteenth century (Northwood and Gallé) differed from the earlier technique in that now top layers of glass or flashes were etched out and the design was finished by engraving.

The glass-cutter used a cutting lathe which was also driven by a treadle, but it had an iron wheel onto which water and sand trickled from a container above it. A tub under the cutting wheel caught the grinding agent. The work of the glass-cutters in Bohemia was sub-divided to such a degree that different men did the coarser work (Eckigreiber) the facetting (Facettenschneider) and the circular cutting (Kugler).

Industrialisation and mechanisation failed to gain control of glass-engraving, which remained an individual artistic skill. Cutting, however, has frequently been imitated by pressed glass; the decoration here may be the result of pressing pure and simple or the glass may be pressed first and cut afterwards.

The technique which was easiest to mechanise was etching. Heinrich Schwanhardt was the first (1670) to employ it. The twentieth century has seen the construction of mechanised pantographs which decorate a number of goblets simultaneously by scratching the pattern in a coat of wax. The glasses are then placed in a corrosive bath. Hydrofluoric acid alone corrodes the glass to give a polished effect, solutions of acid fluorine salts in hydrofluoric acid corrode to give a mat effect. The development of photosensitive glass permits the etching process to be combined with photography; this technique was originally used to prepare glass for technical purposes and has recently been extended, opening up new prospects for decorating glass.

Appendix

Glasshouses: the sites

America (USA)

European emigrants set up a glasshouse at Jamestown in 1608. In 1739 Caspar Wistar's glasshouse in Salem County, South Jersey, 1752 first glasshouse in New York, 1753 first glasshouse in Boston. 1763 Baron Stiegel of Cologne set up Elizabeth Furnace Works and in 1765 established his first glasshouse at Mannheim; the second in 1769. Between the end of the War of Independence (1783) and 1824 some 94 glasshouses were set up. 1797 first fusing furnace fired with coal, in Pittsburgh. From 1823 American glasses exported to South America and the West Indies. During the 19th century pressed glass, including the lace-like type (1825–1850), and glasses blown in the mould became the typical American mass-produced glasses. 1825 John P. Bakewell of Pittsburgh obtained a patent for pressing glass knobs for furniture. 1903 the Steuben glasshouse founded at Corning; taken over in 1918 by

New England Glass Company, Cambridge 1818–80. *Corning, N. Y.:* John L. Gilliland & Co., business moved from New York (see below); Steuben Glass Works 1903 present day. *Frederick, Md.:* New Bremen Glass Manufactory (John Frederick Amelung & Co.) 1785–97. *Jersey City, N. J.:* Jersey Glass Company 1824–62. *Keene, Vt.:* Flint Glass Works 1815–22. *Manheim, Pa.:* Henry William Stiegel's Glasshouse 1765–74 and 1769–74. *New York:* New Windsor Works, Glass House Company of New York 1752–67; Fisher Brothers' Bloomingdale Flint Glass Works 1822–45; John L. Gilliland & Co. 1823–68. *Philadelphia, Pa.:* Philadelphia Glass Works, Kensington 1772–77; Union Glass Works 1826–?. *Pittsburgh, Pa.:* Bakewells' Glass House 1809–80; John Robinsons's Stourbridge Flint Glass Works 1823–45; Curlings' Fort Pitt Glass Works 1826–1900. *Providence, Mass.:* Providence Flint Glass Works

the Corning Glass Works and known as the 'Steuben Division'. (Pages 243, 279, 284.) Important glasshouses. *Boston, Mass.:* Germantown Works 1753–68; South Boston Flint Glass Works (Thomas Cains) 1812–?;

1831–35. *Salem, N. J.:* Wistarburg (Caspar Wistar) 1739–75. *Sandwich, Mass.:* Sandwich Glass Works 1825–88. *Wheeling, W. Va.:* Richies' Works 1829–?; Sweeny's Works 1831–67.

Austria

The earliest documentary evidence records a glasshouse for mirror-glass (?) belonging to Onossorius de Blondi in Vienna. During the 16th century Venetians settled in various places in Austria. Native glasshouses in Henriettental (Carinthia) and Graz (Styrian glassworkers); Augsburg foundation at Hall in Tirol 1534. 1570 Innsbruck court glasshouse founded by Archduke Ferdinand. 1626 Schwaz in Tirol named. Between the 17th and 19th centuries glass-production concentrated in Bohemia. Mildner makes his glasses at Gutenbrunn at the end of the 18th century. Kothgasser's glasses (Vienna) celebrated during the Biedermeier period. In 1836 G. Stölzels Söhne set up two glasshouses in the forest district bordering on the region of the south Bohemian glasshouses. Vienna played a leading part in Art Nouveau and in the modern New Functionalist movement (Adolf Loos). (Pages 125, 269, 270, 280, 284, 309.)

Belgium

By about 1400 there were already glasshouses in the neighbourhood of Genappe and Wavre and in the province of Chimay; about 1475 glasses were being made there on the Venetian pattern. The glasshouse at Bauwelz also worked *à la façon de Venise* using *verre de fougère;* 1550 they began to work in the German manner as well. Venetian *cristallo* was made in Antwerp (from 1525), Liège (from 1550), Brussels, Chatelet, Huy, Barbançon (all from about 1625) until 1700. Liège produced glasses in the German manner too from 1625 until the Thirty Years' War. Glass *à la façon d'Angleterre* was made in Liège (from 1675), Namur (from 1725), Ghent (1700—25) and Vonêche (from 1775). The sheet-glass industry was developed after Belgium became independent (1830). Emile Fourcault, a Belgian (1862—1919), invented the method of perpendicular pulling (his glasshouse: Fourcault-Frison, near Charleroi). The largest Belgian concern making hollow glass during the nineteenth century was the glasshouse at Val Saint-Lambert under its first directors (1826—38) François Kemlin and Auguste Lelièvre.

Bohemia

The earliest glasshouse (at Winterberg) mentioned in 1359. Between four and six glasshouses existed in the 14th century. Production extended during the 16th century to 24 glasshouses. Glass-engraving at the court of Rudolph II in Prague about 1600. 1683 Michael Müller, master of the glasshouse of St Anton (near Winterberg = Vimperk) invents chalk-glass. The new glass extends to northern Bohemia with centres at Böhmisch Leipa, Böhmisch Kamnitz, Steinschönau, Haida, Blottendorf. 1731 Bohemia exported glass to the value of 98,557 florins. 1803 39,000 people working in the glass-industry; annual production worth some 8 million florins; exports amounted to 5 million florins. Peak production reached in 1839 with 19,000 cwt. glass worth 10 million florins. 1814 Josef Mayr set up the Adolfshütte in southern Bohemia (Winterberg estate), named after Prince Johann Adolf von Schwarzenberg. 1822 his son Johann Mayr set up the Eleonorenhain glasshouse (later only tableware). Both concerns made the purest crys-

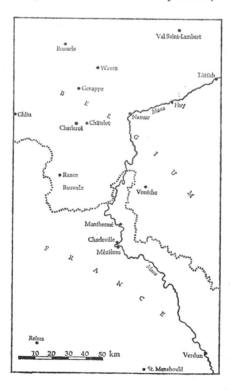

tal-glass of the period. 1830 Johann Lotz and Josef Schmidt set up a glasshouse in Goldbrunn, later known as the factory of Joh. Lötz Witwe in Klostermühle. 1857 L. Moser's glasshouse at Karlsbad, 1826 that of I. Innwald in Deutschbrod. There were 600 glass refineries in Czechoslovakia in 1934. 150,000 people were employed in the country's glass-industry at that time. Between 1920 and 1932 glass to the value of 17.5 milliard crowns was exported (80 per cent of the output). Much of the exported glass went to the East. (Pages 187, 247, 275, 283.)

China

Glass fillets occurred on bronze vessels in China as early as the 3rd century BC. Colour-flashed glass vessels with cameo-engraved decoration during the Ch'ing Dynasty, also opaque-white glass in imitation of porcelain. Blown glasses made in Peking during the K'ang-hsi period (1662—1722) are known. (Page 89.)

Denmark

1552 a glasshouse set up by Eenevold Jensen Seefeld. 1574 a second established near Kolstrup in Nimtofte. 1576 Steen Clausen Bille builds a furnace at Vanås (Skåne); the Victoria and Albert Museum possesses a glass from here (Inv. No. 5231). Work ceased in 1587. Glass-manufacture further patronised by Frederik II who in 1581 appointed a Hessian glassmaker. 1597 30,000 drinking glasses supplied to the court. The glasshouse remained in production until 1630. Other glasshouses in Glaesborg on Djursland (1648—50) and Fjellorup (1650—64). First Venetian glasshouses 1649—50 in Copenhagen. 1652 at the command of Frederick III a glasshouse was built in the palace grounds and remained in operation until 1658 when Copenhagen was occupied by the Swedes. 1690 a glasshouse operating on the Christianshavn in Copenhagen. 1694 an attempt to run a co-operative factory for mirror-glass on the French model fails. 1707 due to lack of wood for fuel the glass-industry has to be transferred to Norway, then a Danish possession. Not until the 19th century did the glass-industry begin to flourish in Denmark itself. Factories set up at Holmegaard (1814) and Copenhagen-Kastrup (1847).

Egypt

Earliest objects made of glass — beads and amulets — 16th cent. BC (New Kingdom). Earliest glass vessels (sand-core glasses) from the tomb of Thotmes I (1508—1493). Glass vessels made only until 970 BC. 'Alexandrian glasses' in great demand during the Roman Empire. After the Arab conquest (639—646 AD) and the founding of Cairo, the capital attracted glassmakers. The Egyptian glassmaker's art came to an end with the Turkish conquest of 1517.

England

13th cent. furnaces have been excavated at Chiddingfold in Surrey. The earliest documentary evidence concerns one Laurence Vitrearius, from the region which later became Normandy, who lived in 1226 at Dyers Cross near Bickhurst. Protestant glassmakers from Lorraine (Jean Carré, d. 1572) and Catholics from Venice (Giacomo Verzelini, d. 1606) arrived in England during the 16th century. Vice-Admiral Sir Robert Mansell in the 17th century bought up all the licences for glassmaking. Manufacture flourishes under the Stuarts (Charles II 1660). 1664 glasshouse for mirror-glass set up at Vauxhall in London. 1674 George Ravenscroft obtains a patent for crystal-glass. By 1695 there were already 47 glasshouses making flint-glass in England. High level of export to the Scandinavian countries and Holland. Bristol (15 glasshouses in 1722) was famous for blue and white glass made in imitation of porcelain (1760—1820), Newcastle for engraved glass (Jacobite glasses c. 1750) and for white enamelled glasses (1720—1800), Neilsea (1788—1873, founded by John Robert Lucas) and Birmingham (founded in 1824 by Robert Lucas Chance) for polychrome decorative glass. The most ubiquitous of English glass was brilliant-cut lead-crystal during the 19th century. Two factories at Stourbridge became noted during the last quarter of the 19th century for their cameo-glasses: Stevens & Williams with the artist John Northwood and Thomas Webb & Sons with Thomas and George Woodall (page 306).

Finland

The factory set up in Stockholm in 1640 by Melchior Jung was transferred by his son to Nystad (Savonlinna) which at that time still belonged to Sweden. Finnish glass became important in fairly recent times, its centres being Iittala, Notsjo and Helsinki (page 310).

France

Lorraine, Normandy and Poitou can be traced back to the 15th century as centres of both indigenous and Venetian glassmaking. Indeed, mirrors were made in Lorraine as long ago as the 13th century. 1693 a glasshouse for making mirror-glass set up in Picardy and amalgamated with Colbert's factory in the Faubourg Saint-Antoine. 1698 removed to Cherborne in Normandy. 1765 glasshouse set up at Baccarat and still in operation. Glassmaking in France began to flourish during the early 19th century. Glass-wares to the value of only 6 million francs were produced over the whole country in 1789 while by 1834 the value of the output had risen to 29 and by 1860 to 50 million francs. Principal products were tableware and mirror-glass. The most important areas where hollow glass was made were in the vicinity of Paris (glasshouses and refineries) and in the Mouse and Moselle valleys. In the late 19th century Nancy became the centre of Art Nouveau (Pages 102, 278, 280, 285). Important glasshouses. *Baccarat:* Compagnie des Cristalleries de Baccarat, founded in 1764 as a royal project. Began to flourish under the directorship of Jean-Baptiste Toussaint (coloured glasses 1850—70). *Paris:* Choisy-le-Roi, set up in 1821 by M. Grimbolt. 1823—48 Georges Bontemps director. Closed down 1851. *Clichy:* set up in Billancourt in 1837 by M. M. Rouyer and Maes, removed to Clichy-la-Garenne in 1844. Coloured glass, high quality. 1875 the concern was merged with the Sèvres glassworks. Pantin, set up by E. S. Monot in 1851 at La Vilette, 1855 removed to Pantin. Reached its peak 1865—1900, when the glasshouse signed itself Stumpf, Touvier, Violett & Co. *Saint-Louis:* Cristallerie de Saint-Louis, founded in 1767; originally a royal glasshouse, run on a commercial basis from 1782.

Germany

Earliest documentary records: 1340 Bischofsgrün in the Fichtelgebirge and Reichswald, near Nuremberg, 1350 Suhl in Thuringia, 1397 Solling on the Weser and 1406 Spessart. Glassmaking spreads to other places during the 15th century, Venetian influence (enamel-painting) in the 16th century. Nuremberg the main centre in the 17th century. The Potsdam glasshouse, set up in 1679, becomes famous for Kunckel's ruby glass. Outstanding Baroque glasses in Brandenburg (page 191), Hesse (page 226), Brunswick, Lauenstein, Thuringia (page 227), Saxony (page 227). Of 107 glasshouses in 1834, 21 were in Silesia, 11 in Hanover, 4 in Brunswick, 5 in Hesse, 45 in Bavaria, 10 in Thuringia, 6 in Baden and 5 in Wurttemberg (page 310).

Holland

An English document of 1485 mentions Dutch glass being imported into England. Dutch glassmaking and decorating are closely bound up with Belgium, England, France, Venice and Germany. 1531 the first Venetian glasshouse set up in Middelburg, 1549 a second established in Antwerp; after this and until the end of the 17th century glass *à la façon de Venise* was the principal Dutch ware. During the 18th century the decorating of glass outstripped manufacture of the raw metal. One reason for this was lack of wood. Typical of the glass decorated in Holland were the styles of ornamentation executed with the diamond-point. English glasses were favoured for the purpose (pages 157, 311).

Hungary

The early Slovakian glasshouses belonged to Hungary. Other glasshouses in the 18th century at Munkács, in the Gömör and Szathmár combine. During the 19th century glass was decorated in Budapest.

Ireland

Captain Philip Roche set up the first Irish glasshouse making flintglass in Dublin c. 1690. It continued until 1755, after which no

337

flintglass was made in Ireland until 1764, when it began to be made at the bottle-factory at Marlborough Green in Dublin. After the 1770s this factory belonged to Richard Williams & Company. Between 1780 and 1801 there was a glasshouse making flint-glass at Newry, a new factory from 1824 until 1847. 1783 Benjamin Edwards set up a glasshouse in Belfast which continued until 1829. 1784 glasshouse established at Waterford by George and William Penrose with the collaboration of John Hill of the Coalbournhill glasshouse near Stourbridge; it was acquired in 1799 by Ramsay, Gatchell and Barcroft. Barcroft built a new factory in Old Tan Yard, where in 1817 a water-driven cutting-mill was installed. 1784—97 Chesby & Co.'s glasshouse in Dublin. The main Dublin wares were flint-glass candle-sticks and vessels. There were 9 glasshouses in Ireland in 1785. 1793 the first glasshouse in Cork (Cork Glass Co.), a second set up in 1815 by Daniel Foley (Waterloo Glass-House Co., until 1835), a third in 1819 established by Edward and Richard Ronayne (Cork Terrace Glasshouse, until 1841). Cork produced mostly roemers and decanters. Irish glass after 1800 was particularly clear and suitable for cutting.

Italy

By the 13th century the Venetian glass-industry was already in a position of eminence. Glass exported to Holland from 1317. Glassmaking concentrated in northern Italy (Altare, near Genoa, Bologna, Florence, Pisa and elsewhere, see pages 95, 103). Venetian glass flourished again for a short period during the 19th century reaching its peak in 1867 with the work of A. Salviati (page 312).

Lithuania

A glasshouse is supposed to have operated in Lithuania during the 15th century.

Mexico

Records name the Puebla glasshouse as having been established by Spaniards in 1648. For two centuries it was the only glasshouse in Latin America.

Norway

Three glasshouses superseded one another: 1741—77 Nöstetangen, set up under the patronage of King Christian VI of Denmark and Norway, reorganised 1753. 1777—1809 Hurdal, 1809—47 Gjorvik. Johann Albrecht Becker, a glass-engraver, was brought from Saxony (active 1767—73), instructor at the Villa Vinter (from 1770). Heinrich Gottlob Kohler active 1757—70 at Nostetangen. 1755 James Keth of Newcastle, blower of crystal-glass went to Norway.

Persia

Little is known about glassmaking in Persia before the 7th century. Glasses of the Sassanian period (AD 224—650) have survived. Glassmaking flourished during the Islamic period. Received special encouragement from Shah Abbas I (1587—1629), who resided in Isfahan. A glass-industry arose in that city and maintained its importance into the 18th century (pages 74, 76).

Poland

Glassmaking was concentrated in the south-west bordering upon Upper Silesia. 1763 11 Polish glasshouses are mentioned in the vicinity of the Prussian frontier. Some raw glass exported to Prussia.

Portugal

During the 17th century glass was made in Portugal by Muranese glassmakers, Altarists and Flemings. 1731 government prohibition on the import of Bohemian glass.

Russia

Earliest records (glass jewellery) date from the 11th century. 12th century Hedwig glasses at Novo Grudok (White Russia). 1635 a glasshouse set up at Dukanino near Voskressensk, a second about 1650 at Ismailov near Moscow. Glassmaking flourishes in the 18th century thanks to princely patronage and the part played by M. V. Lomonossov (1711—65) who established a glasshouse making coloured glass at Ust Rudiza in 1754. Royal foundations: Jamburg, by Peter I (1672—1725), St Petersburg (1743) by Elisabeth Petrovna (Czarina 1741—62). The largest private factories belonged to the Bachmetjev (from 1764) and Malzov (from 1760) families at centres named after them. Subanov, considered the greatest Russian engraver of glass, worked at the Malzov factory at Gusj. Other glass-engravers were Guskov, Kalmykov, Lebedev, Novskij, Opantin and Skatchkov. Engraved decoration stained black (from 1743) is typical 18th century Russian work; this form of decoration was revived in the 19th century. There were 156 glasshouses in 1812 and 275 employing 75,000 workers in 1913; annual output worth 75 million roubles. Industry modernised after 1928.

Silesia

The earliest records of glassmaking in Silesia (Riesengebirge) date from the mid-14th century. A glasshouse of this period has been identified near Schreiberhau. There were at least three glasshouses in Silesia in the 15th century, 7 in the 17th and by 1740 the number had increased to 11. During the 17th and 18th centuries there was a prominent glass-decorating industry at Warmbrunn (pages 190, 229).
In 1763 there were 12 glasshouses in Prussian Silesia and one in Austrian Silesia; by about 1780 there were 30 in all. The largest, at Friedrichsgrund, produced 11 crucibles of glass per week worth 500 *Reichstaler*. In 1837 of 25 Silesian glasshouses, 5 were in the district of Breslau, 13 in that of Oppeln and 7 in that of Liegnitz. In 1890 there were 56 glasshouses in Silesia employing 6,024 workers, as well as 31 concerns where glass was decorated. The most important of the Silesian glasshouses in the 19th century was the Josephinenhütte at Schreiberhau under its manager Franz Pohl.

Slovakia

Earliest documentary evidence of a glasshouse 1360: Glaserhau, near Kremnitz, named after the master, Peter Glaser. 1630 a glasshouse set up at Neuschl (Nová Baňa) by one Master Uhub. 1678 a glasshouse near Modern (Modrá) belonging to the Counts Palffy leased by Georg Bauer. 1707 Prince Rakoczy ordered the removal of the Stampfen (Stupava) glasshouse to Munkács. There were some 70 glasshouses during the 18th century, most of them in the Luče-Detva district. 1892 Josef Schreiber founded the glasshouse at Lednicke Rovné. In 1918 there were 10 glasshouses in Slovakia.

Spain

Glass was being made in Spain in pre-Roman times. During the Islamic period there were glasshouses in southern Spain and in Valencia and Barcelona (Mudejar style) during the 15th century. The glass-industry developed under Venetian influence in Andalusia, Catalonia and Castile during the 16th century. Barcelona is famous for enamelled glasses. 1728 royal glass-factory founded in Cranja de San Ildefonso, where glass was also made in the Bohemian manner (page 76).

Sweden

There seem to have been glassmakers in Stockholm, Uppsala, Kalmar and Visby as far back as the 14th century. Earliest factories of which the foundations have been authenticated date from the 17th century: Pafrel in Kronborg, Melchior Jung in Stockholm in 1640; the latter's son transferred the factory to Finland. Giacomo Scapitta, a mendicant friar, established a glasshouse on Kungsholm, which remained in operation until 1815. Charles XI (1660—97) was a patron of glassmaking. Glasshouses in Goteborg, Henrikstorp, Kosta (established 1742), Skånska Glasbruket (1691—1762). The industry spread during the 18th century to become concentrated in the 19th in Varmland and Smaland. Mutual marketing organisations in the 20th century.

Switzerland

Switzerland reflected the development of glassmaking in southern Germany and the Alps and in the 17th century produced enamelled glass.

Syria

The Phoenicians were the first to make the coast of Syria important in the history of glass. Glassmakers' tubes came into use here before the Christian era. The art of glass-making in the ancient world was strongly influenced by Syrian work. Flourished again under Islam between the 13th and 15th centuries, the main centres being Damascus and Aleppo. These cities lost their position in 1402 after Tamerlaine had laid them waste and their glass-manufacture came to a standstill in 1517.

Turkey

During the 4th century Byzantium was a centre of glass-production, particularly of glass mosaic. Byzantium was called upon to supply 36 million *tesserae* (= the small blocks used in mosaic) for the Cathedral of St George at Saloniki. To all intents and purposes glassmaking ceased when Enrico Dandolo conquered Constantinople in 1204. Mosque lamps were decorated in Constantinople during the 16th century.

Index and glossary

The following groups have been set out in tabular form elsewhere in the book and therefore do not appear in this index:

painters (page 155)
diamond-engravers (page 158)
glass-engravers (page 192)
Art Nouveau artists and factories (page 280)
glasshouses and their sites (page 333)

The modern artists named on pages 309 and 312 are not mentioned in the index. Pagenumbers in italics refer to illustrations.

Calligraphic glass. Glass decorated with calligraphic flourishes *164, 173*

Camaïeu painting, monochrome painting 156, *178*

Cameo-engraving *(Hochschnitt)* 47, *79, 81, 200, 288*

Cameo glasses. Cameo-engraved glasses made at Stourbridge, 19th–20th century 288, 306

Cántaro. Spanish jug *75*

Carré, Jean. Glassmaker from Arras, 1570 (d. 1572). Glasshouse in Crutched Friars, London 102

Celtic glasses 26, *44*, 329

Chalk-glass, 'chalk crystal'. Glass with an admixture of chalk, 1683 by M. Müller at Winterberg 316

Chameleon-glass. Type of Lithyalin, 1835 283

Chinoiseries. Exotic, 'Chinese', style of decoration *167, 178, 185, 210*

Chrysophrase-glass. Pale green opaque glass containing uranium. 1831, Neuwelk, Schreiberhau 274

Circus, ancient Roman glasses carrying scenes from *50, 51*

Club-shaped glass. One of the forms of *Waldglas 139*

Coal-firing. In England from 1615 104, 326

Cold-painting. Painting in oil-colour *142, 267*

Craquelé lustre. 1900

'Cristallo'. Venetian straw-coloured glass of the Renaissance. Soda-glass 96, *104, 107, 114, 115*

Crown-glass, manufacture of 36, 102

Cutting-lathe 330

'Cyptus' glasses. Green, with exotic decoration. 1889. Petersdorf 284

Damascened bronzes. Bronzes with inlays of gold or silver wires. Islam 76

Desprez. Artist-glassmaker, Paris 1806–58 269

Diamond-engraving 89, *107, 121, 122, 157, 172, 259*

Diatreta, vasa. Ancient Roman network bowls 33, *35, 55*

Dichroic glass. Glass which shows different colours according to how the light falls. (19th century, contains uranium) 33

Double flashing 283

Drinking horn. Frankish 38, *39*

'Edenhall, The Luck of'. Syrian enamelled glass cup *68*, 76

Egermann, Friedrich (1777–1864). North Bohemian artist-glassmaker 262, *263*, 277, 283

'Eleonorengrün'. A green colour obtained from uranium *(Annagrün)*

Elstermann, Kristoffer. Glass-engraver in Kungsholm 1698–1715 (d. 1721)

Enamelled glass. Glass with fired painted decoration in opaque colours 42, 67, 77, *83, 86*, 97, *104, 132, 140*, 153, *223*, 232, 274

Encrusted cameos. Silvery relief portraits enclosed in the glass walls of a vessel. 19th century *265*, 269, 274

Ernst I, Duke of Saxe-Coburg-Gotha (1826 to 1844) 272

Etching. Technique of decoration by corrosion. Etching can produce mat, coloured, deeply engraved and frosted effects 183, 330

Facet-cutting. Flat cutting *35, 199*

Favrile glass. Tiffany's lustre-glass *239*, 307

Filigrane glass. See thread-glass.

Fino, Abraham (d. 1657). An Italian who introduced blowing 'at the lamp' into Nuremberg in the 17th century 329

'Fichtelgebirger' glasses. Fichtelgebirge *147*, 153

Fire-polish. Brilliant fused surface 224

Flash. Surface layer of glass of a different colour from that of the vessel 274

Flint-glass. Glass made of calcined flint, 1647 by Ravenscroft 231

Flute. Drinking-glass of Dutch origin *120*, 159

Frankish glasses (400–700) 37, *39, 57*

Friedrich II of Prussia (Frederick the Great) (1712–86) 230, 330

Frit. a) Sand-mass calcined from having been subjected to partial fusing (when glazed known as 'Egyptian faience'). b) Unrefined glass-flux which a second fusing converts into the finished glass-flux 14, *15*, 317

Gallé, Emile (1846–1904). Art Nouveau artist-glassmaker in Nancy 306

Glass-blowing. A Syrian invention 27, 316

Glass-disease ('crisselling'). A symptom of decomposition 317

Gold relief. Raised gilding on a ground of stucco or enamel. Venice, Saxony *118, 268*, 274

Götze, Adam. Hessian glassmaker. 17th century 132

'Graalglas'. Type of glass made at Orrefors 310

Gundelach, Gondelach. Hessian family of glassmakers 130, *145*, 196, 216, 226

Monastic glasshouses, medieval   62, 90

Mosaic glass. *Millefiori* glass   25, *45*

'Mousseline' glass. Very thin glass, from 1823, France   274

Mycenaean plaque beads. Blue glass jewellery, 16th–13th century BC   18

Mirrors, manufacture of   101, 102

Nautilus beaker. Beaker, with foot, in the form of a ship   229

Neri, Antonius: *L'arte vetraria, distinta in libri VII,* Florence 1612 and 1661, Venice 1663 and 1678, Amsterdam 1668 and 1686, English trsl. by Merret 1662, German trsl. by Kunckel 1679 and 1689   316

Network beaker. See *distreta, vasa*

'Netzglas'. See *latticino*

Nimrod glasses. Assyrian, sea-green   22, 24, *60*

Northwood, John (1837–1902). English engraver of glass. Son John Northwood active 1888–1906   306

'Ochsenkopf'. Mountain in the Fichtelgebirge shown in painted decoration of Fichtelgebirge Glass   *147*, 153

Onyx-glass. Antique agate-glass   25, *45*

Pallada, Giovanni. Venetian in Berlin   126

'Passglass'. Drinking-glass divided into measures by an applied glass thread   93, *129*, *150*

Pellatt, Apsley (1791–1863). Invented 'cameo incrustations'

Perrot, Bernard. Invented the casting process, 1662, Orléans   102

Pliny, Gaius P. Secundus (24 BC–AD 79): *Naturalis historia*   23

Pohl, Franz. Director of the Gräfliche Schaffgotsche Josephinenhütte in Schreiberhau   283

Porron. Spanish drinking-flask   75

Portland Vase. Ancient cameo-engraved vase   30, *47*, 305

Porcelain imitated. Milk-glass and cobaltglass   73, 89, 156, *178*, 179, *180*, 232

Pot or crucible. Fire-resistant vessel in which glass is fused   324, 327

Potash. Potassium carbonate   317

Powell, Harry (1835–1922). English engraver of glass

Pressed glass, American, with lacy pattern, 1828–40   235

'Putti' with fruit   *204*, 225

Puzzleglasses, glasses for practical jokes. Mainly glass figures, blown, and drinking-glasses. Common in 17th–18th centuries   138

'Ranftbecher'. Beaker with thick cut foot-ring   *249*, *255*

'Rautenglas'. Made by the Lausitz glass-works   310

Ravenscroft, George. English glassmaker 1618 to 1681   125, 231, 318

Richter, Hans Christoph. Engraver of glass at Warmbrunn. c 1700   190

Riedel, Franz Anton (1786–1844), engraver of glass. Josef (1816–94) 'Glass-king of the Isergebirge'   272, 311

'Ringelbecher, -pokal'. Beaker or goblet with moveable rings   *112*, *134*

'Römer'. Originally a form of *Waldglas*   94, *129*, 153

Rosler, Bartholomäus. Director of Buquoy's factory in southern Bohemia, 19th century   283

Rosbach, Elias (1700–65). Engraver of glass in Berlin and Zechlin   159, *207*, 226

Rousseau, Eugène. Designer for Appert Frères, Paris 1875–85

Ruby glass. Red glass containing gold or copper. From the 17th century   *188*, *203*, *205*, *266*, 318

'Rüsselbecher'. Frankish   *39*, 40, *59*, 61

Sand-core glass. Opaque coloured glasses shaped over a sand-core. Egypt, Mesopotamia, Syria   19, *43*

Saroldi. Venetian family of glassmakers in Nevers and Cologne   102, 126

Scapitta, Giacomo. Venetian in Stockholm   127

Scarpoggiato, Giovanni. Venetian in Munich   126

Schaffgotsch. Counts with estates in the Hirschberger Tal   187, 190

'Scheuer'. Medieval drinking-glass   92, *137*

Schindler, Caspar, Georg and Wolfgang. Glass-engravers of Dresden, 17th century   181

Schneider, Christian Gottfried (1710–73). Engraver of glass at Warmbrunn   208 f., 229

Schwanhardt, Georg (1601–67). Engraver of glass in Nuremberg   157, *162*, 182, 183

Schwartz, Samuel (1681–1737). Thuringian engraver of glass   185, *221*, 227, 228

'Schwarzlot' painting   *150*, 154, *178*

Semi-precious stones, glasses imitating opaque coloured glasses   262, *263*, 269

Shell-fish beaker. Beaker with applied shell-fish motifs   40, *58*

Siebel, Franz Anton (1777–1842). Miniature-painter at Lichtenfels a. M. Daughter Klara   277

Siemens, brothers. Furnace-builders   328

Bibliography

Angus-Buttterworth, L. M., 'Glass'. In: *A history of technology*, Vol. IV., Oxford, Clarendon Press, 1958 (see also Charleston, R. J.).

Barrelet, J., *La verrerie en France de l'époque Gallo-Romaine à nos jours*, Paris: Larousse, 1953.

Barrington Haynes, E., *Glass through the ages*. Harmondsworth: Penguin, 1959.

Barzakowsky, V. P., 'Zur Entwicklungsgeschichte der Vorstellungen über die chemische Natur des Glases im 19. Jahrhundert'. *Glastechn. Berichte* 32 (1959) pp. 464—6.

Besborodow, M. A., *Das Glaswesen im alten Rußland*. Minsk: Academy of Science, 1956.

Biesantz, Hagen, 'Rätsel Portlandvase'. *Werkzeitschrift Jenaer Glaswerk Schott & Gen., Mainz* (1965), No. 3, pp. 6—13.

Boesen, Gudmund, *Venetianske Glas paå Rosenborg*. Copenhagen, 1960.

Bott, Gerhard, 'Kunsthandwerk um 1900'. *Jugendstil* (Exhibition catalogue). Darmstadt: Eduard Roether, 1965.

Bremen, Walther, *Die alten Glasgemälde und Hohlgläser der Sammlung Bremen in Krefeld* (Beihefte der Bonner Jahrbücher, Bd. 13). Catalogue Cologne, Graz: Böhlau, 1964.

Steuben Glass: *British artists in crystal*. New York, 1954.

Buckley, Francis, *A History of old English Glass*. London, 1925.

Buckley, Wilfred, *The Art of Glass*. New York, 1939.

Chambon, Raymond, *L'histoire de la verrerie en Belgique du IIᵐᵉ siècle à nos jours*. Brussels: Edition de la Librairie Encyclopédique, 1955.

Charleston, R. J., and Angus-Butterworth, L. M., 'Glass'. In: *A history of technology*, Vol. III. Oxford: Clarendon Press 1957.

Charleston, R. J., 'The Monogrammist HI: A Notable German Engraver'. *Journal of Glass Studies* IV (1962) pp. 67—84.

Czihak, E. v., *Schlesische Gläser*. Breslau: Verlag des Museums schlesischer Altertümer, 1891.

Dexel, Walter, 'Glas'. *Werkstoff und Form*, Vol. I. Ravensburg: Otto Maier, 1950.

Doppelfeld, Otto, 'Der Muschelpokal und das neue Diatretglas von Köln'. *Glastechn. Berichte* 34 (1961) pp. 563—6.

Douglas, R. W., 'Glass technology'. In: *A history of technology*, Vol. V. Oxford, 1958.

Drahotova, Olga, *Cristal de Bohème*. Prague, June 1965, p. 29.

Dreier, Franz-Adrian, 'Geschnittene Gläser von Charpentier. Ein Beitrag zum Pariser Glasschnitt des Empire'. *Glastechn. Berichte* 34 (1961) pp. 282—5.

Dreier, Franz-Adrian, 'Stichvorlagen und Zeichnungen zu Gläsern Gottfried Schneiders'. *J. Glass Studies* VII (1965) pp. 66—78.

Eckstein, Hans, 'Die gute Form. Begriff, Wesen, Gefährdungen und Chancen in unserer Zeit'. *Glastechn. Berichte* 34 (1961) pp. 567—70.

Egg, Erich, 'Die Glashütten zu Hall und Innsbruck im 16. Jahrhundert'. *Tiroler Wirtschaftsstudien* 15 (1962).

Elville, E. M., *English and Irish cut glass 1750—1950*. London: Country Life Limited, 1953.

Flinders Petrie, W. M., *Tell el Amarna*. London: Methuen, 1894.

Franceschini, Felice, 'Die Glasindustrie in Italien'. *Glastechn. Berichte* 27 (1954) pp. 166—9.

Fremersdorf, Fritz, *Die Denkmäler des römischen Köln*. Cologne: Verlag der Löwe. Six vols, since 1928.

Fremersdorf, F., 'Zur Geschichte des fränkischen Rüsselbechers'. *Wallraf-Richartz-Jb. N. F.* 2—3 (1933—1934).

Fuchs, Ludwig F., *Die Glaskunst im Wandel der Jahrtausende*. Darmstadt: Schneekluth, 1956.

Ganzenmüller, Wilhelm, *Beiträge zur Geschichte der Technologie und der Alchemie*. Weinheim: Verlag chemie 1956.

Gardi, Rene, 'Die Glasmacher von Bida'. *Werkzeitschrift Jenaer Glaswerk Schott & Gen., Mainz* (1964), Nr. 2, S. 6—11.

Gasparetto, F. Astone, *Il vetro di Murano*. Venice, 1958.

Gasparetto, Astone, 'Die Zusammenarbeit zwischen Künstlern und der Industrie in der venezianischen Glasmacherkunst'. *Silikattechnik* 12 (1961) pp. 380—4.

Geilmann, Wilhelm (and others), 'Beiträge zur Kenntnis alter Gläser'. *Glastechn. Berichte* 26 (1953) pp. 259—63 (phosphate content); 27 (1954) pp. 456—9 (manganese content); 28 (1955) pp. 146—56 (German glasses 10th—18th cent.); 29 (1956) pp. 145—68 (decomposition in ground); 33 (1960) pp. 213—19 (products of decomposition on window-panes); 33 (1960) pp. 291—6. (A curious phenomenon of decomposition on Roman glass cullet.)

Gelder, H. E. van, 'Achttiende-eeuwse glassnijders in Holland'. *Oud-Holland* 73 (1958) pp. 1—17, 90—102, 148—55, 211—19.

Günther, Rudolf, 'Rauchgaskegel auf alten Glashütten'. *Glastechn. Berichte* 34 (1961) p. 559.

Haberey, Waldemar, 'Der Werkstoff Glas im Altertum'. *Glastechn. Berichte* 30 (1957) pp. 505—9 and 31 (1958) pp. 188—94.

Haevernick, Thea-Elisabeth, 'Mykenisches Glas. Beiträge zur Geschichte des antiken Glases'. *III. Jahrbuch des röm.-german. Zentralmus. Mainz* 7 (1960) pp. 36—58.

Harden, D. B., 'Glass and Glazes'. In: *A history of technology*, Vol. II. Oxford 1957.

Harden, D. B., 'New Light on Roman and Early Medieval Window-Glass'. *Glastechn. Berichte* 32 K (1959) pp. VIII/8—VIII/16.

Harden, D. B., 'The Rothschild Lycurgus Cup: Addenda and Corrigenda'. *Journal of Glass Studies* V (1963) pp. 9—17.

Harro, Ernst, *Moderne Gläser*. Darmstadt: Schneekluth, n. d.

Heinemeyer, Elfriede, *Glas*, Vol. I of the catalogue of the Kunstmuseum Düsseldorf, 1966.

Hettes, Karel, 'Venetian Trends in Bohemian Glassmaking in the Sixteenth and Seventeenth Centuries', *Journal of Glass Studies* V (1963) pp. 39—53.

Honey, W. B., *Glass*, London, 1946.

Hughes, Bernard G., *English, Scottish and Irish table glass. From the Sixteenth Century to 1820*, London: B. T. Batsford, 1956.

Jebsen-Marwedel, Hans, 'Die Freunhofer-Glashütte in Benediktbeuren — heute'. *Glastechn. Berichte* 33 (1960) pp. 132—6.

Kampfer, Fritz, *Viertausend Jahre Glas*, Munich and Dresden, 1966.

Kahlert, Wolfgang, Die Wärmewirtschaft mittelalterlicher Glasschmelzofen. *Glastechn. Berichte* 28 (1955) pp. 483—5.

Kachalov, N. N., and Vargin, V. V., 'Antike russische Gläser'. *Glass and ceramics (Russian)* 11 (1954) pp. 11—13.

Killing, Margarete, *Die Glasmacherkunst in Hessen*, Marburg: N. C. Elwert, 1927.

Kisa, A., *Das Glas im Altertume*, Leipzig: Hiersemann, 1908.

Klesse, Brigitte, *Glas*. (Catalogue of the Kunstgewerbemuseum der Stadt Köln), 1963.

Klesse, Brigitte, *Glassammlung Helfried Krug*, Munich: Lambert Müller, 1965.

Klinckowstroem, Carl Graf von, *Knaurs Geschichte der Technik*, Munich: Droemer, 1959.

Kühnel, Ernst, *Islamische Kleinkunst*, Braunschweig: Klinkhardt & Biermann, 1963.

La Baume, Peter, *Römisches Kunstgewerbe zwischen Christi Geburt und 400*, Brunswick: Klinkhardt & Biermann, 1964.

Lamm, Carl Johan, *Mittelalterliche Gläser und Steinschnittarbeiten aus dem Nahen Osten*, Berlin, 1930.

Larsen, Alfred, Riismøller, Peter, and Schluter, Mogens, *Dansk Glas 1825—1925*, Copenhagen: Nyt Nordisk Forlag Arnold Busk, 1963.

Lauer, Otto, see Streit, Julius.

Liederwald, Anna Elisabeth, 'Niederländische Glasformen des 17. Jahrhunderts', *Diss. Freiburg*, 1962/64.

Löber, Hans, 'Guttrolfe, Formgebung und Herstellungstechnik', *Glastechn. Berichte* 39 (1966) pp. 539—48.

Lobmeyr, L., and Ilg, A., *Die Glasindustrie*, Stuttgart, 1874.

Mariacher, Giovanni, *Edle Gläser von der Antike bis Murano*, Munich: Bruckmann, 1962.

Mason, Stefen F. (Übersetzung Bernhard Sticker), *Geschichte der Naturwissenschaft in der Entwicklung ihrer Denkweisen*, Stuttgart: Alfred Kroner, 1961.

Meister, Peter Wilhelm, Nah- und fernöstliches Glas, *Glastechn. Berichte* 31 (1958) pp. 463—6.

347

Meyer-Heisig, Erich, *Der Nürnberger Glasschnitt des 17. Jahrhunderts,* Nuremberg: Verlag Nürnberger Presse, 1963.

Muschalek, L., 'Geschichtliche Entwicklung der Glasverarbeitungsmaschinen', Giegerich/Trier: *Glasmaschinen* pp. 119–42, Berlin: Springer, 1964.

Neuburg, Frederic, *Antikes Glas,* Darmstadt: Eduard Roether, 1962.

Oliver, Prudence, 'Islamic Relief Cut Glass: A Suggested Chronology', *Journal of Glass Studies* III (1961) pp. 9–30.

Pazaurek, Gustav E., *Moderne Gläser,* Leipzig: Hermann Seemann, 1901.

Pazaurek, Gustav E., *Kranke Gläser,* Reichenberg, 1903.

Pazaurek, Gustav E., *Glasperlen und Perlen-Arbeiten in alter und neuer Zeit,* Darmstadt: Alexander Koch, 1911.

Pazaurek, Gustav E., *Glaser der Empire- und Biedermeierzeit,* Leipzig: Klinkhardt & Biermann, 1923.

Pazaurek, Gustav E., *Franz Gondelach,* Berlin, 1927.

Pazaurek, Gustav E., 'Alt-thüringischer Glasschnitt', *Glastechn. Berichte* 11 (1933) p. 325.

Pesatova, Suzanna, 'Dominik Biemann', *Journal of Glass Studies* VII (1965) pp. 83–106.

Pesatova, Suzanna, and Brok, Y., *Böhmisches graviertes Glas,* Prague: Artia, 1965.

Pfeffer, Waltraud von, 'Fränkisches Glas', *Glastechn. Berichte* 33 (1960) pp. 136–42.

Polak, Ada Buch, *Gammelt norsk glass,* Oslo: Gyldendal Norsk Forlag, 1953.

Raban, Josef, *Modernes böhmisches Glas,* Prague, 1963.

Rademacher, Franz, *Die deutschen Gläser des Mittelalters,* Berlin: Bruno Hessling, 1963.

Refior, Birgit, *Altägyptisches Glas.* Münchner ägyptologische Studien, Berlin: Bruno Hessling, 1967.

Renaud, J. C. N., 'Das Hohlglas des Mittelalters unter besonderer Berücksichtigung der neuesten in Holland und anderswo gemachten Funde', *Glastechn. Berichte* 32 (1959) p. VIII/29.

Reuter, Willy, 'Aus der Geschichte des Glashandels', *Glastechn. Berichte* 30 (1957) pp. 514–19.

Riismøller, Peter, see Larsen, Alfred.

Roselt, J. Christof, 'Samuel Schwartz, Glasschnitt-Meister in Thüringen', *Journal of Glass Studies* IV (1962) pp. 85–102.

Röver, Fritz, 'Caspar Lehmann aus Uelzen'. *Niederdeutsche Beiträge zur Kunstgeschichte IV,* Munich and Berlin: Deutscher Kunstverlag, 1965.

Ruckert, Rainer, Venezianische Moscheeampeln in Istanbul'. *Festschrift für Harald Keller,* Darmstadt, 1963.

Saldern, Axel v., 'Die Bedeutung der Ausgrabungen in Gordion für die Geschichte des Luxusglases', *Glastechn. Berichte* 32 K (1959) pp. VIII/1–VIII/8.

Saldern, Axel von, *German Enameled Glass.* New York: Corning Museum, 1965.

Savage, George, *Glas.* Frankfurt: Ariel, 1966.

Schebeck, Edmund: *Bohmens Glasindustrie und Glashandel,* Prague, 1878.

Schelkownikow, W. A., *Vortragsprotokoll des Internat. Glaskongresses Sektion B Nr. 246,* Brussels, 1965.

Schelkownikow, W. A., 'Russian glass of the eighteenth century'. *Journal of Glass Studies* II (1960) pp. 95–111.

Schenk zu Schweinsberg, Eberhard, 'Glas aus vier Jahrtausenden'. *Glastechn. Berichte* 29 (1956) pp. 400–3.

Schenk zu Schweinsberg, Eberhard, 'Der Becher des Lykurg'. *Glastechn. Berichte* 31 (1958) pp. 470–2.

Schlosser, I., *Das alte Glas,* Brunswick: Klinkhardt & Biermann, 1965.

Schluter, Mogens, see Larsen, Alfred.

Schmidt, Robert, *Brandenburgische Glaser.* Berlin: Verlag für Kunstwissenschaft, 1914.

Schmidt, Robert, *Das Glas.* Berlin und Leipzig: De Gruyter, 1922.

Schröder, K., 'Die UMBS. Eine vollautomatische Glasverarbeitungsmaschine mit Saugspeiseanlage und Drehpfeifen zur Herstellung dünnwandiger Hohlgläser'. *Sprechsaal 96* (1963), No. 10 pp. 231–5, No. 11 pp. 264–9, No. 18 pp. 432–7.

Schulz, Hans: *Die Geschichte der Gläserzeugung.* Leipzig: Akademische Verlagsges. 1928.

Seitz, F., *Äldre svenska glas med graverade dekor.* Stockholm, 1936.

Simmingskold, Bo, see Steenberg, Elisa.

Sotheby & Co. Sale catalogue *English and continental glass.* London, 1965.

Steenberg, Elisa, *Modern Swedish glass,* Stockholm: Lindqvist, 1949.

Steenberg, Elisa, und Simmingskold, Bo: *Glas.* Stockholm: Natur och Kultur, 1958.

Stein, Günther, 'Johann Kunckels Ars Vitraria als Synthese internationalen Glaswissens im 17. Jahrhundert'. *Glastechn. Berichte 25* (1952) pp. 411—6.

Stein, Günther, 'Aus der Geschichte des Wannenofens'. In Günther, *Glasschmelz-Wannenöfen.* Frankfurt a. M.: Deutsche Glastechnische Gesellschaft, 1954.

Stein, Günther, 'Die Erfindung der automatischen Flaschenblasmaschine von Owens um die Jahrhundertwende'. *Glastechn. Berichte 27* (1954) pp. 15—17.

Stein, Günther, 'Die Brüder Siemens und das Glas'. *Glastechn. Berichte 27* (1954) pp. 449—56.

Stein, Günther, 'Johann Kunckel im Dienste des Großen Kurfürsten, die Glanzzeit seines glastechnologischen Wirkens'. *Glastechn. Berichte 28* (1955) pp. 121—4.

Stein, Günther, 'Das Thema Glas in der Physik des 17. und 18. Jahrhunderts'. *Glastechn. Berichte 28* (1955) pp. 486—90.

Stoevesandt, Wilhelm, 'Glasmacherkunst als Gleichnis bei Nicolaus von Cues'. *Glastechn. Berichte 33* (1960) pp. 142—3.

Streit, Julius, and Lauer, Otto, *Dominik Biemann, Lebensbericht und Meisterarbeiten des besten Porträtgraveurs.* Leutelt-Ges., Schwab. Gmund, 1958.

Turner, William Ernest Stephen, 'Studies of ancient glass and glassmaking processes'. *Journal of the Society of Glass Technologists 38* (1954) pp. 436—44, 445—6; 40 (1956) pp. 162T—86T; 40 (1956) pp. 277T—300T; 40 (1956) No. 192 pp. 39T—52T.

Turner, William Ernest Stephen, 'Glas bei unseren Vorfahren'. *Glastechn. Berichte 28* (1955) pp. 255—9.

Turner, William Ernest Stephen, 'Die Leistungen der alten Glasmacher und ihre Grenzen'. *Glastechn. Berichte 30* (1957) pp. 257—65.

Turner, William Ernest Stephen, 'The Technical Study of Ancient Glasses. A Review of Progress and a Plan for the Future'. *Glastechn. Berichte 32 K* (1959) pp. VIII/57—VIII/58.

Vargin, V. V., see Kachalov, N. N.

Vavra, J. R., *Das Glas und die Jahrtausende.* Prague: Artia, 1954.

Wakefield, Hugh, *Nineteenth Century British Glass.* London: Faber and Faber, 1961.

Wiedmann, Karl, 'Das römische Distret, mit den Augen des Hohlglastechnikers gesehen'. *Glastechn. Berichte 27* (1954) pp. 33—40.

List of references

page 128 Passage from Spessart charter of 1406, cited after Magarete Killing, *Die Glasmacherkunst in Hessen,* Marburg, 1927, p. 175.

page 130 Passage from letter of 1537 of the Hessian *Bund,* cited after M. Killing, *op. cit.,* p. 176.

pages 160 and 181 f. Account by Joachim von Sandrarts in *Academie der Bau-, Bild- und Mahlerey-Künste,* 1675, cited after Erich Meyer-Heisig, *Der Nürnberger Glasschnitt des 17. Jahrhunderts,* Nuremberg, 1963, p. 218.

pages 183 f. Information concerning the Schwanhardt family from I. G. Doppelmayr, *Historische Nachricht von den Nürnbergischen Mathematicis und Künstlern* Nürnbergs, 1730, cited after E. Meyer-Heisig, *op. cit.,* pp. 219 f.

page 190 Letter of 1686 from Friedrich Winter, steward to Count Christoph Leopold Schaffgotsch, cited after E. von Czihak, *Schlesische Gläser,* Breslau, 1891, p. 130.

page 230 Pronouncement by Frederick II to the Silesian glass-industry, cited after E. von Czihak, *op. cit.,* pp. 152 f.

pages 230 f. *Règlement für die Glas-Meistere und Glas-Arbeitere im Konigreich Böheim* of 5 October 1767, from the original in the possession of the Spezial-Farbglashütte Mittinger und Co. KG, Darmstadt.

page 231 Observation by Goethe concerning the gem-cutters of Warmbrunn, cited after E. von Czihak, *op cit.,* p. 135.

page 271 M. A. Gessert's opinion of Samuel Gottlob Mohn from *Geschichte der Glasmalerei,* 1839, cited after Gustav E. Pazaurek, *Gläser der Empire- und Biedermeierzeit,* Leipzig, 1923, p. 158.

page 271 Announcement in the *Franzensbader Kurlisten* of the years 1851–4, cited after Suzanno Pesatovo, 'Dominik Biemann', in *Journal of Glass Studies,* 1965, pp. 83—106.

page 276 Verses of 1807 by Samuel Mohn on the occasion of the birthday of Duke Friedrich Franz I of Mecklenburg, cited after G. E. Pazaurek, *op. cit.,* p. 160.

page 280 Signatures of Art Nouveau artists after Gerhard Bott, *Kunsthandwerk um 1900. Jugendstil.* (Exhibition catalogue). Darmstadt, 1965.

page 308 Comment of Hans Eckstein, cited from *Die Neue Sammlung,* Munich, n. d. p. 13.

page 308 From Van de Velde's *Vom neuen Stil,* Leipzig, 1907, cited after Julius Posener, *Anfänge des Funktionalismus.* Bauwelt Fundamente Vol. 11, Berlin, 1964, p. 18.

page 310 Comment by Paul Reilly, 1953, cited after Harro Ernst, *Moderne Gläser,* Darmstadt, n. d., p. 7.

page 318 Statement by Kunckel referring to his discovery of ruby glass, cited after Robert Schmidt, *Brandenburgische Gläser,* Berlin, 1914 (appendix).

page 320 Passage from Johann Mathesius, *Sarepta oder Bergpostill,* 1562, cited after Wilhelm Ganzenmüller, *Beiträge zur Geschichte der Technologie und der Alchemie,* Weinheim, 1956, p. 137.

Acknowledgements of illustrations

Jacket Museum für Kunst und Gewerbe, Hamburg, Münze von Hautsch: Badisches Landesmuseum, Karlsruhe.

page 41 Verlag Electa, Milan.

page 42 left Metropolitan Museum of Art, New York. *Right* The British Museum, London.

page 43 left Wilhelm Henrich Antiquitäten, Frankfurt/M. *Right* The British Museum, London.

page 44 top The British Museum, London. *Bottom left and right* Naturhistorisches Museum, Vienna, Department of Pre-history.

page 45 top The British Museum, London. *Bottom* Victoria and Albert Museum, London.

page 46 top and bottom Wilhelm Henrich Antiquitäten, Frankfurt/M.

page 47 The British Museum, London.

page 48 top left Wilhelm Henrich Antiquitäten, Frankfurt/M. *Top right* Kunstmuseum Düsseldorf. *Bottom left and right* Wilhelm Henrich Antiquitäten, Frankfurt/M.

page 49 Wilhelm Henrich Antiquitäten, Frankfurt/M.

page 50 top and bottom left The Corning Museum of Glass, Corning New York. *Bottom right* Wilhelm Henrich Antiquitäten, Frankfurt/M.

page 51 top Rheinisches Landesmuseum, Trier. *Bottom* Römisch-Germanisches Museum, Cologne, Photo: Rheinisches Bildarchiv, Cologne.

page 52 Wilhelm Henrich Antiquitäten, Frankfurt/M.

page 53 Wilhelm Henrich Antiquitäten, Frankfurt/M.

page 54 left Römisch-Germanisches Museum, Cologne, Photo: Rheinisches Bildarchiv, Cologne. *Right* Wilhelm Henrich Antiquitäten, Frankfurt/M.

page 135   Hessisches Landesmuseum Darmstadt. Photo: Rudolf Dobrick, Darmstadt.

page 136   Museum für Kunsthandwerk, Frankfurt/M.

page 137 top   Kunstgewerbemuseum der Stadt Köln. *Bottom* Kunstsammlungen der Veste Coburg.

page 138 left   Museum für Kunsthandwerk, Frankfurt/M. *Right* Wilhelm Henrich Antiquitäten, Frankfurt/M.

page 139 left and right   Museum für Kunsthandwerk, Frankfurt/M.

page 140 left and right   Kunstsammlungen der Veste Coburg.

page 141 left and right   Kunstsammlungen der Veste Coburg.

page 142 left   Kunstmuseum der Stadt Düsseldorf. Photo: Landesbildstelle Rheinland.

page 142 right   Museum für Kunsthandwerk, Frankfurt/M.

page 143 left   Museum für Kunsthandwerk, Frankfurt/M. *Right* Stiftung Kunsthaus Heylshof, Worms.

page 144 left   Kunstsammlungen der Veste Coburg. *Right* Staatliche Galerie Moritzburg, Halle.

page 145   Staatliche Kunstsammlungen Kassel.

page 146 left   Museum für Kunsthandwerk, Frankfurt/M. *Right* Museen für Kunst und Kulturgeschichte, Lübeck. Photo: Wilhelm Castelli, Lübeck.

page 147 left and right   Kunstsammlungen der Veste Coburg.

page 148 left   Museum für Kunsthandwerk, Frankfurt/M. *Right* Stiftung Kunsthaus, Heylshof, Worms.

page 149 left   Kunstsammlungen der Veste Coburg. *Right* Marburger Universitätsmuseum für Kunst und Kulturgeschichte. Bildarchiv Foto Marburg.

page 150 left   Helfried Krug, Mülheim. Photo: Gerd Richter, Essen. *Top right* Museum für Kunst und Gewerbe, Hamburg. *Bottom right* Kunstgewerbemuseum, Cologne. Photo: Rheinisches Bildarchiv, Cologne.

page 151   Museum für Kunsthandwerk, Frankfurt/M.

page 152   Museum für Kunsthandwerk, Frankfurt/M. Photo: Ruth und Helmut Dornauf, Frankfurt/M.

page 161   Bayerisches Nationalmuseum, Munich. Photo: Sophie-Renate Gnamm, Munich.

page 162 left and right   Kunstsammlungen der Veste Coburg.

page 163 left   Kunstsammlungen der Veste Coburg. *Right* Museum für Kunst und Gewerbe, Hamburg.

page 164 left and right   Bayerisches Nationalmuseum, Munich.

page 165 left   Bayerisches Nationalmuseum, Munich. *Right* Kestner-Museum, Hanover. Photo: Hermann Friedrich, Wulferod-Hanover.

page 166 left   Museum für Kunst und Gewerbe, Hamburg. *Right* Helfried Krug, Mülheim. Photo: Gerd Richter, Essen.

page 167   Helfried Krug, Mülheim. Photo: Gerd Richter, Essen.

page 168 left   Helfried Krug, Mülheim. Photo: Gerd Richter, Essen. *Right* Kunstsammlungen der Veste Coburg.

page 169 left and right   Kunstsammlungen der Veste Coburg.

page 170 left   Staatliche Kunstsammlungen Kassel. *Right* Kunstsammlungen der Veste Coburg.

page 171 top and bottom right   Kunstsammlungen der Veste Coburg.

page 172 left   Rijksmuseum, Amsterdam. *Right* Wilhelm Henrich Antiquitäten, Frankfurt/M.

page 173   Helfried Krug, Mülheim. Photo: Gerd Richter, Essen.

page 174 left   Museum für Kunst und Gewerbe, Hamburg. *Right* Museum für Kunsthandwerk, Frankfurt/M.

page 175 left and right   Rijksmuseum, Amsterdam.

page 176 left and right   Helfried Krug, Mülheim. Photo: Gerd Richter, Essen.

page 177   Helfried Krug, Mülheim. Photo: Gerd Richter, Essen.

page 178 left   Wilhelm Henrich Antiquitäten, Frankfurt/M. *Top right* Helfried Krug, Mülheim. Photo: Gerd Richter, Essen. *Bottom left* Kunstsammlungen der Veste Coburg. *Bottom right* Wilhelm Henrich Antiquitäten, Frankfurt/M.

page 179 top   Kunstsammlungen der Veste Coburg. *Bottom* Wilhelm Henrich Antiquitäten, Frankfurt/M.

page 256 top left Hessisches Landesmuseum Darmstadt. Photo: Rudolf Dobrick, Darmstadt. *Top and bottom right* Helfried Krug, Mülheim. Photo: Gerd Richter, Essen. *Left* Kunstmuseum der Stadt Düsseldorf. Photo: Landesbildstelle Rheinland.

page 257 Kunstsammlungen der Veste Coburg.

page 258 top left Museum für Kunst und Gewerbe, Hamburg. *Top right* Kunstgewerbemuseum der Stadt Köln. Photo: Rheinisches Bildarchiv, Cologne. *Bottom left* Wilhelm Henrich Antiquitäten, Frankfurt/M. *Bottom right* Rijksmuseum, Amsterdam.

page 259 Museum für Kunsthandwerk, Frankfurt/M.

page 260 Helfried Krug, Mülheim. Photo: Gerd Richter, Essen.

page 261 left Helfried Krug, Mülheim. Photo: Gerd Richter, Essen. *Right* Wilhelm Henrich Antiquitäten, Frankfurt/M.

page 262 top and bottom left Sammlung R., Frankfurt/M. *Top right* Helfried Krug, Mülheim. Photo: Gerd Richter, Essen. *Bottom right* Kunstsammlungen der Veste Coburg.

page 263 Sammlung R., Frankfurt/M.

page 264 top and bottom Sammlung R., Frankfurt/M.

page 265 top left Museum für Kunsthandwerk, Frankfurt/M. *Top right* Hessisches Landesmuseum Darmstadt. Photo: Rudolf Dobrick, Darmstadt. *Bottom left* Sammlung R., Frankfurt/M. *Bottom right* Helfried Krug, Mülheim. Photo: Gerd Richter, Essen.

page 266 top left and right Kunstgewerbemuseum, Köln. Photo: Rheinisches Bildarchiv, Cologne. *Bottom left* Helfried Krug, Mülheim. Photo: Gerd Richter, Essen. *Bottom right* Wilhelm Henrich Antiquitäten, Frankfurt/M.

page 267 left and right Sammlung R., Frankfurt/M.

page 268 Kunstgewerbemuseum Köln. Photo: Heinz Doppelfeld, Cologne.

page 288 Sotheby & Co., London.

page 289 Hessisches Landesmuseum Darmstadt. Photo: Rudolf Dobrick, Darmstadt.

page 290 Wilhelm Henrich Antiquitäten, Frankfurt/M.

page 291 left Hessisches Landesmuseum Darmstadt. Photo: Rudolf Dobrick, Darmstadt. *Right* Wilhelm Henrich Antiquitäten, Frankfurt/M.

page 292 Hessisches Landesmuseum Darmstadt. Photo: Rudolf Dobrick, Darmstadt.

page 293 Hessisches Landesmuseum Darmstadt. Photo: Rudolf Dobrick, Darmstadt.

page 295 left and right Museum für Kunsthandwerk, Frankfurt/M.

page 296 left and right Hessisches Landesmuseum Darmstadt. Photo: Rudolf Dobrick, Darmstadt.

page 297 Photo: Eta Lazi, Stuttgart.

page 298 August Warnecke, Hamburg. Works photo: Paolo Venini, Murano, Venice.

page 299 top and bottom August Warnecke, Hamburg. Works photo: Cristallerie Baccarat.

page 300 Civici Musei Venezia d'Arte e di Storia, Venice.

page 301 left Museum für Kunsthandwerk, Frankfurt/M. *Right* Tiroler Glashütte Claus Josef Riedel KG, Kufstein (August Warnecke, Hamburg).

page 302 August Warnecke, Hamburg. Works photo: Orrefors.

page 303 Die Neue Sammlung, München. Photo: Sophie-Renate Gnamm, Munich.

page 304 Sammlung R., Frankfurt/M. Photo: Ruth und Helmut Dornauf, Frankfurt/M.